Year 2000 Solut... For Dummies

KU-122-697

Sheet

Methods of Handling Year 2000 Problems

Date expansion. In this method, two-digit year values are expanded to four-digit values. For example, suppose the date November 20, 1957, is currently stored as 112057. After being expanded, the value would be 11201957.

Fixed window. You define a static 100-year period, and all dates that your programs reference exist in that window. One possible fixed window is 1940 through 2039. If this window is chosen, the year value in the date 112057 refers to the year 1957. The year value in the date 103027 refers to the year 2027.

Sliding window. You define a 100-year period, and all dates that your programs reference exist in that window. Every year, the window slides forward a single year. One possible sliding window is 1940 through 2039. A date with a year of 40 refers to 1940. The next year, the window slides forward to include the years 1941 through 2040. At that point, a date with a year of 40 refers to 2040.

Date compression. This technique compresses a four-digit year value and stores it where the current two-digit year is stored. This technique is also referred to as *date encoding*. Frequently the year is expressed as a hexadecimal value. The date 112057 could be stored as 112039 in a compressed date format because the hexadecimal value 39 is equivalent to the decimal value of 57.

Encapsulation. The Gregorian calendar repeats itself every 28 years. For example, the years 1998 and 1970 are identical. In both of these years, January 1st is a Thursday and December 31st is a Tuesday. Encapsulation stores dates after subtracting 28 years from them. When dates are retrieved from storage, the 28 years are added back. This avoids the problem of comparing dates across a millennium boundary for the next 28 years. Assume a new employee is hired on 1/1/1998 and her date of birth is 7/4/1976. The values stored in the computer would be 1/1/70 for her hire date and 7/4/48 for her birth date if encapsulation was used.

Bridge programs. A bridge program translates data from different formats. A bridge can convert data from its old format to a new format or from a new format to the original format. The bridge allows both old and new programs to use the data. A bridge program runs online, performing conversions as programs request data. A data conversion program, on the other hand, runs infrequently or offline.

Types of Year 2000 Testing

Unit testing. The act of testing a single program module. Usually performed by the programmer who wrote or modified the module.

Integration testing. Testing to verify that all individual modules in a subsystem will work together. Frequently performed by the testing team or the quality assurance (QA) group.

System testing. Testing the entire system at one time to verify that it functions as intended. Usually performed by the testing team or the QA (Quality Assurance) group.

Acceptance testing. Testing performed by the client or the customer before they accept the system. Acceptance testing is similar to system testing in scope but is performed by different individuals.

Regression testing. Testing performed to determine whether modifications to the system have introduced new errors. Usually performed by the testing team or the QA group.

YR2K Web Sites

www.year2000.com

www.software.ibm.com

www.yr2k.com

www.spr.com

www.mitre.org/research/yr2k/

...For Dummies: #1 Computer Book Series for Beginners

Year 2000 Solutions For Dummies®

Cheat Sheet

Important Year 2000 Terms and Definitions

BIOS (basic input/output system). The part of a PC operating system that controls reading data from and writing data to the external world.

Century window. A 100-year interval, usually crossing a century boundary, within which all data lies.

COBOL (Common Business Oriented Language). A widely used computer language in which many programs have been written. The majority of COBOL programs were written for mainframe computers.

Critical event horizon. The date on which a hardware or software component first fails to process dates properly.

DASD (direct access storage device). A fancy term for a hard drive. This term is most frequently used in a mainframe environment.

Embedded systems. Products that contain a computer chip that has hard-coded programs onboard. Some examples are microwave ovens, VCRs, automobiles, cellular phones, and elevators.

Encoding. Compressing year values to a format other than decimal to fit a four-digit year into a two-digit field.

Event horizon. How far into the future a system or a program "sees." A computer program that calculates 30-year mortgages deals with dates 30 years into the future. It could encounter year 2000 problems as early as 1970.

Expansion. Expanding two-digit year fields to contain four-digit year values.

Gregorian calendar. A reformed Julian calendar. Leap years occur every year that is divisible by 4 except centenary years (that is, years that are multiples of 100) that are not divisible by 400. The year 2000 will be a leap year, but 1700, 1800, and 1900 are not leap years.

Julian calendar. Calendar system established by Julius Caesar in 46 B.C. This calendar contains 12 months totaling 365 days. It established the practice of a leap year, with 366 days occurring every fourth year.

Julian date. A dating system that counts the number of days past a base date. The inventor of this system was Joseph Scaliger, who invented it in 1582 and named it in honor of his father, Julius Caesar Scaliger.

Leap year. A year that contains 366 days instead of the normal 365. Leap years are used to keep the Gregorian calendar in sync with the solar year.

LOC (lines of code). One way to measure the size of computer programs.

Millennium. A period of one thousand years.

RTC (real-time clock). A chip in a PC that uses a battery to maintain the current time whether or not the computer is turned on.

SCM (software configuration management). A tool to maintain track of and control of software libraries.

Solar year. The time it takes for the Earth to travel around the sun once. This is approximately 365.25 days.

Standardization. The use and enforcement of standard date formats, names, and routines.

UTC (Universal Time Coordinated). A time scale based on both atomic and astronomic measurements.

Three Primary Year 2000 Problems in a Nutshell

#1: Many computer systems have abbreviated the year value when dates are stored. Instead of storing four-digit values (like 1957), only two digits were stored (like 57). The assumption is that the other two digits will always be 19. With the arrival of the year 2000, this assumption will no longer be true. After this date, arithmetic performed on date values will no longer be correct.

#2: The year 2000 will be a leap year. There will be 29 days in February and 366 days in the year. Not all computer programs have been written to recognize this fact. This problem can occur on both mainframes and PCs.

#3: On many PCs, the day December 31, 1999, will not be followed by January 1, 2000. The next day on many of these computers will be January 1, 1980. This will cause a number of problems for programs that run on PCs.

...For Dummies: #1 Computer Book Series for Beginners

References for the Rest of Us! ®

COMPUTER BOOK SERIES FROM IDG

Are you intimidated and confused by computers? Do you find that traditional manuals are overloaded with technical details you'll never use? Do your friends and family always call you to fix simple problems on their PCs? Then the *...For Dummies*® computer book series from IDG Books Worldwide is for you.

...For Dummies books are written for those frustrated computer users who know they aren't really dumb but find that PC hardware, software, and indeed the unique vocabulary of computing make them feel helpless. *...For Dummies* books use a lighthearted approach, a down-to-earth style, and even cartoons and humorous icons to diffuse computer novices' fears and build their confidence. Lighthearted but not lightweight, these books are a perfect survival guide for anyone forced to use a computer.

> *"I like my copy so much I told friends; now they bought copies."*
>
> **Irene C., Orwell, Ohio**

> *"Quick, concise, nontechnical, and humorous."*
>
> **Jay A., Elburn, Illinois**

> *"Thanks, I needed this book. Now I can sleep at night."*
>
> **Robin F., British Columbia, Canada**

Already, millions of satisfied readers agree. They have made *...For Dummies* books the #1 introductory level computer book series and have written asking for more. So, if you're looking for the most fun and easy way to learn about computers, look to *...For Dummies* books to give you a helping hand.

YEAR 2000
SOLUTIONS
FOR
DUMMIES®

YEAR 2000 SOLUTIONS FOR DUMMIES®

by K. C. Bourne

IDG Books Worldwide, Inc.
An International Data Group Company

Foster City, CA ♦ Chicago, IL ♦ Indianapolis, IN ♦ Southlake, TX

Year 2000 Solutions For Dummies®

Published by
IDG Books Worldwide, Inc.
An International Data Group Company
919 E. Hillsdale Blvd.
Suite 400
Foster City, CA 94404
www.idgbooks.com (IDG Books Worldwide Web site)
www.dummies.com (Dummies Press Web site)

Library of Congress Catalog Card No.: 97-80212

ISBN: 0-7645-0241-7

Printed in the United States of America

10 9 8 7 6 5 4 3 2 1

1DD/RX/QZ/ZX/IN

Distributed in the United States by IDG Books Worldwide, Inc.

Distributed by Macmillan Canada for Canada; by Transworld Publishers Limited in the United Kingdom; by IDG Norge Books for Norway; by IDG Sweden Books for Sweden; by Woodslane Pty. Ltd. for Australia; by Woodslane Enterprises Ltd. for New Zealand; by Longman Singapore Publishers Ltd. for Singapore, Malaysia, Thailand, and Indonesia; by Simron Pty. Ltd. for South Africa; by Toppan Company Ltd. for Japan; by Distribuidora Cuspide for Argentina; by Livraria Cultura for Brazil; by Ediciencia S.A. for Ecuador; by Addison-Wesley Publishing Company for Korea; by Ediciones ZETA S.C.R. Ltda. for Peru; by WS Computer Publishing Corporation, Inc., for the Philippines; by Unalis Corporation for Taiwan; by Contemporanea de Ediciones for Venezuela; by Computer Book & Magazine Store for Puerto Rico; by Express Computer Distributors for the Caribbean and West Indies. Authorized Sales Agent: Anthony Rudkin Associates for the Middle East and North Africa.

For general information on IDG Books Worldwide's books in the U.S., please call our Consumer Customer Service department at 800-762-2974. For reseller information, including discounts and premium sales, please call our Reseller Customer Service department at 800-434-3422.

For information on where to purchase IDG Books Worldwide's books outside the U.S., please contact our International Sales department at 415-655-3200 or fax 415-655-3295.

For information on foreign language translations, please contact our Foreign & Subsidiary Rights department at 415-655-3021 or fax 415-655-3281.

For sales inquiries and special prices for bulk quantities, please contact our Sales department at 415-655-3200 or write to the address above.

For information on using IDG Books Worldwide's books in the classroom or for ordering examination copies, please contact our Educational Sales department at 800-434-2086 or fax 817-251-8174.

For press review copies, author interviews, or other publicity information, please contact our Public Relations department at 415-655-3000 or fax 415-655-3299.

For authorization to photocopy items for corporate, personal, or educational use, please contact Copyright Clearance Center, 222 Rosewood Drive, Danvers, MA 01923, or fax 508-750-4470.

is a trademark under exclusive license to IDG Books Worldwide, Inc., from International Data Group, Inc.

About the Author

K. C. Bourne is a software developer and consultant with extensive experience in client/server systems, GUI systems, and relational databases. This is K. C.'s second book; his first is *Testing Client/Server Systems* (published by McGraw-Hill). He has also written many articles for *DBMS, Database Programming,* and *Database Design* magazines. K. C.'s next goal in life is to become a contestant on the TV game show Jeopardy!

ABOUT IDG BOOKS WORLDWIDE

Welcome to the world of IDG Books Worldwide.

IDG Books Worldwide, Inc., is a subsidiary of International Data Group, the world's largest publisher of computer-related information and the leading global provider of information services on information technology. IDG was founded more than 25 years ago and now employs more than 8,500 people worldwide. IDG publishes more than 275 computer publications in over 75 countries (see listing below). More than 60 million people read one or more IDG publications each month.

Launched in 1990, IDG Books Worldwide is today the #1 publisher of best-selling computer books in the United States. We are proud to have received eight awards from the Computer Press Association in recognition of editorial excellence and three from *Computer Currents'* First Annual Readers' Choice Awards. Our best-selling *...For Dummies®* series has more than 30 million copies in print with translations in 30 languages. IDG Books Worldwide, through a joint venture with IDG's Hi-Tech Beijing, became the first U.S. publisher to publish a computer book in the People's Republic of China. In record time, IDG Books Worldwide has become the first choice for millions of readers around the world who want to learn how to better manage their businesses.

Our mission is simple: Every one of our books is designed to bring extra value and skill-building instructions to the reader. Our books are written by experts who understand and care about our readers. The knowledge base of our editorial staff comes from years of experience in publishing, education, and journalism — experience we use to produce books for the '90s. In short, we care about books, so we attract the best people. We devote special attention to details such as audience, interior design, use of icons, and illustrations. And because we use an efficient process of authoring, editing, and desktop publishing our books electronically, we can spend more time ensuring superior content and spend less time on the technicalities of making books.

You can count on our commitment to deliver high-quality books at competitive prices on topics you want to read about. At IDG Books Worldwide, we continue in the IDG tradition of delivering quality for more than 25 years. You'll find no better book on a subject than one from IDG Books Worldwide.

John Kilcullen
CEO
IDG Books Worldwide, Inc.

Steven Berkowitz
President and Publisher
IDG Books Worldwide, Inc.

*Eighth Annual
Computer Press
Awards ≥1992*

*Ninth Annual
Computer Press
Awards ≥1993*

*Tenth Annual
Computer Press
Awards ≥1994*

*Eleventh Annual
Computer Press
Awards ≥1995*

IDG Books Worldwide, Inc., is a subsidiary of International Data Group, the world's largest publisher of computer-related information and the leading global provider of information services on information technology. International Data Group publishes over 275 computer publications in over 75 countries. Sixty million people read one or more International Data Group publications each month. International Data Group's publications include: **ARGENTINA:** Buyer's Guide, Computerworld Argentina, PC World Argentina; **AUSTRALIA:** Australian Macworld, Australian PC World, Australian Reseller News, Computerworld, IT Casebook, Network World, Publish, Webmaster; **AUSTRIA:** Computerwelt Osterreich, Networks Austria, PC Tip Austria; **BANGLADESH:** PC World Bangladesh; **BELARUS:** PC World Belarus; **BELGIUM:** Data News; **BRAZIL:** Annuário de Informática, Computerworld, Connections, Macworld, PC Player, PC World, Publish, Reseller News, Supergamepower; **BULGARIA:** Computerworld Bulgaria, Network World Bulgaria, PC & MacWorld Bulgaria; **CANADA:** CIO Canada, Client/Server World, ComputerWorld Canada, InfoWorld Canada, NetworkWorld Canada, WebWorld; **CHILE:** Computerworld Chile, PC World Chile; **COLOMBIA:** Computerworld Colombia, PC World Colombia; **COSTA RICA:** PC World Centro America; **THE CZECH AND SLOVAK REPUBLICS:** Computerworld Czechoslovakia, Macworld Czech Republic, PC World Czechoslovakia; **DENMARK:** Communications World Danmark, Computerworld Danmark, Macworld Danmark, PC World Danmark, Techworld Denmark; **DOMINICAN REPUBLIC:** PC World Republica Dominicana; **ECUADOR:** PC World Ecuador; **EGYPT:** Computerworld Middle East, PC World Middle East; **EL SALVADOR:** PC World Centro America; **FINLAND:** MikroPC, Tietoverkko, Tietoviikko; **FRANCE:** Distributique, Hebdo, Info PC, Le Monde Informatique, Macworld, Reseaux & Telecoms, WebMaster France; **GERMANY:** Computer Partner, Computerwoche, Computerwoche Extra, Computerwoche FOCUS, Global Online, Macwelt, PC Welt; **GREECE:** Amiga Computing, GamePro Greece, Multimedia World; **GUATEMALA:** PC World Centro America; **HONDURAS:** PC World Centro America; **HONG KONG:** Computerworld Hong Kong, PC World Hong Kong, Publish in Asia; **HUNGARY:** ABCD CD-ROM, Computerworld Szamitastechnika, Internetto online Magazine, PC World Hungary, PC-X Magazin Hungary; **ICELAND:** Tolvuheimur PC World Island; **INDIA:** Information Communications World, Information Systems Computerworld, PC World India, Publish in Asia; **INDONESIA:** InfoKomputer PC World, Komputek Computerworld, Publish in Asia; **IRELAND:** ComputerScope, PC Live!; **ISRAEL:** Macworld Israel, People & Computers/Computerworld; **ITALY:** Computerworld Italia, Macworld Italia, Networking Italia, PC World Italia; **JAPAN:** DTP World, Macworld Japan, Nikkei Personal Computing, OS/2 World Japan, SunWorld Japan, Windows NT World, Windows World Japan; **KENYA:** PC World East African; **KOREA:** Hi-Tech Information, Macworld Korea, PC World Korea; **MACEDONIA:** PC World Macedonia; **MALAYSIA:** Computerworld Malaysia, PC World Malaysia, Publish in Asia; **MALTA:** PC World Malta; **MEXICO:** Computerworld Mexico, PC World Mexico; **MYANMAR:** PC World Myanmar; **NETHERLANDS:** Computer! Totaal, LAN Internetworking Magazine, LAN World Buyers Guide, Macworld Netherlands, Net, WebWereld; **NEW ZEALAND:** Absolute Beginners Guide and Plain & Simple Series, Computer Buyer, Computer Industry Directory, Computerworld New Zealand, MTB, Network World, PC World New Zealand; **NICARAGUA:** PC World Centro America; **NORWAY:** Computerworld Norge, CW Rapport, Datamagasinet, Financial Rapport, Kursguide Norge, Macworld Norge, Multimediaworld Norge, PC World Ekspress Norge, PC World Nettverk, PC World Norge, PC World ProduktGuide Norge; **PAKISTAN:** Computerworld Pakistan; **PANAMA:** PC World Centro Panama; **PEOPLE'S REPUBLIC OF CHINA:** China Computer Users, China Computerworld, China InfoWorld, China Telecom World Weekly, Computer & Communication, Electronic Design China, Electronics Today, Electronics Weekly, Game Software, PC World China, Popular Computer Week, Software Weekly, Software World, Telecom World; **PERU:** Computerworld Peru, PC World Profesional Peru, PC World SoHo Peru; **PHILIPPINES:** Click!, Computerworld Philippines, PC World Philippines, Publish in Asia; **POLAND:** Computerworld Poland, Computerworld Special Report Poland, Cyber, Macworld Poland, Networld Poland, PC World Komputer; **PORTUGAL:** Cerebro/PC World, Computerworld/Correio Informático, Dealer World Portugal, Mac*In/PC*In Portugal, Multimedia World; **PUERTO RICO:** PC World Puerto Rico; **ROMANIA:** Computerworld Romania, PC World Romania, Telecom Romania; **RUSSIA:** Computerworld Russia, Mir PK, Publish, Seti; **SINGAPORE:** Computerworld Singapore, PC World Singapore, Publish in Asia; **SLOVENIA:** Monitor; **SOUTH AFRICA:** Computing SA, Network World SA, Software World SA; **SPAIN:** Communicaciones World España, Computerworld España, Dealer World España, Macworld España, PC World España, PC World Korea; **SRI LANKA:** Infolink PC World; **SWEDEN:** CAP&Design, Computer Sweden, Corporate Computing Sweden, Internetworld Sweden, it.branschen, Macworld Sweden, MaxiData Sweden, MikroDatorn, Nätverk & Kommunikation, PC World Sweden, PCAktiv, Windows World Sweden; **SWITZERLAND:** Computerworld Schweiz, Macworld Schweiz, PCtip; **TAIWAN:** Computerworld Taiwan, Macworld Taiwan, NEW ViSiON/Publish, PC World Taiwan, Windows World Taiwan; **THAILAND:** Publish in Asia, Thai Computerworld; **TURKEY:** Computerworld Turkiye, Macworld Turkiye, Network World Turkiye, PC World Turkiye; **UKRAINE:** Computerworld Kiev, Multimedia World Ukraine, PC World Ukraine; **UNITED KINGDOM:** Acorn User UK, Amiga Action UK, Amiga Computing UK, Apple Talk UK, Computing, Macworld, Parents and Computers UK, PC Advisor, PC Home, PSX Pro, The WEB; **UNITED STATES:** Cable in the Classroom, CIO Magazine, Computerworld, DOS World, Federal Computer Week, GamePro Magazine, InfoWorld, I-Way, Macworld, Network World, PC Games, PC World, Publish, Video Event, THE WEB Magazine, and WebMaster; online webzines: JavaWorld, NetscapeWorld, and SunWorld Online; **URUGUAY:** InfoWorld Uruguay; **VENEZUELA:** Computerworld Venezuela, PC World Venezuela; and **VIETNAM:** PC World Vietnam.   3/24/97

Dedication

This book is dedicated to my wife Liz and our children. Our wedding anniversary came and went while I was writing this book, and we didn't celebrate as fully as we should have. I'll make it up to you next year. Our children, Aaron, Burke, and Keelin, were very cooperative during this project. Although they were out of school and I was working on the book at home, they understood that "Daddy was working" and didn't interrupt me. Thanks. And now you can use the "good" computer.

Author's Acknowledgments

Books, like computer systems, are seldom the product of a single mind or a single pair of hands. My name appears as the author, but numerous people made significant contributions along the way. Gareth Hancock spent a great deal of time helping turn my initial outline into something that IDG Books Worldwide deemed to be publishable. Darlene Wong always answered my questions promptly and accurately. My project editor, Susan Pink, helped me turn a mass of words into a real, live book. As technical reviewer, Colin Banfield kept me honest when I strayed from the path or neglected to cover a topic thoroughly or accurately. My thanks to you all.

Publisher's Acknowledgments

We're proud of this book; please send us your comments about it by using the IDG Books Worldwide Registration Card at the back of the book or by e-mailing us at feedback/dummies@idgbooks.com. Some of the people who helped bring this book to market include the following:

Acquisitions, Development, and Editorial

Project Editor: Susan Pink

Acquisitions Editor: Gareth Hancock

Technical Editor: Colin Banfield

Editorial Manager: Mary C. Corder

Editorial Assistant: Donna Love

Special Help

Suzanne Thomas, Associate Editor; Andrea Boucher, Copy Editor; Elizabeth Kuball, Copy Editor; Stephanie Koutek, Proof Editor

Production

Project Coordinator: Regina Snyder

Layout and Graphics: Lou Boudreau, Linda M. Boyer, Angela Bush-Sisson, J. Tyler Connor, Angela F. Hunckler, Heather N. Pearson, Brent Savage, Kate Snell

Proofreaders: Henry Lazarek, Carrie Voorhis, Michelle Croninger, Joel K. Draper, Rebecca Senninger, Robert Springer

Indexer: Sharon Hilgenberg

General and Administrative

IDG Books Worldwide, Inc.: John Kilcullen, CEO; Steven Berkowitz, President and Publisher

IDG Books Technology Publishing: Brenda McLaughlin, Senior Vice President and Group Publisher

Dummies Technology Press and Dummies Editorial: Diane Graves Steele, Vice President and Associate Publisher; Kristin A. Cocks, Editorial Director; Mary Bednarek, Acquisitions and Product Development Director

Dummies Trade Press: Kathleen A. Welton, Vice President and Publisher

IDG Books Production for Dummies Press: Beth Jenkins, Production Director; Cindy L. Phipps, Manager of Project Coordination, Production Proofreading, and Indexing; Kathie S. Schutte, Supervisor of Page Layout; Shelley Lea, Supervisor of Graphics and Design; Debbie J. Gates, Production Systems Specialist; Robert Springer, Supervisor of Proofreading; Debbie Stailey, Special Projects Coordinator; Tony Augsburger, Supervisor of Reprints and Bluelines; Leslie Popplewell, Media Archive Coordinator

Dummies Packaging and Book Design: Patti Sandez, Packaging Specialist; Lance Kayser, Packaging Assistant; Kavish + Kavish, Cover Design

♦

The publisher would like to give special thanks to Patrick J. McGovern, without whom this book would not have been possible.

♦

Contents at a Glance

Cartoons at a Glance

By Rich Tennant

"After working on the VR2000 problem, I've decided it'll probably function better as a paperweight than as a computer."

page 7

"IT'S CHAOS — BUT IT'S CHAOS THAT WORKS."

page 73

"'MORNING, MR. DREXEL. I HEARD YOU SAY YOUR COMPUTERS ALL HAD BUGS; WELL, I FIGURE THEY'RE CRAWLING IN THROUGH THOSE SLOTS THEY HAVE, SO I JAMMED A COUPLE OF ROACH-DISKS IN EACH ONE. LET ME KNOW IF YOU HAVE ANY MORE PROBLEMS."

page 135

"OH SURE, IT'LL FLOAT ALRIGHT, BUT INTEGRATION'S GONNA BE A KILLER."

page 239

"WELL, SYSTEMS INTEGRATION ISN'T PERFECT. SOME DEPARTMENTS STILL SEEM TO GET MORE INFORMATION THAN OTHERS."

page 269

Fax: 508-546-7747 • E-mail: the5wave@tiac.net

Table of Contents

- -

Introduction

● ●

*W*elcome to *Year 2000 Solutions For Dummies,* the book for those who are curious about or terrified of how the year 2000 will affect their computer systems.

Anyone who meets even a single one of the following criteria can benefit by reading this book:

- ✔ You own a computer.
- ✔ You use a computer at work or your employer owns one or more computers.
- ✔ In an organization chart, your name appears above, below, or anywhere near the acronyms MIS (Management Information Services), IS (Information Services), or IT (Information Technology).
- ✔ Your home or apartment has any of the following modern conveniences: running water, electricity, telephone service, or natural gas.
- ✔ Any of your personal assets are in a bank, a savings & loan, a mutual fund, or common stocks.
- ✔ FICA withholding has been withdrawn from your paycheck.
- ✔ You've written a check to the IRS.
- ✔ You enjoy watching TV, listening to the radio, or going to a movie.
- ✔ You prefer that your life continue pretty much as it is now.

People who don't need to worry about the year 2000 problem have a different set of criteria. If you meet *all* the following criteria, don't bother reading this book:

- ✔ You live on an otherwise uninhabited island.
- ✔ You travel to and from your island in a catamaran you carved from a coconut tree trunk.
- ✔ You grow, catch, or barter for all your food.
- ✔ You make your own clothing from palm fronds, fig leaves, or animal skins.
- ✔ Your wealth is measured in chickens, cattle, or shiny beads.
- ✔ You never intend to move from your island.

Seriously, if you program computers, manage programmers, use computers in your job, or interact with other organizations that use computers, you need to educate yourself on what is going to happen.

This book provides a great deal of information about how the year 2000 will affect computers. Specifically, it deals with potential errors that could occur as January 1, 2000, approaches. Predictions about the seriousness of this event range from The Second Great Depression to merely a blip on the radar screen. I can assure you that if individuals throughout our country and around the world continue to ignore this problem, its effect will be closer to the former than the latter.

Some groups of people unquestionably need to be aware of this problem. Some of these groups follow:

- Directors and officers of a corporation, who could be held liable for any losses that the corporation experiences
- Owners or managers of businesses that don't have an MIS department
- Purchasing managers within organizations
- Managers of groups of users who depend heavily on computers to fulfill their jobs
- Those in management or programming positions in banks, insurance companies, and telecommunications firms
- Employees of a government entity, a nonprofit organization, or an institute of higher education that uses computers

If you expect this book to contain references to a computer named HAL, robots, Big Brother, or travel to Mars, you've picked up the wrong book. Put it back on the shelf quickly before you read something that upsets you. If you've already purchased it, save the receipt and return it to where you purchased it. If the store's computers aren't messed up, they'll probably refund your money.

About This Book

Like all ...For Dummies books, Year 2000 Solutions For Dummies explains a technical subject in a way that the average person can understand. I've tried to fully explain all the major points in lay terms without watering down their meaning or importance.

Depending on your situation, you can safely skip certain chapters. If you don't deal with mainframe computers, for instance, feel free to read past references to them. If your organization doesn't use any PCs, you can safely omit Chapter 2. However, you might want to read the chapter on fixing PCs so that you can discuss this topic at cocktail parties, backyard cookouts, and corporate meetings.

How this book is organized

This book is divided into a number of parts, each of which deals with a specific area of the year 2000 situation. These parts are arranged in the order in which a year 2000 project manager would address the problem. This sequence is understanding the problem, developing a plan for dealing with the problem, implementing this plan, and then assessing where the plan gets you.

Within each part are a number of chapters. Each chapter is self-contained, so you don't necessarily have to read them in order or even read all of them.

Part I: The Year 2000 Crisis

This part consists of chapters that explain what the year 2000 problem is all about. It discusses the worst-case scenario. Why we are in this position is also explained. If you are seeking to familiarize yourself with the year 2000 problem, make sure you read Part I.

Part II: Developing a Year 2000 Plan

Dealing with a potential year 2000 problem requires detailed thinking, orderly steps, and coordinated activity. In other words, you need a plan. This plan will lay out what needs to be accomplished, in what order it will be accomplished, and who will do it. Your plan should also cover what you'll do if things go wrong.

Read Part II if you are developing such a plan or approving or paying for a year 2000 project. In addition, those who will be directly affected by the year 2000 problem would benefit from reading this part. Examples of this last group include major users of the computer systems, directors and officers of the corporation, and anyone assigned to the project team.

Part III: Implementing Your Plan

A plan that has been written down on paper isn't worth much until it is carried out. Part III provides information on how your plan can be implemented, discussing each phase of the project in detail.

Check out this part if you're a project manager, a project team member, or a representative of the user community who will be working on this effort.

Part IV: The Good, the Bad, and the Ugly

Part IV focuses on the gains your organization will experience by addressing its year 2000 problems. The first benefit is fairly obvious, but some of the secondary benefits aren't so obvious.

Project managers, corporate directors and officers, and managers of the user communities should read Part IV. You can also use the information in this part to convince upper management that this project needs to be adequately funded.

Part V: The Part of Tens

All ...*For Dummies* books include a Part of Tens, although the actual content of this part varies from book to book. The Part of Tens in this book can be broken down into two different types of information.

The first type is information that will help you deal with the year 2000 problem. The two main sources of information described are Web sites and year 2000 user groups. (No one is likely to succeed on a year 2000 project without some extra help or information.) The second type of information is advice to help prevent you from straying off the year 2000 path: situations to avoid, preparations to make, and questions to ask.

Icons Used in This Book

I feel compelled to warn you in advance that I have been known to climb up on my soapbox and give unsolicited opinions. I try to control this urge, but when it takes over I can't control myself. When you see this icon, it means that that urge has overpowered me once again. You're free to agree with me or simply shake your head and feel sorry for me.

This icon alerts you to a way of doing something easier or faster. Every tip won't be applicable to every reader's year 2000 project, but you should read it and carefully consider whether it applies to you or not.

When this icon appears, it's time to put on your thinking cap. The information is likely to show up on a test at some time. The test might take the form of your boss asking you how you are handling a certain facet of the year 2000 problem.

When this icon appears, you need to pay special attention to the text! It's used to point out ways in which you could seriously affect your year 2000 project, your organization's ongoing operations, or your future with that organization. Ignore these warnings at your own peril.

Where to Go from Here

The year 2000 will arrive sooner than you think. No amount of denial will delay it for even a single day. You *can* successfully prepare your organization for this date with destiny. All it will take is an open and inquisitive mind, a well-thought-out plan, a little resolve, and a lot of hard work.

When you successfully complete your year 2000 project, you can be proud of yourself and everyone who participated in the effort. You have overcome the most complex software problem in the history of computers. Congratulations!

Part I
The Year 2000 Crisis

The 5th Wave   By Rich Tennant

"After working on the YR2000 problem, I've decided it'll probably function better as a paperweight than as a computer."

In this part . . .

The year 2000 will poke up its ugly head in a lot of places. Some of those places will be unexpected. Your first step in correcting the year 2000 problem is to understand how it will affect your organization.

The chapters in Part 1 provide a high-level view of the year 2000 situation. They describe why we are in this situation and how to identify and correct problems with a PC. They also describe the effect this problem has on data received by and exported by your organization.

Chapter 1

What's It All About, Alfie?

· ·

In This Chapter

▶ Uncovering the potential threats of the year 2000

▶ Understanding why year values have been stored in two digits

▶ Discovering whether your PC will be affected

▶ Understanding that 2000 is a leap year and how this might affect programs

▶ Finding out how the year 2000 can affect you

▶ Protecting your organizations from potential lawsuits

▶ Recognizing how both hardware and software will be affected

▶ Starting early is crucial

· ·

The year 2000 represents a threat to computer systems worldwide on a scale that has never been experienced. When the calendar is flipped from December 31, 1999 to January 1, 2000, a high percentage of computers and computer systems will probably experience severe problems. Projections are that many computer systems and the companies that rely on them will fail. Software expert Capers Jones, Chairman of Software Productivity Research, Inc. estimates that 5 percent of all U.S. businesses will go out of business because of this problem. If anything close to the worst-case scenario should occur, we're all in for a very rough ride.

This rendezvous is approaching quickly, but you still have time to address the situation in your professional as well as personal life. You need to become familiar with the issues, identify how they will affect you, and plan the steps to mitigate or eliminate their effect on you and your organization. This book helps you prepare for this date with destiny. Good luck.

The Triple Threat

The year 2000 poses at least three distinct problems for computers, as shown in Figure 1-1. Two of these are software problems, and the third is essentially a hardware problem. Depending on the hardware platforms and software in your computer systems, you can be affected by one, two, or all three of these problems:

- Many computer applications store year values in two digits instead of four.
- Not all software recognizes that the year 2000 is a leap year.
- Not all PCs "know" that 01/01/2000 is the day after 12/31/1999.

Software Stores Year Values in Two Digits

The problem that has captured the most limelight is that year values in many computer systems are stored in two digits. The root of the problem is that it takes four digits to completely express the year portion of a date value: one digit each for the year, the decade, the century, and the millennium.

At least this has been the case for the last 998 years. Before the year 1000, only three digits were needed, but that's ancient history. Figure 1-2 demonstrates how year values have been traditionally stored in computer systems.

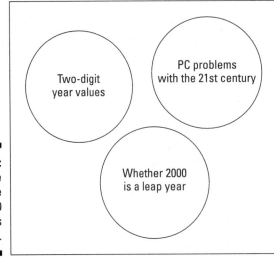

Figure 1-1:
Three separate year 2000 problems exist.

Two-digit year values

PC problems with the 21st century

Whether 2000 is a leap year

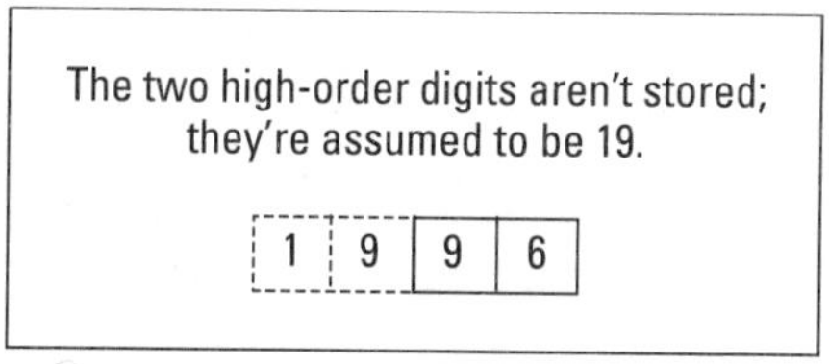

Figure 1-2:
How year
values are
stored.

The two high-order digits aren't stored;
they're assumed to be 19.

```
1 : 9 | 9 | 6
```

You may be wondering how such a problem could be allowed to occur. The industry knew that the year 2000 would arrive, so why didn't they design programs to handle it? I'll try to provide an answer in this section.

The most common way of expressing a date value in a computer system has been in the form: YYMMDD. Two digits store the year (YY), two digits store the month (MM), and the final two digits store the day of the month (DD). An example might make this storage format more understandable. The date of the first moon landing was July 20, 1969. This date would be stored as 690720 in YYMMDD format.

The business of business includes a lot of dates. Order dates, hire dates, shipping dates, payment dates, and many other types of dates exist in the business world. Computer systems handle information that generally includes a considerable number of date fields. The layout of two data processing records is presented in Figure 1-3.

Some variation exists in the ordering of the particular date units. In some systems, the format is MMDDYY. Other systems, particularly European ones, store dates in the format DDMMYY. All these formats, however, store the date in six characters instead of eight. This tiny piece of thriftiness is causing thousands of companies, government agencies, and other organizations to spend millions of dollars before the clock rolls over to 1/1/2000.

Figure 1-3:
Typical
layouts for
data
processing
records.

ID#	NAME	ADDRESS	DATE OF BIRTH	DATE OF HIRE
137658	Peterson, Amy	37 Hollyhock Lane	01 14 60	05 30 93
180637	Miller, Reginald	173 No. 155 Ave.	07 13 63	08 14 94
191945	Billings, Fredrick	145 East St.	11 20 55	01 31 96

ACCOUNT NUMBER	NAME	ADDRESS	EXP DATE	CARDHOLDER SINCE...
4423 0812 3314	Jones, Tabitha	52 Adams Lane	01 30 99	01 07 90
4455 0937 1351	Walker, Ima	1145 Shamrock Road	05 01 97	10 30 89
6776 0141 1562	Carlson, Chet	1906 Fontenelle Blvd	09 15 95	12 05 70

Saving two digits

It might sound unbelievable that developers would deliberately scrimp on the amount of space for storing dates. It stretches the imagination even further if you consider that programmers must have known that the day of reckoning would arrive. Why would intelligent people make such a catastrophic decision? Well, compelling reasons did exist for the decisions that modern-day MIS professionals are now saddled with.

Hardware was king; programmers weren't

The world of computers thirty or forty years ago was vastly different from the way it is now. During the early days of the industry, hardware costs far surpassed all other expenditures. The labor costs of programmers were minimal compared to the cost of a computer. Efforts were placed on anything that could conserve or more fully utilize this precious commodity. Storing the year in two digits instead of four saved both memory and long-term storage space. If extra programming was required to write code to handle a two-digit year value, that price was paid willingly.

Today, when the typical home computer has 8, 16, 24, or even 32 megabytes of memory, it's difficult to grasp how precious memory and other hardware resources were. The first computer system I worked on after graduating

How to display a date field

How should date values be stored in a computer? By now I hope I've convinced you that the entire four-digit year value should be stored. This defines what should be stored, but doesn't address the format in which a date should be displayed.

The method of expressing dates varies widely from country to country. The date November 18, 1989 is usually expressed as 11/18/89 in the United States. In the United Kingdom, it's written as 18/11/89. In Switzerland, it's expressed as 18.11.89.

Can we all agree on a single format? The ISO (International Standards Organization) is attempting to get agreement on a single format for expressing dates. ISO 8601 is this attempted standard, and it addresses the following:

✔ The order in which components of a date are expressed. The standard order will be year, month, and day.

✔ The character that will be used to separate date values. Currently, people use just about any character, such as a slash (/), a backslash (\), a period (.), or a hyphen (-). The standard character will be a hyphen (-).

✔ Should single-digit values be preceded by a zero? For example, should January 1, 2000 be expressed as 1-1-2000 or 01-01-2000? Including a leading zero will be the standard.

If all countries agree to follow these standards, everyone will be able to understand what dates other individuals are referring to.

from college included five computers. Three were online at any given time, and the remaining two were backup machines. Each computer had 256K words of memory. Each word was 3 bytes, so the amount of memory in each computer was 768K bytes. An additional 768K of memory was shared between the five computers in this SCADA (Supervisory Control and Data Acquisition) system. With only 1.5 megabytes of memory, the system sounds primitive, yet it controlled most of the oil pipelines in a major oil-producing country.

The following table demonstrates how the price of memory has plummeted over the last 30 or so years. When the price of memory was over $3,000,000 per MB, is it any wonder that programmers tried to save as much as possible?

Year	RAM ($/MB)
1970	$3,200,000 (no, this is not a misprint)
1980	$64,000
1990	$120
1995	$30
1997	$5

Saving two characters adds up

It's easy to forget that in the 1960s, when these decisions were made, the current plethora of storage options weren't available. You couldn't buy a multi-gigabyte hard drive, a 1.4 megabyte floppy drive, or a DAT tape drive, which holds tens of gigabytes. Mass storage, as today's users and developers know it, didn't exist. Storage technology was initially limited to paper tape, cards, magnetic tape, and core memory.

The Hollerith card (also known as the IBM or punched card) was one of the most common early storage methods. An example of a computer punch card is shown in Figure 1-4. Each rectangular card had the capacity to store 80 characters, or bytes, worth of data. Eighty bytes! A $3^1/_2$-inch diskette today can store 1.44 million bytes, or more data than 18,220 punch cards. And a single CD-ROM can contain more data than 8.5 million Hollerith cards.

The effect of storing dates in six characters instead of eight can be shown with the following example. Assume that one data record is stored on a single computer card. This data record holds three date fields: an employee's date of birth, hire date, and date of last review. These date fields together exhaust 18 bytes (3 date fields times 6 bytes per field). If the year had been stored in 8 bytes instead of 6, the total would have been 24 bytes (3×8).

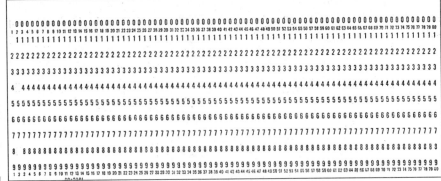

Figure 1-4:
A computer
punch card.

So, the difference between storing a two-digit year value and the fully expanded year format in this example is 6 bytes. These 6 bytes are the equivalent of 7.5 percent of the total storage capacity of each punched card. That's a lot of real estate on a punched card. It's also a tremendous amount of space to tie up to designate a value that won't be needed for almost forty years.

Saving two characters in each date field can quickly add up. The computer system for a large insurance company, bank, or credit card issuer could easily contain tens of millions of records. If each record in one of these systems contains even half a dozen date fields, you can save hundreds of millions of bytes by storing two-digit years. That figure may not be a significant amount of storage today, but it represented an enormous resource when these systems were developed.

When put in this context, it shouldn't be surprising that the decision was made to store dates in YYMMDD format. The developers were neither stupid nor shortsighted. They weighed the alternatives and took the one that seemed optimal under the circumstances.

In addition to the storage space saved, there was also the effect on processing speed. Even today, the input/output (I/O) system is the major bottleneck for most computer systems. If the date had been expanded to eight characters, the system would be required to read in 7.5 percent more cards to input the same data. Surely this scenario wouldn't be looked on with favor by management, developers, or the operations staff.

Storing the year as two characters saved corporations a significant amount of storage. It also saved money by avoiding the need to buy additional hardware. One estimate is that the typical organization saved more than $1 million per billion bytes of storage between the years 1963 and 1992. If these calculations are accurate, the decision to abbreviate the date being stored was justified.

Systems wouldn't be around in 40 years

Another reason why systems were developed with an embedded date problem is simply that no one expected these systems to survive this long. How could a COBOL programmer or project manager in the mid-1960s have ever imagined that his or her program would still be running three and a half decades later?

Programmers expected these systems to be in production for a limited time, perhaps five or ten years, before they were replaced by something newer, bigger, and better. Unfortunately, inertia set in. Instead of systems being replaced, they were simply modified, enhanced, and kept around.

The more cynically minded have a different explanation for why this decision was made. In their scenario, the decision maker didn't care because he or she expected to be happily retired (or at least to have changed companies) long before the millennium crisis raised its ugly head.

Maintaining backward compatibility

As new programs were added, they needed to access existing data. The only way this could be accomplished was to continue to store dates in the same (two-digit year) format. To store it any other way would create compatibility problems. In this way, the need to maintain links to older data and programs perpetuated the two-digit year problem.

Reusing software

Reusing code has always been the Holy Grail of software development. Reusing code has the following advantages over developing new code:

- Faster
- Cheaper
- Results in fewer errors

Although reusing software has many advantages, it has a significant drawback: It tends to continue the status quo. Any problems in current software libraries are perpetuated in new systems when you reuse software.

Effect on the bottom line

When programmers and management thought about the problem, they knew that it would need to be handled eventually. Time and money, however, were never budgeted for the effort. Correcting the problem would be time-consuming and expensive, but it wouldn't directly improve the bottom line. Management chose not to direct resources toward this problem until the impending disaster couldn't be ignored.

Insufficient staff also contributed to this problem. Even if management were willing to pay for this effort, there simply weren't enough programmers to write new programs, enhance current programs, and correct all the date problems.

Other places where dates are stored

Punched cards and disk files aren't the only locales where dates are stored. A slightly looser definition of the term *stored* yields two additional, significant storage locations. Date fields are stored also on computer screens (well, stored temporarily) and in printed reports. In each of these locations, the tendency has been to condense year values to two digits.

Computer screens

The majority of date values on computer screens include two-digit year values, primarily because so many computer terminals in the field still consist of "dumb" terminals. A dumb terminal usually refers to a monochrome terminal with a green screen connected to a mainframe computer. The IBM 3270 terminal is a classic example of this type of computer hardware.

Screens associated with this class of terminal are smaller and have a lower resolution than modern monitors. A typical dumb terminal screen, as shown in Figure 1-5, displays 80 columns and 24 rows.

When space is at a premium, users and developers alike tend to pack as much as possible into the available real estate. Trimming two digits from every date on a screen can save a lot of screen space.

Perhaps the most important reason for having two-digit year fields on computer screens is that the user is required to enter less data. Why have the user enter all four year digits when the two century digits are always the same? Fewer digits to enter means data can be entered more quickly and with less chance for data entry errors.

Printed reports

Programmers and users always seem to want to cram as much data as possible onto a report. Traditional mainframe line printers have a maximum width of 132 columns, and reports tend to use every one of these columns.

Reports seem to represent the ultimate in data processing tar pits. Once a column appears on a report, it never seems to come off. Additional columns may be added, but seldom are any removed. In my almost twenty years of software development, I can count on one hand the number of times a user has requested that the number of columns on a report be reduced.

```
Stewardson, Marjory A 010467 7416 South 34 St.      Hastings           NE68901
Stewart, Ronald J       050179 1009 West George Blvd Greenwood          NE68366
Stickman, Laura C       120190 1253 Hillsborough      Bennington         NE68007
Stier, Hattie G         072865 28140 Bluff Road        Omaha              NE68114
Stiefel, Phyllis R      030476 1174 Pasadena Blvd      Council Bluffs     IA51510
Stienblock, Richard C   102182 206 Shillaelagh Lane    Minden             IA51501
Stiens, Denny R         050778 13133 Calhoun Road      California Junction IA51623
Stier, James T          062397 1943 Burdette St.       Blair              NE68008
Stierman, Roger E       041268 7557 Josephine Lane     Springfield        NE68059
Stigge, William J       033056 13350 Meadows Parkway   Tekamah            NE6801
Stika, Dennis A         021563 1101 Conestoga Road     Malvern            IA51534
Stilen, Jake W          122465 2050 Roundup Cirle      Strahan            IA51578
Stiles, Steve P         110923 13940 Woolworth St.     Murdoch .          NE68407
Stillman, Debra W       070483 13496 Jefferson         Weeping Water      NE68463
Stillwell, Shirley O    081224 1205 Castana Circle     Memphis            NE68042
Stine, Joseph T         012078 18440 Fairview Road     Elk City           NE68022
Stinson, Katrina I      091280 53190 Boyd St.          Pisgah             IA51576
Stirling, Jerome V      032945 9209 Jackson Drive      West Point         NE68788
Stoakes, Susan P        022996 15656 Anderson Way      Wisner             NE68791
Stock, Benjamin F       013159 3344 Corby St.          Neligh             NE68756
Stockton, Jerry B       112233 1943 Woodcrest Lane     Elliott            IA51587
Stockwell, Tonya L      061854 13039 Drexel Plaza      Manning            IA51512
Stoffel, Evert U        022897 5314 Quail Ridge Road   Papillion          NE68046
Stohlman, Frederick S   113067 11890 Mason Drive       Boys Town          NE68010
```

Figure 1-5:
See how little space exists on a typical 80-x-24 terminal?

So simple, so much trouble

Storing the year in two digits instead of four may have saved a significant amount of storage. But it also created the potential to cause momentous problems when date comparisons or calculations are performed. The root of the problem is that a baseline assumption will soon be invalid. When systems were designed with dates stored in two digits, an implied understanding was that the value in the two century positions was 19. When the clock advances past 12/31/1999 into the 21st century, programs and systems based on that assumption will no longer function correctly.

After 12/31/1999, date comparisons based on two-digit year values will probably be incorrect. Take a hypothetical case of an insurance policy application. One of the dates provided by the applicant is date of birth. If the applicant was born on November 22, 1956, this is coded and stored as 561122.

To calculate the applicant's age, the program subtracts the year of birth from the current year (such as 99 - 56, which results in 43). If the current year is 1999 or less, this algorithm works as intended. The calculation, however, is slightly more complicated than this. Here's the pseudocode for the complete calculations that must be performed:

```
IF Present Month > Month of Birth THEN
     Age = Present Year - Year of Birth
ELSEIF Present Month = Month of Birth AND
          Present Day >= Day of Birth THEN
     Age = Present Year - Year of Birth
ELSE Age = Present Year - Year of Birth - 1
```

If this hypothetical application were processed on or after 1/1/2000, the results would differ significantly. The calculation during the year 2000 becomes 00 - 56, which results in a value of -56. The insurance company won't write premiums for people who haven't been born yet, so the application would almost certainly be rejected. If the software isn't corrected, it could be some time before the company can issue new policies. When an insurance company is unable to write new policies, how can it stay in business?

Two bytes seem like such a small thing. Indeed, by themselves they are fairly insignificant. When multiplied millions (or billions) of times, however, they become very significant. Likewise, the programming statements to subtract or accurately compare dates is trivial. Only when it is repeated hundreds (or thousands) of times in hundreds of programs does it cause trouble.

PC Problems with the 21st Century

The second year 2000 problem is a hardware problem. Every PC contains instructions permanently written (burned) into memory. These instructions control the most primitive functions of the system and are collectively called the basic input/output system, or BIOS.

System date #1

PCs from the AT class onwards store and maintain dates in two locations. One copy of the system date is stored in the CMOS real-time clock chip. This piece of hardware is normally located on the computer's motherboard. The date maintained in this chip is in the form of a one-digit century and two digits each for the year, the month, and the day (CYYMMDD). An onboard battery maintains this time even when the computer is turned off or unplugged.

System date #2

The other place where your PC stores a date value is in the operating system software. Each time DOS boots, it reads the current date and time from the real-time clock chip. DOS then converts this date to a format that includes a four-digit year value (YYYYMMDD). Figure 1-6 shows how both dates are stored in an IBM-compatible PC.

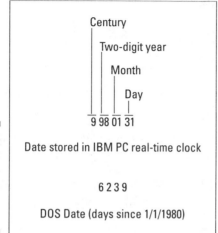

Century

Two-digit year

Month

Day

9 98 01 31

Date stored in IBM PC real-time clock

6 2 3 9

DOS Date (days since 1/1/1980)

Figure 1-6:
CMOS
system time
and DOS
system
time.

Never the twain shall meet

Representing the year in three digits (CYY) in the real-time clock is the cause of PC-related date problems. When the year 1999 rolls over to 2000, the date in the clock will be 0000101. There's no placeholder for the millennium digit, so this information is lost. The next time the operating system requests the date, it will be passed an incorrect value.

In many PCs, if the BIOS code receives a flawed date, the code converts the date to an incorrect system date. The most common incorrect date is January 1, 1980.

You will be confronted with this problem the first time your computer is rebooted in the year 2000. The operating system will likely act as though the year is 1980. How many applications will be relying on this flawed date? Each is likely to behave in an unpredictable and essentially incorrect manner.

The Leap Year Conundrum

The third year 2000 problem addressed here won't show up on January 1, 2000. In fact, you won't experience it until two months after New Year's Day. This problem is concerned with whether or not the year 2000 is a leap year.

On a collision course with complacency

One of the biggest contributing factors to the year 2000 situation is complacency. Too many MIS directors, managers, and their organizations aren't convinced that their organization will encounter problems with the year 2000. They are basing their confidence not on research but on secondhand knowledge or wishful thinking.

Another justification for delaying immediate action is the belief that a "silver bullet" will become available between now and January 1, 2000. Some individuals hope that all their year 2000 problems will be solved by the development of a powerful tool — like the legendary weapon that could kill werewolves. Sorry, folks. It isn't going to happen!

The problem is too complex and the software is too diverse to be corrected by a single tool. Although better tools are constantly being developed, the correction of each problem still requires substantial time and effort as well as the intervention of a human being. Waiting for a one-size-fits-all solution isn't a prudent plan; it simply wastes the precious little time still available to you.

A leap year doesn't occur every four years. It occurs every year that is divisible by 4 and also divisible by 400 if the year ends in two zeros. For example, 1700, 1800, 1900, 2100, and 2200 are divisible by 4, but are not leap years because they are not divisible by 400. On the other hand, 1600, 2000, and 2400 are divisible by 4 and 400 and are therefore leap years. See the "Who put the leap in leap years?" sidebar for all the exciting details.

What does this definition of a leap year have to do with computer programs? Programmers can implement the first part of the leap year rule easily, by determining whether the year is evenly divisible by 4. If the year is divisible by 4, February in that year has 29 days. And, because a leap year occurs every fourth year, it's easy to determine whether the logic has been implemented correctly.

Slightly more complicated logic must be used to determine whether a year meets the second aspect of the leap year requirements: If a year ending in 00 isn't evenly divisible by 400, it isn't a leap year. The problem is determining whether or not this part of the procedure has been properly implemented. The year 2000 will be the first time the second part of the leap year rule has occurred since computers were invented. A lot of programs out there haven't exercised that piece of code in a production environment. Have they all correctly included and accurately programmed the second part of the leap year rule? You'll find out on February 29, 2000 — or will it be March 1, 2000?

Who put the leap in leap years?

In 46 B.C. Julius Caesar, the Emperor of Rome, took action to correct the calendar then used by Rome. At that time, the calendar was so far out of sequence with the sun that winter was arriving in October. He decreed that the year 46 B.C. should have 445 days to properly align the calendar with the sun. He also made a permanent change to the calendar. Old Julius established that every fourth year should include 366 days instead of the normal 365. This additional day was his attempt to keep the calendar synchronized with the sun. The year with an extra day is what we call a leap year.

Unfortunately, the calculations used by Julius Caesar's astronomers were close, but not perfect. The Earth doesn't take 365 1/4 days to circle the sun. The precise time is 365 days, 5 hours, 48 minutes, and 45.66 seconds. Although this difference is small, over the centuries it adds up. Every 128 years, the Julian calendar is in error by one day.

By the year 1582, another adjustment was needed. Pope Gregory XIII decreed that the date October 5 would be followed by October 15. This corrected errors in the calendar system that had accumulated over the previous centuries. This new calendar was referred to as the Gregorian calendar.

To prevent further occurrences of this problem, the original implementation of leap year was slightly modified. Exceptions would be made to the rule that a leap year occurs every four years. Now, leap years would occur every year that is evenly divisible by 4, except for years ending in two zeros (1800, 1900, 2000) that are not evenly divisible by 400. Thus, the years 1800 and 1900 are not leap years because they aren't evenly divisible by 400. The year 2000 is evenly divisible by 400 and therefore is a leap year.

The Worst That Could Happen

I hope I've convinced you that the year 2000 is a significant problem. You might question whether it will be as big a problem as people are making it out to be. Reset the dates in a few PCs. Expand some dates in some files. Verify that leap years are being properly identified. That doesn't sound too complicated, does it?

To truly judge the potential effect of this problem, you need to think big and bad, really big and bad. Imagine the computers that enable the stock market to function shutting down. What if the phone system collapsed? The computers that make up the FAA air traffic control system are shaky already. Will they be able to function in the year 2000? Speaking of shaky, how about the IRS computer systems! What if all credit card processing suddenly halted? Some industry experts predict that many American companies could go bankrupt due to this problem.

The year 2000 problem won't affect just impersonal corporations. It has the potential to affect each of us in our personal lives. Suppose that your bank account and stock brokerage account records were lost. Imagine Social Security and other government checks not being issued to their intended recipients. What if every bill you received after 1/1/2000 (such as mortgage, credit card, utilities, and insurance premiums) declared that your account is decades overdue? How many credit records would be ruined by such an occurrence? This is the sort of worst-case scenario you need to envision.

The U.S. auto industry has moved from a practice of stockpiling needed parts to relying on a "just in time" delivery from their suppliers. If the supplier of crucially needed parts doesn't deliver them on time, the entire production line could be shut down. How many suppliers do the major automakers depend on? Isn't it likely that one or more of these suppliers will be unable to make deliveries due to year 2000 problems? How many auto workers will be laid off until production is restored?

These are just a few of the most significant catastrophes that could happen. If even one of them were to come true, our modern, highly efficient world could quickly degenerate into chaos.

You could be affected in a myriad of other unpredictable ways. Is your place of employment in a multistory office building? Some computerized elevators in office buildings turn off every weekend to save energy. They also shut down if they haven't been serviced on predefined maintenance schedules. If these elevators don't correctly handle the year 2000, they might miscalculate the day of the week or when they require their next periodic maintenance servicing. That means they probably won't function as expected on the first workday in the year 2000.

Who Will Get Sued?

Few people will disagree with the assertion that we live in the most litigious society that has ever existed. Add to this the potential for serious financial damages from the year 2000 situation. Many organizations and individuals will be saying, "Who can I sue?" (Hey, programmers and managers knew that the year 2000 would arrive eventually.)

The Gartner Group estimates that it will cost American organizations up to $600 billion to correct the year 2000 problem. They further estimate that litigation resulting from this problem could reach $1 trillion!

Some grounds for lawsuits include:

- ✓ Credit card holders suing card issuers for damaging their credit history
- ✓ Homeowners suing utilities for improperly cutting off utility services

Year 2000 problems that are already here

Year 2000 problems are already occurring. The examples listed here were reported in both the computer trade press as well as general interest sources such as magazines and newspapers.

Computers have refused to accept credit cards because the expiration date on them is 00. This has happened both when the cardholder tried to use the card in a store and when the card was inserted into an ATM. The short-term solution was to recall all credit cards with this expiration date.

Senior citizens have been sent letters stating that they have been enrolled in kindergarten. The computer has mistaken people born in 1892 to be 5 years old in 1997. Along the same lines, senior citizens have also been sent to pediatric wards in hospitals.

An aluminum refinery in New Zealand experienced a computer date-related problem that cost over $1 million (New Zealand currency) to correct. The problem was that the computer didn't recognize that the year 1996 was a leap year. Due to this, the computers hung up and several pot cells overheated and were damaged beyond repair. Although this problem wasn't specifically year 2000 related, it is indicative of problems that will occur.

People attempting to rent cars have been refused because their driver's license expired in the year 2000. The computers at these car rental companies interpret licenses with dates beyond 1999 as being expired.

Computer systems have already attempted to dispose of food that they interpreted as having exceeded its legal expiration date because the expiration date was in 2000 or later.

Criminals have been released from prison due to year 2000 date problems. Their release date was in the next century (for example, 2005), but the computer system stored it as 05. Another program read the 05 value and assumed that it meant 1905. Because the present date is after 1905, the computer acted as though the criminals had already served their entire sentences.

At a local year 2000 user group, one of the attendees told of a year 2000 incident. A friend of his was purchasing a new truck. He looked at the printout of the loan repayment schedule. The last payment was scheduled for June 1, 2103. That is one long-term truck loan!

At this point, the problems are fairly uncommon, but how much more severe will these problems become before they are corrected?

  ✔ Stockholders suing corporate officers for loss of their investment

  ✔ Customers suing suppliers for not providing materials on schedule

Almost any organization with computers is a potential target, but you will be at less risk if you have solved your year 2000 problems or made good faith efforts towards doing so. You should discuss your year 2000 liability exposure with an experienced attorney.

Affected Hardware and Software

Just about every piece of hardware and software you own is a potential victim of this problem! You can't assume that any piece of computer equipment is safe until it has been tested and cleared. Affected hardware ranges from the smallest computers to the largest. Software embedded on chips, desktop PCs, database and file servers, network routers, and mainframe computers needs to be examined.

Mainframe computers

Many people think that the year 2000 problem will affect only COBOL programs running on mainframe computers. This misconception does have a grain of truth. Mainframe computers and the applications that run on them will be heavily affected by the year 2000. Almost all these systems use six digits to store dates. They also need to be examined for proper leap year calculations.

Embedded microcomputers and microcontrollers

Microchips are embedded in a plethora of consumer products, including microwave ovens, VCRs, fax machines, automobiles, security systems, and automatic sprinkler systems. These chips contain software. Because the chips are inside other devices, it will be very difficult to find, test, and correct all such devices.

An article in the May 19, 1997, issue of *Computerworld* highlighted some of the potential problems with embedded chips, including the following:

- Some elevators have embedded chips that monitor the last time the elevator was serviced. If the maintenance schedule isn't maintained, the elevator shuts down.

- Security systems rely heavily on date and time values. If their embedded chips haven't been properly programmed to handle the year 2000, you might not be as safe as you thought you were.

- Bank vaults are locked and unlocked based on the time and date. If you're planning on accessing your safety deposit box on January 3, 2000, you might have to wait a while.

- One manufacturer of heart defibrillators recalled a shipment of their product. According to congressional testimony, these devices wouldn't work if the date was advanced into the year 2000.

Microcontrollers are used to control a variety of industrial equipment in nuclear power plants, security systems, petrochemical refineries, and water purification systems, among many others. Will these be able to function in the year 2000? No one knows for sure. What will the impact be if they don't function correctly? No one knows the answer to that question either.

How many microchips are hidden under the hood of a modern automobile? The answer might surprise you. An article in the June 2, 1997, issue of *Newsweek* stated that as many as 100 chips are in some cars. If one chip fails, what's the effect — simply an inconvenience or a life-threatening situation? Would the car not start or would the brakes not work? The same *Newsweek* article quoted experts who said that if those chips aren't year 2000 compliant, you can forget about driving.

If your organization produces systems of this type, you must test them thoroughly. If you use these products (and who doesn't?), you should contact the manufacturer. See the "Can you trust your vendor?" sidebar in this chapter.

PCs and their applications

One class of software frequently overlooked consists of applications running on PCs. Your accounts payable system, developed in-house, may not be able to properly function into the next century due to two-digit year limitations. The Human Resources Information System (HRIS) package you just purchased may reference library modules that aren't year 2000 compliant. Any application that deals with dates is suspect until it's been proved otherwise.

Even your spreadsheet and personal finance tools are potential sources of problems come January 1, 2000. A number of packages used on PCs have known year 2000 problems. Some now have workarounds. Other products will need to be upgraded.

Networks

Computer networks are another source of year 2000 problems. Network bridges, routers, and gateways frequently maintain tables based on the time stamps embedded in communications packets. Only the most recent routing information is kept in these tables. Statistics gathered from older packets are discarded. If the time stamps are incorrect due to a year 2000 problem, how accurate will the resulting tables be? An incorrect year value might result in the most recent information being thrown out.

To make matters worse, network computers are rarely (if ever) accompanied by their source code. Identifying, testing, and correcting problems without the source code is significantly more difficult. If problems are uncovered, you have to rely on the vendor to correct them.

Each network computer must be identified and individually tested. Due to the large number of platforms, packages, and versions, it isn't safe to test a single computer and assume that if it works, so will other computers by the same vendor.

Servers

Many computer systems include two types of computers: servers and clients. A server provides services for client computers. The PC on your desktop is a client. When you use an application on your PC, it requests the necessary information from the server.

As the world of computers becomes more interconnected, the importance of servers becomes paramount:

- ✔ **File servers and print servers** have been around since the beginning of the network. They enable multiple users to share expensive pieces of equipment, such as big disk drives and printers.

- ✔ **Fax servers** allow a group of users to share a pool of telephone lines for fax operations. This avoids having to run telephone lines to each user's desk.

- ✔ **Database servers and application servers** are part of client/server computer systems. Database servers receive and process requests from client machines for information from a common database. Application servers contain programs that provide a way to centralize all business rules in a single location. (Some examples of business rules are: Don't extend additional credit to a customer whose account is overdue, don't ship and order if a method of payment hasn't been defined, and don't issue a refund if the client owes you money.) This allows enterprise-wide systems to share the same business rules without duplicating them on every user's computer.

Any computer that acts as a server must be rigorously tested for year 2000 related problems. Why the extra attention? If a server is unavailable, it affects a large number of users. An entire department could be idled if the database server isn't operational.

Can you trust your vendor?

I hate to sound like a rabble-rouser, but it isn't completely safe to rely on a vendor's verbal assurances that his or her product is year 2000 compliant. (A vendor's representative assured me that a certain application package was capable of operating on dates into the next millennium. The first time a user tried to schedule an event to occur after 12/31/99, the system displayed an invalid date message. I'm not implying that the vendor purposefully lied to me; I think the vendor had an unrealistic amount of confidence in the product's obviously untested year 2000 capabilities.)

When (not if) a vendor gives you automatic assurances that a product is year 2000 compliant, ask for proof of this claim. Your attitude should be one of "trust but verify." Request a summary of the testing that has been performed on the product or system. Ask the vendor to demonstrate the product's capabilities on your system. If everything works as claimed, wonderful. If it isn't quite as capable as the vendor thought, you've both discovered something.

In an article in the June 9, 1997, issue (page 6) of *Computerworld,* some analysts predict that up to 35 percent of vendor software might not work in the year 2000. Isn't it likely that your systems might be included in this 35 percent of the software? You can find out in two ways. The first is to test the software now. The second is to wait until January 1, 2000, and be surprised.

Start Early

Starting early on your year 2000 problem is the most important decision you can make. Here are some reasons why you should start your year 2000 project as early as possible:

- **You can't postpone the date.** This project is one of the few in your data processing or business career with a deadline that can't be postponed. No matter how much you pay or pray, the first day of the year 2000 will follow the last day of December 1999.

- **The sooner you start, the sooner you can discover what you must do**. The year 2000 project, like most software projects, will probably require more time, effort, and people than your initial estimates. If you start early and run into problems, you'll have a chance to still finish before the deadline.

- **Resources may be unavailable later.** There's a physical limit to the human resources available to solve this problem. In simpler terms, only so many programmers (COBOL or otherwise) are out there. Delaying your start makes it all the more likely that this pool of valuable resources will be occupied by the time you attempt to hire from it. You may be forced to pay higher wages, get by with fewer people, or accept personnel with less experience than you expected.

✔ **A limit exists to the number of people you can add to shorten the timetable.** Software projects can't be subdivided into an indefinite number of tasks, with each task performed simultaneously. Two classic examples in everyday life illustrate this principle. The first is that one woman can bear a child in nine months, but nine women can't give birth to a child in a single month. The other example is that if a cake bakes for 35 minutes at 350 degrees (Fahrenheit), you can't double the temperature to halve the baking time. So too with software projects — their schedules can be compressed only so much, even if you throw unlimited resources at them.

✔ **Adding people to a late project may make it even later.** Even if you can locate and afford more resources to your project team, a limit exists to how quickly the work can be accomplished. Adding staff to a project requires a corresponding increase in the level of intrateam communications. In the classic book on software development, *The Mythical Man-Month* (published by Addison Wesley Longman), Frederick Brooks states that adding people to a late project can make it later.

Start early, and you can avoid many of these problems.

Chapter 2

Correcting Problems with PCs

· ·

In This Chapter

▶ Setting the time on your PC

▶ Correcting your PC

▶ Identifying BIOS chips

▶ Testing all your PCs

▶ Keeping track of which PCs have been corrected

· ·

*I*f any single part of the year 2000 problem can be considered simple, it's testing individual PCs. Identifying PCs with BIOS problems consists of a few easy steps. When you've finished this chapter, you'll be able to identify PCs that need correcting and understand the steps you can take to repair them.

Testing and repairing an individual PC is easy to do, and you'll know quickly whether or not the machine has a problem. When your organization has hundreds, thousands, or even tens of thousands of PCs, however, testing becomes time-consuming.

Testing a PC's BIOS

A survey conducted by the year 2000 consulting group headed by Peter de Jager estimates that 95 percent of all PCs will fail a simple year 2000 test. This failure occurs because the computer's BIOS (basic input/output system) doesn't properly handle a four-digit year value. *ComputerWeekly,* a British publication, tested 500 PCs containing BIOS chips marked with a manufacture date of 1997. The test found that 47 percent were not year 2000 compliant. The article further stated that 97 percent of pre-1997 BIOS chips couldn't correctly roll over from 1999 to 2000. These results emphasize how important it is to test all PCs in your organizations.

Actually, two tests should be performed. The first determines whether the real-time clock (RTC) chip maintains a millennium value when the year rolls over from 1999 to 2000. The second test verifies that the real-time clock (RTC) will maintain a year value of 2000 across a reboot operation.

Before running either test, I recommend taking some precautions. First, disconnect the PC if it is connected to a network or any other system. (The PC might obtain a time and date value from another network device instead of its own RTC when it boots, which invalidates the year 2000 testing.) Second, close all applications running on the computer. If any problems do occur, you want to minimize their effect. Invalidating data files, spreadsheets, and so on won't make the testing go any faster or easier — and it surely won't make you popular with the computer's owner.

Setting the time on your PC

The PC tests described here all require that you change the time on your PC. You can set the time and date on a PC in at least three ways. I describe them from the least difficult to the most difficult.

Here's the easiest way to change the current time and date:

1. **Go to the Control Panel.**

2. **Click on the Date/Time icon.**

    The Date/Time Properties dialog box appears.

3. **Click on the Date & Time tab.**

4. **In the Date section, change the date to December 31, 1999.**

    See Figure 2-1.

5. **In the Time section, change the time to something close to midnight, such as 11:58:00 PM.**

6. **Click on OK.**

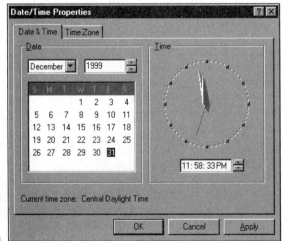

Figure 2-1:
Setting the
date using
the Control
Panel.

The next easiest way to change the time and date is with DOS commands:

1. **Open a DOS session. In Windows 95, click on Start, choose Programs, and then choose MS-DOS Prompt. On a Windows 3.1 system, open the Main program group and double-click on MS-DOS Prompt.**

2. **Type the command** `time` **and press Enter.**

   The command echoes the current time and requests that you enter a new time value.

3. **Enter a time in the format hh:mm:ss. You can specify an *a* or a *p* to designate AM or PM, respectively.**

4. **Next, type the command** `date` **and press Enter.**

   The command echoes the current date and requests that you enter a new date value.

5. **Type a date in the format mm-dd-yy and press Enter.**

   See Figure 2-2.

6. **Close the DOS session by typing** `exit` **and pressing the Enter key.**

The third way to set the time on your computer isn't a pretty sight. You must get into the setup screen when your computer boots. The technique for doing this differs depending on the machine you have, so you'll need to

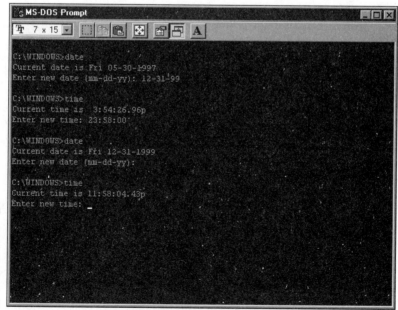

Figure 2-2:
Setting
the date
using DOS
commands.

consult your documentation. (For many machines, getting into the setup screen requires that you press a specific key at a designated time during the boot process.) After you get into the setup screen, follow the instructions for setting the date and time.

Real-time clock rollover test (test #1)

Here are the steps to take to test whether your IBM-compatible PC will properly roll over from 12/31/1999 to 1/1/2000:

1. **Set the system date to December 31, 1999.**
2. **Set the system time to 11:58:00 PM.**

   That's 23:58 for you 24-hour-clock types.

3. **Verify that you set the time and date accurately by going back to the Control Panel Date/Time window and examining the time and date.**
4. **Shut down Windows.**
5. **Turn off your computer.**
6. **Wait at least five minutes.**
7. **Turn on your computer.**
8. **After your computer finishes booting, check the date and time. (To do so, see Step 3.)**

   The current date and time should be the values you just entered.

Real-time clock year 2000 (test #2)

Your PC might be able to roll over from 1999 to 2000, but not be able to retain the year 2000 across the next reboot. Therefore, you should follow the next steps to test whether or not your IBM-compatible PC will maintain a date beyond 12/31/1999 across a reboot operation:

1. **Set the system date to January 1, 2000.**
2. **Verify that the date was set by going into the Date/Time window in the Control Panel.**
3. **Exit from Windows.**
4. **Turn off your computer.**
5. **Wait at least two minutes.**
6. **Turn on your computer.**

7. **After your computer finishes booting, check the date and time by going to the Date/Time window in the Control Panel. (You can check the date and time also by opening a DOS session and using the date and time commands.)**

The time displayed should be the same as before, but the date should now be January 1, 2000.

A software consulting firm I interviewed while researching this topic suggested that the second test (to test whether the PC can maintain the date over a reboot) be performed several times. The consultants said they have encountered PCs that pass this test after the first reboot, but fail the test after subsequent reboot operations. To verify that your PC doesn't have this problem, you should repeat Steps 1 through 7 of the second test several times.

If either of the two tests failed to display the year 2000 after being rebooted, the PC will have a problem when the real year 2000 arrives. If your PC performed flawlessly, you can skip the rest of this chapter because your PC won't require any of the corrections that I describe here.

When I ran these tests on the two PCs I own, one failed both and the other passed both. The PC that passed is a Pentium-based machine; the other is a 486 machine. The date displayed on the 486-based machine after rebooting the first time was 1/4/80.

To see how a common Windows program handles the year 2000, create a file with Notepad, Paint, Write, or another program. Then go into File Manager (or Windows Explorer for Windows 95 and NT) and examine the creation date for the file.

In File Manager for Windows 3.1, the date you see will be 1/1/:0, as shown in Figure 2-3. The date displayed in Windows 95 Explorer is 1/1/00, as shown in Figure 2-4. Neither File Manager nor Explorer displays four-digit year values. Sounds like an upgrade problem to me.

Reset your computer to the current date and time. You don't want to annoy or inconvenience the next user of the computer.

Correcting Year 2000 Problems

Okay, you've established that one or more of your PCs has a year 2000 related problem. Where do you go from here? You're going to correct the problem, of course. This section outlines three ways to do so — I hope your PC can be solved the easy way.

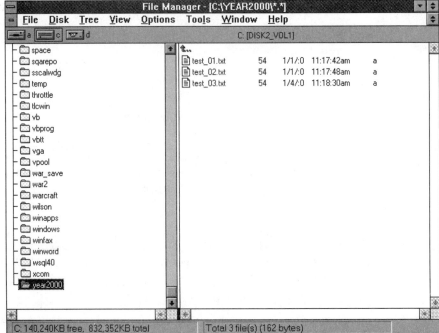

Figure 2-3:
File
Manager
displaying
the year
2000.

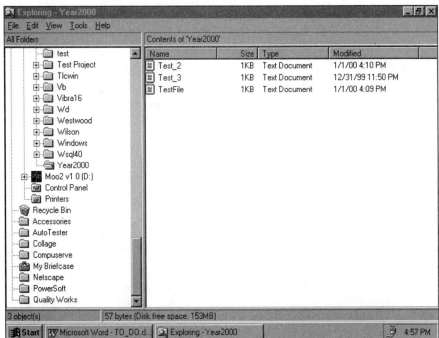

Figure 2-4:
Explorer
displaying
the year
2000.

Manually updating the year

If the PC you just tested failed the first test but passed the second one, congratulations. This machine is in fairly good shape. Although the PC won't correctly roll over the year value from 1999 to 2000, it can maintain the year 2000 across a reboot.

The only action you need to take on this PC is to reset the year to 2000 on (or after) New Year's Day 2000. If this is your machine, leave yourself a note. If it belongs to someone else, remind the owner on the first working day of the year 2000. If you have e-mail, you can send a message on New Year's Eve 1999 or on January 3, 2000.

 You may want to test one more little thing on this machine. Set the time and date to December 31, 2000, at 23:58:00. Turn off the power and wait a few minutes. When you reboot, what's the date? If it's 2001, great. If it isn't, you'll probably have to reset the year value every January 1 from now on. Make a note of this in your records, too.

Replacing the BIOS in a flash

All BIOS chips were not created equal. Some memory chips that hold BIOS information can be written to more than once; others cannot be written to after they have been initialized (burned). A BIOS chip that can be modified without being physically replaced is referred to as a *flash BIOS*. Changes can be made permanently through software procedures. This is much better than having to replace the chip with a new one.

You can tell whether your computer contains a flash BIOS in several ways. If you saved the documentation that came with the PC, check it out. It might tell you exactly what type of memory chip the BIOS is using.

The second method is simple but takes more time. Ask the computer's manufacturer. If you provide the model number and the serial number of your PC, the manufacturer should be able to tell you what's inside.

 The final method is for only the most adventurous. It requires that you remove the cover of the computer and physically examine the BIOS chip. When doing this, make sure that you follow the instructions that accompany the machine. Don't forget to unplug the computer and discharge any static electricity your body might have built up. Static electricity can be discharged by touching the chassis of the computer. Forgetting to unplug the computer could be fatal to you; forgetting to discharge any static electricity could prove fatal to your PC.

Because of the great variety of personal computer manufacturers and models, I can't describe the exact location of the BIOS chip in your computer. Its location should be provided in your system documentation.

After you locate the BIOS chip, notice the markings on its back. The following is a list of designations that identify flash memory chips:

- 28Fxxx — 12-volt flash memory
- 29Cxxx — 5-volt flash memory
- 29LVxxx — 3-volt flash memory
- 28Cxxx — EEPROM memory, similar to flash memory
- 27Cxxx — EPROM memory, requires a UV light source to modify
- PH29EE010 — Flash memory
- 29EE011 — 5-volt flash memory
- 29C010 — 5-volt flash memory

If the chip has one of these codes, you should be able to update its BIOS instructions. Next, you need a computer file containing the new BIOS commands for your computer. The file must come from the computer maker or company that produced the BIOS program.

You might also be able to get this upgrade file from the Internet. First, look under the Support area of your PC manufacturer's home page on the World Wide Web (WWW). I provide the Web pages of a number of computer manufacturers here. Figure 2-5 shows IBM's Web page for downloading BIOS files. Compaq's Web page is displayed in Figure 2-6. The Web page provided by Gateway 2000 is shown in Figure 2-7, and the Web page offered by Acer is shown in Figure 2-8.

If an update is available, the manufacturer should also provide detailed instructions on how you go about installing it.

Here are addresses for some of the more popular PC manufacturers:

Manufacturer	Web Address
IBM	www.ibm.com
Compaq	www.compaq.com
Gateway	www.gw2000.com
Dell	www.dell.com
Packard Bell	www.packardbell.com

If the file is not available on the Internet, the manufacturer might provide the upgrade program on a disk. Contact the PC manufacturer for instructions on getting the upgrade program. They may direct you to the BIOS vendor. Either way, follow the installation instructions exactly.

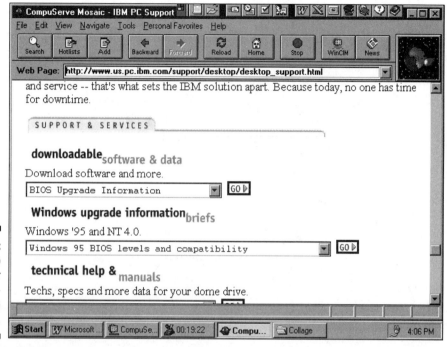

Figure 2-5:
IBM Web page for downloading BIOS files.

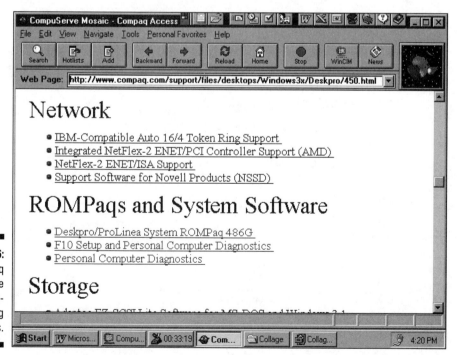

Figure 2-6:
Compaq Web page for downloading BIOS files.

Figure 2-7:
Gateway
2000 Web
page for
down-
loading
BIOS files.

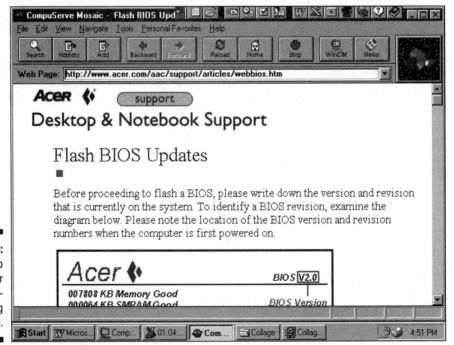

Figure 2-8:
Acer Web
page for
down-
loading
BIOS files.

After you complete the flash upgrade, your PC should be capable of recognizing when it has rolled over to 1/1/2000. Repeating the year 2000 tests would be a smart thing to do.

Flipping in a new chip

If you have determined that your PC's BIOS can't be upgraded with a software update, you need to replace the chip itself. Contact the manufacturer; it'll provide the chip as well as instructions on how to install it. As always, follow the installation instructions exactly.

Installing memory chips, I've found, is harder than adding a card to your PC but easier than changing your spark plugs. Having small hands and strong fingernails helps, too.

After you've installed the new chip, repeat the year 2000 BIOS tests. (See the section, "Testing a PC's BIOS.") If it appears that the problem hasn't been corrected, contact the manufacturer again.

Handling the year 2000 problem with software

If your BIOS can't be replaced, or you simply don't feel like getting under the hood of your PC, the problem can be addressed another way. The fundamental problem you're dealing with is that, after 12/31/1999, the date DOS calculates is incorrect. One solution is to let DOS calculate that incorrect date and then moments later overwrite it with the correct one. A number of software products claim to correct the problem in this manner. Figure 2-9 illustrates how such a program works. These types of programs can be initiated by the autoexec.bat file or via the Startup folder, whichever is more appropriate.

One software package that claims to correct the dates in PCs is Y2KPCPro from The RighTime Company. Its phone number is 305-644-6500. Its Web address is www.RighTime.com.

If you decide to take this approach, you have a few decisions to make. First, choose and acquire the program you'll be using. Don't settle on a program until you've had the chance to test it thoroughly. If the program is freeware, you'll have the opportunity to test it before paying for it. If the program is a commercial product, make sure that it comes with a money back guarantee before you break open the shrink wrap.

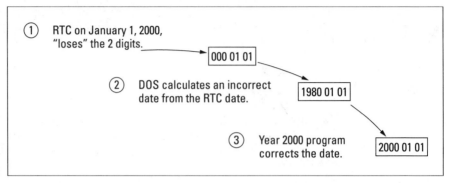

Figure 2-9:
Using
software
to correct
an invalid
real-time
clock date.

Your testing should include installing the product on a representative selection of the PCs in your organization. You might also want to test it across a number of year-end situations, both 1999 and otherwise.

If you plan on installing the product on more than one PC, find out whether your license allows this. Frequently, software products offer a corporate license, which is significantly less costly than purchasing a bunch of individual licenses.

After you're properly licensed, install the product on all PCs that exhibit this problem. If you're dealing with a large number of PCs, you may want to distribute the tool to users instead of installing the product on all PCs yourself. The installation procedure can be as simple as copying the file onto the hard drive and inserting an entry in the AUTOEXEC.BAT file. If you go this route, write explicit instructions telling users what they need to do. Emphasize that they shouldn't hesitate to contact you if they have any questions.

Here's a hypothetical entry in an AUTOEXEC.BAT file that initiates the correction program. It assumes that the program is named fix2000.exe and is located in the root director of the C drive:

```
c:\fix2000.exe
```

Like Snowflakes, No Two PCs Are Alike

From the outside, most PCs look similar. Almost all are painted the same off-white color. Some PCs stand on their sides, and others lay flat on your desk, but they all have pretty much the same boxy look about them.

Spreading the wealth

If your organization has a lot of PCs, you need to develop a schedule for testing each of them. Identifying and correcting any one PC may take only a short time, but doing the same for hundreds of PCs means that your evenings will be booked for a long, long time. If you don't have a count of how many machines there are, you won't be able to make an accurate estimate of how long it will take you to perform this task.

One way to handle this effort is to divide the work among all PC "owners" in your organization. You can consider sending each PC user explicit instructions on how to test his or her own machine. You should instruct them to respond to you whether or not their PC appears to have a problem. You can then schedule a visit to each machine identified as possibly having a year 2000 problem. This approach

at least saves you from the effort of testing each PC.

This approach involves some risk. Users who don't understand your instructions might be reluctant to admit it. They also might not get around to running the test and not respond to your requests.

When should you begin testing PCs? As soon as possible. The only downside to starting early is that you might test PCs that will be retired before the year 2000. I don't think you should skip the testing of older PCs unless you are absolutely certain that they will be replaced. (Remember, computer hardware designated for replacement often ends up hanging around for a long time.) If you don't test early, you might have an overwhelming task right before the crucial date.

Although most PCs are similar on the outside, they can be surprisingly different inside. Once inside that off-white metal shell, you never know which corporation has supplied which parts. Motherboards, chips, and the BIOS software may have been obtained from a variety of sources.

In addition, you may not know the history of each PC. Hardware problems or user requests may have resulted in change. Most upgrades involve parts from different vendors. As a result, each PC becomes a nonstandard, unique piece of equipment.

Even two computers from the same manufacturer can contain significantly different parts inside. Most PC manufacturers rely on suppliers for their low-level components. Moreover, the same manufacturer might use a number of different suppliers over time. Therefore, you can't guarantee that two PCs from the same manufacturer will respond the same way to your year 2000 testing.

It's time to get up on my soapbox. PC manufacturers are doing the industry and themselves a disservice by not providing more assistance in this area. They should be contacting PC owners and informing them as to whether or not their PC is compliant. For PCs that aren't, they should provide assistance in meeting this requirement. When the consumers bought these computers, they had every right to assume that the machines would continue to function beyond the year 2000.

This means that you need to test every PC in your organization. Even when two PCs appear to be identical, they can still be significantly different on the inside. One may pass your year 2000 testing, but the other may fail. You won't know which is which until you test them all.

Desktop PCs

Desktop PCs should be easy to find and test. They sit up so proudly in people's offices or cubicles. You just need to look around to find all these specimens.

Laptop PCs

Laptop PCs will be a smidgen harder to corner because they are frequently not in the office. Laptop owners are always on the go. They drag the poor things home at night and on the road during the day. It may take some time to coordinate testing, but all laptop computers need to be tested just as much as their desk-locked brethren.

Forgotten PCs

When you're inventorying the PCs in your organization, it's easy to concentrate on the ones immediately visible, that is, the ones right there on everyone's desks. These are easy to spot unless they're covered with post-its and pictures of kids.

When you start snooping around less-frequented areas of the building, you might be surprised what turns up. Many organizations have PCs that are only used for specific purposes. It's easy to overlook computers like this because they don't "belong" to anyone in particular and they may not be used daily. Here are a few examples:

- PCs dedicated to printing labels or specialized forms. These PCs may be tucked away in the back of the mail room. You may find a machine that hasn't been updated in years.

✔ Machines dedicated to printing employee badges. These may be snug as a bug in that little windowless, white room in the Human Resources Department. You haven't been in that room since the day you were hired, but that machine is still there making employee badges every day.

✔ The LAN or server closet. Although the computers here are critical to the organization's mission, they are "out of sight, out of mind." You may be able to test these PCs only when users aren't utilizing them. You may even have to schedule a time when these network computers can be taken out of service to be examined and potentially upgraded.

Tracking Your Efforts

No matter how you plan to handle individual PCs, you must implement one thing from day one. You must keep records on which machines have been tested, which have failed, and which have been corrected. If you don't keep records, you will be unable to track your progress. Figure 2-10 shows a spreadsheet that includes some of the information you might want to consider tracking for each PC.

Tracking this information by manufacturer may provide you with some insight into which PCs are having the most trouble. You shouldn't discontinue testing a particular model, however, just because it has had few or no problems to date. All PCs need to be tested.

See whether your company has a group who tracks furniture, telephones, fixtures, computer equipment, and anything else of value that belongs to the company. (They're often called the "Furniture Police" — or something worse.) They might be able to provide you with a current list of PC hardware. If so, you won't have to prepare the list yourself, and there may be less chance of missing some PCs that need to be tested.

Figure 2-10:
Keeping
track of PCs
that have
been
tested and
corrected.

Manu-facturer	Serial#	Model/Speed	Owner	Location	Network ID	Phone	Tested By	Test Date	Pass/Fail	Corrective Action
Gateway	4825198	P5-120	KCB	M-23	kbourne	7823	KCB	1/5/98	Pass	N/A
Gateway	3132342	4DX-33	ACB	M-15	abourne	4290	ACB	2/1/98	Fail	BIOS upgrade
Gateway	4840678	P5-120	LAG	M-20	lguest	5342	LAG	1/15/98	Pass	N/A
IBM	132450	760ED	EFH	M-33	fjones	4132	KCB	2/1/98	Pass	N/A
IBM	451942	AT 33	TAL	M-17	tlangtry	3190	KCB	2/2/98	Fail	Software fix
IBM	453145	AT 33	ERH	M-45	ehaus	5495	ERH	3/1/98	Fail	Software fix

PC Tools

A number of tools are available that can automatically perform the tests required to identify PCs that will encounter problems rolling over to the year 2000.

One such tool is YR2K Management System from Double E Computer Systems. This tool performs two functions. The first is to determine whether the PC can recognize and retain dates greater than 12/31/1999. The other function is to perform an inventory of all the software loaded onto that machine. The telephone number for Double E Computer Systems is 402-334-7870.

Another tool that can identify PCs with year 2000 problems is Test2000.exe from The RighTime Company. The phone number is 305-644-6500. The web address is www.RighTime.com.

Chapter 3

Protecting Your System from Incoming Data

● ●

In This Chapter

▶ Identifying data that your systems receive from external sources

▶ Analyzing incoming data

▶ Communicating with personnel at the external sources

▶ Scheduling when each data source will be ready

▶ Trusting isn't enough

▶ Agreeing on a common data format

▶ Recognizing and handling "bad" date values

▶ Preparing for potential litigation

● ●

*Y*ou've laid out your plans to locate, correct, and test your systems for the year 2000 crisis. You're hoping that, after this effort is complete, you'll be in good shape for 1/1/2000. Sorry, but you may be in for an awful surprise.

Many pundits feel that data coming into your systems from external sources represents the ultimate year 2000 Trojan Horse. You may have modified your systems, but you need to be aware that not everyone is as conscientious as you and your organization. This chapter addresses what you need to know about the potential for "bad" data coming into your cozy little world from outside sources that aren't so well behaved. The applications that access and process this data are frequently written in-house in languages like COBOL, C, or PL/1.

Electronic Data Interchange: A Way of Life for Computers

It's common for computer systems to receive a significant portion of their input data from other computers. This electronic data interchange, or EDI, has three benefits:

- ✔ It's more efficient to receive data electronically than to manually enter it into your system.
- ✔ Incoming data is available almost immediately.
- ✔ Errors that might be introduced by an additional data entry process are eliminated.

The types of data transferred between computers is limited only by the analyst or developer's imagination. Following are some examples of the types of data moved between different systems:

- ✔ Timekeeping data is transferred between an organization and the vendor who processes the payroll and prints paychecks. The organization has thousands of employees. Every employee is expecting his or her check to be both accurate and on time.
- ✔ The personnel department prepares data pertaining to its payroll savings plan and passes this information to a broker who handles employee mutual fund accounts. If this isn't handled accurately and promptly, the employee, the corporation, and the IRS will be asking the broker a lot of questions.
- ✔ A law firm creates a data file listing billing hours and rates, and then passes it to a client. Each transferred file may contain thousands of records billed to hundreds of different cases. If this information isn't passed correctly, the law firm won't be paid in a timely manner.
- ✔ A state government requires mail order companies to provide a list of its residents who purchased items through the mail. This enables the state to tax its residents who make mail order purchases. Without EDI, the amount of paper involved would swamp both the state's department of commerce and the mail order companies.
- ✔ A franchisee is required to order supplies from the franchise company. There might be thousands of different franchisees around the country. If a paper system were relied on, the orders for replacement supplies couldn't possibly be filled in time.

Data sources for a computer system can be quite varied. Low volumes of data can be contained on $3^1/_2$-inch disks. Larger data volumes can enter the system through communications lines, ranging from dial-up modems to T1 lines. Computer tapes are another avenue for the arrival of large amounts of data. Popular sizes for tapes are 4mm, 8mm, quarter-inch cartridge, and 9-track. Figure 3-1 illustrates some of these types of data sources.

Electronic data interchange also has potential downsides. To some degree, you're at the mercy of the quality of someone else's data. If another company's data is riddled with errors, your computer operations should be prepared to deal with it. One approach is to clean up the errors at the time the data is brought in. You could do this by reading the data into a temporary area and scanning it for mistakes. One example of this is in reconciling area codes and cities. If a credit card applicant lists 712 as the telephone area code and Dallas, Texas, as the zip code, a discrepancy exists. It might be an honest mistake, or it might indicate attempted credit card fraud.

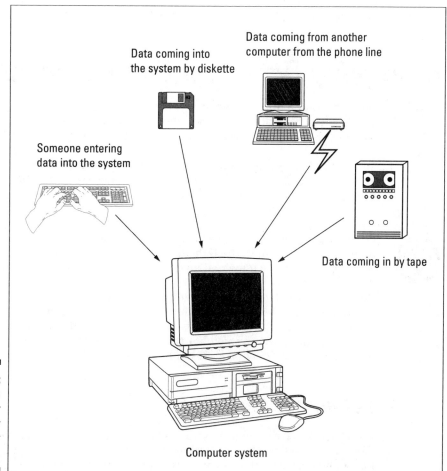

Data coming into the system by diskette

Data coming from another computer from the phone line

Someone entering data into the system

Data coming in by tape

Figure 3-1: Data sources for your computer system.

Computer system

Another method is for users to identify and correct errors as they interact with the system. For example, the customer representative examining this credit card application would be depended upon to recognize the discrepancy between the area code and city.

Neither approach is desirable. Scanning the data as it is brought into the system requires your site to perform one extra step before the data can be used. Relying on the customer representative is risky because some discrepancies will inevitably slip through. It would be so much easier if you could count on receiving error-free data.

The year 2000 has the potential to raise your bad data problems by an order of magnitude or two. Every data source coming into your system must now be examined to determine whether it contains date related information. You must plan how you will handle each individual date field — at both the sending and receiving ends of the data communications transfer.

Identifying Data from External Sources

You know that a potential year 2000 problem exists with data received by your system. How do you begin to deal with it? Your first step is to examine where and how data comes into your computer systems.

To identify external sources, the year 2000 team members need to scrutinize your systems. They must talk to programmers, users, and managers about where the systems get their data. No single group is likely to remember all external sources, so talk to everyone.

People tend to overlook external sources that have been in place for a long time. This is especially true if the data source has been well-behaved — working without much manual intervention and relatively error free.

Another way to identify external sources is to examine system documentation of programs developed by your internal staff. Diagrams of computer systems typically show all input sources, with cute little symbols of tapes, disks, or punch cards (remember those?). This information can be very useful for tracking down sources of data.

Follow the data

During the Watergate investigation, informant Deep Throat, told reporters Woodward and Bernstein to "follow the money." My advice to you is to follow the data. To get into your system, data must arrive on some kind of medium. Look around for those arrival methods, and you'll locate the external sources.

Computer tapes

Computer tape is a common method for inputting data. Examples of computer tape are the following:

> ✔ Nine-track reels of tape are commonly associated with mainframe computers.
>
> ✔ Quarter-inch cartridge tapes are used on midrange computers. Many UNIX platforms have tape drives that read this size of cartridge tapes.
>
> ✔ 8 mm and 4 mm tapes are now being used on PCs as well as servers.

Identifying systems that receive tapes as input shouldn't be too hard. Just look for computers with stacks of tapes next to them! This may sound trite, but it's a realistic statement. Incoming tapes need to be stored somewhere, and that somewhere is frequently close to the computer on which the data is loaded.

Electronic transfers

Direct electronic transfers between computers are another common method of transferring data. In many cases, these transfers are completely automated — they're both initiated and received without manual intervention. The biggest advantage to this is that people don't have to remember to kick off the transfer.

Unfortunately, this automation also makes it more difficult to locate instances of electronic transfers. The major clues you have are wiring circuits and people's memories. If the connection is a special circuit (for example, a T1 line), it shouldn't be too hard to identify.

Systems that receive their data by modem and a regular phone line are the sneaky ones. It's hard to identify this type of external data source simply because so many desktop PCs are attached to modems and phone lines. If every computer in the office includes a modem, it would be easy to forget that one or two are regularly used to bring in data files from an external source.

Floppy diskettes

Floppy diskettes are the stealth bomber of incoming data. Any computer with a floppy drive can be used to import data. With this many potential targets, it's extremely easy to overlook one in your search.

CD-ROMs

CD-ROMs are the newest entry in the data medium sweepstakes. One of their primary strengths is their large capacity (650MB). Another advantage is that they are inexpensive to produce and easy to transport. Finally, virtually all new PCs include a CD-ROM. All the these virtues make them excellent candidates for use as an input data device. Because so many PCs include a CD-ROM drive, it is difficult to determine which PCs are using the drives for inputting data from external sources.

Tracking input sources

It would be a waste of time and effort to identify data sources and then lose track of them. It also wouldn't impress your supervisor. So as you locate and identify external sources of data coming into your computer systems, make sure that you track them.

You need to maintain a number of pieces of information for every external data source you locate. Figure 3-2 lists items to track.

Figure 3-2: Data to track for each data source.

System	Application	Name of Source	Input Type	Frequency	Volume	Description
Production1	Accts/Recv	Southwest	9-track tape	weekly	10,000	Receivables from Southwest division
Production1	Accts/Recv	Southeast	1/4" cartridge	weekly	15,000	Receivables from Southeast division
Production1	Accts/Recv	Northeast	9-track tape	weekly	12,500	Receivables from Northeast
Production1	Accts/Recv	Northwest	CD-ROM	weekly	8,750	Receivables from Northwest
Production1	Accts/Recv	Midwest	electronic download	daily	500	Receivables from Midwest
Production1	Accts/Recv	Alaska	diskettes	monthly	1,000	Receivables from Alaska

The spreadsheet has rows for every data source you identify. Each row denotes one data source. The columns contain different pieces of information that you collect on each data source. Figure 3-3 shows an example of such a spreadsheet. If your company has a lot of data sources, you may break this information down further. You can, for instance, create separate spreadsheets and dedicate one spreadsheet to each major application or department. Examples of the applications that can be tracked include payroll, accounts payable, and accounts receivable. The applications were likely developed in COBOL by in-house personnel.

Source Identifier	Field#	Begin Col#	End Col#	Data Type	Length	Description
Southwest A/R Data Feed	1	1	8	char	8	Customer ID
Southwest A/R Data Feed	2	9	16	char	8	Invoice Number
Southwest A/R Data Feed	3	17	22	date	6	Date Invoice was sent (YYMMDD)
Southwest A/R Data Feed	4	23	30	real	8	Invoice Amount
Southwest A/R Data Feed	5	31	36	date	6	Date invoice is due (YYMMDD)
Southwest A/R Data Feed	6	37	38	integer	2	Discount if paid early
Southwest A/R Data Feed	7	39	44	date	6	Early Pay Date to qualify for discount (YYMMDD)
Southwest A/R Data Feed	8	45	51	char	7	Type of Purchase
Southeast A/R Data Feed	1	1	8	char	8	Customer ID
Southeast A/R Data Feed	2	9	16	char	8	Invoice Number
Southeast A/R Data Feed	3	17	22	date	6	Date Invoice was sent (YYMMDD)
Southeast A/R Data Feed	4	23	30	real	8	Invoice Amount
Southeast A/R Data Feed	5	31	36	date	6	Date invoice is due (YYMMDD)
Southeast A/R Data Feed	6	37	38	integer	2	Discount if paid early
Southeast A/R Data Feed	7	39	44	date	6	Early Pay Date to qualify for discount (YYMMDD)
Southeast A/R Data Feed	8	45	51	char	7	Type of Purchase
Northeast A/R Data Feed	1	1	8	char	8	Customer ID
Northeast A/R Data Feed	2	9	16	char	8	Invoice Number
Northeast A/R Data Feed	3	17	22	date	6	Date Invoice was sent (YYMMDD)
Northeast A/R Data Feed	4	23	30	real	8	Invoice Amount
Northeast A/R Data Feed	5	31	36	date	6	Date invoice is due (YYMMDD)
Northeast A/R Data Feed	6	37	38	integer	2	Discount if paid early
Northeast A/R Data Feed	7	39	44	date	6	Early Pay Date to qualify for discount (YYMMDD)
Northeast A/R Data Feed	8	45	51	char	7	Type of Purchase

Figure 3-3: This spreadsheet lists a company's external sources of data.

Analyzing incoming data

After you identify all the data sources that feed into your system, you're halfway home. Your next task is to analyze the incoming data. By *analyze,* I mean dig through the stream of incoming data looking for data fields that may be date related.

For each identified data source, you need to decipher and translate individual data fields. I use the word *decipher* because in many cases you'll be moving into unknown territory. For many applications and data sources, the documentation may be lost, outdated, poorly indexed — or it may never have existed outside the developer's head. (*Poorly documented* would be a compliment.)

If the data source isn't adequately documented, how can you identify what's a date and what isn't? With a lot of hard work! You can start either at the data end or by looking at the programs that use the data. Think of these two approaches as the Scylla and Charybdis of this project. In the *Odyssey,* if Odysseus approached too close to one side, his crew would be eaten. Too far the other way, and they'd be drawn into a whirlpool. Sounds a lot like some of the projects you've worked on, doesn't it?

Starting with the data

To examine data sources for date values, first you need a sample of the data. You need to obtain permission to access the data. Then you must get this data in a format that you can read and examine. This process may involve having to beg, grovel, or otherwise humiliate yourself to get access to the required computer, disk volumes, or hardware. People in control of these resources aren't disposed to allowing riff-raff such as yourself access to their kingdom. Plan on starting early — it will take longer than you expect.

After you have access to the data and have recovered your dignity, begin eyeballing the data. If you're fortunate, the data can be viewed in a standard word processor program. If you're not, read on.

Many times, the data format makes it difficult to examine the data. For example, if the data was produced by a COBOL program, it might have been written in a packed format. A standard word processor would display data in this format as meaningless control characters. Other problems you might encounter when examining data files include

✔ Special characters

✔ Long records

✔ Very large data fields

If the data includes control characters that regular word processors can't handle, you'll need an editor that can display control characters in another format, perhaps hexadecimal. Some editors display records in a split screen — one screen shows ASCII characters, and the other shows the same file in a hexadecimal format.

Another problem might be a record's length, which can easily exceed what a word processor or text editor can handle. Your editor might truncate (cut off) long records or arbitrarily split them into multiple records. The solution is to get a text editor specifically geared for software developers. This type of text editor doesn't provide attractive fonts and pretty formatting and doesn't print envelopes. It will, however, handle very large records and files.

A second length related problem has to do with the size of the entire file. Some simpler text editors and word processors can't open extremely long files. The solution, again, is to obtain a developer-oriented text editor.

Looking for date formats

Now that you can view records, how do you know what you're looking at or looking for? When approaching the problem from the data end, you should be looking for values that appear to be dates. Normally (and I'm stressing the word *normally*), you'll look for strings of characters that are in the following formats:

MMDDYY

DDMMYY

DDMONYY

MMDDYYYY

DDMMYYYY

JULMM

where the symbols represent the following:

MM	Two-digit month value
DD	Two-digit day value
YY	Two-digit year value
YYYY	Four-digit year value
MON	Three-letter month value (JAN, FEB, and so on)
JUL	Julian day of the year (1/1 is 001, 1/31 is 031, 2/1 is 032, 2/28 is 59, and so on)

There's no guarantee, however, that one of these formats will be used. For example, the developer might have separated the parts of the date field by positioning other fields between them.

Document everything you decipher from the data sources. A spreadsheet is a very good tool for this purpose. The spreadsheet outlined in Figure 3-4, for example, has a row to track each of the columns in the data source. For example, row 1 in the spreadsheet contains data from column 1 in the data file. Row 2 in the spreadsheet contains information from column 2 in the data file.

Source Identifier	Field#	Original Begin Col#	Original End Col#	Original Data Type	Original Length	New Begin Col#	New End Col#	New Data Format	New Length	Modified On	Modified By	Tested On	Tested By	Certified On	Certified By
Southwest A/R Data Feed	1	1	8	char	8	1	8	char	8						
	2	9	16	char	8	9	16	char	8						
	3	17	22	date	6	17	24	date	8	1/2/98	KCB	3/1/98	WVA	3/5/98	LEP
	4	23	30	real	8	25	32	real	8						
	5	31	36	date	6	33	40	date	8	1/2/98	KCB	3/1/98	WVA	3/5/98	LEP
	6	37	38	integer	2	41	42	integer	2						
	7	39	44	date	6	43	50	date	8	1/2/98	KCB	3/1/98	WVA	3/5/98	LEP
	8	45	51	char	7	51	57	char	7						
Southeast A/R Data Feed	1	1	8	char	8	1	8	char	8						
	2	9	16	char	8	9	16	char	8						
	3	17	22	date	6	17	24	date	8	1/5/98	KCB	3/1/98	GAS	3/5/98	CHC
	4	23	30	real	8	25	32	real	8						
	5	31	36	date	6	33	40	date	8	1/5/98	KCB	3/1/98	GAS	3/5/98	CHC
	6	37	38	integer	2	41	42	integer	2						
	7	39	44	date	6	43	50	date	8	1/5/98	KCB	3/1/98	GAS	3/5/98	CHC
	8	45	51	char	7	51	57	char	7						

Figure 3-4:
Details on
input
sources.

If the data source has preexisting documentation, you can use it to help fill out this spreadsheet. Specifically, the data source can provide the following information:

- ✔ Field number
- ✔ Beginning column number
- ✔ Ending column number
- ✔ Data type
- ✔ Date length
- ✔ Description

This spreadsheet can also become a progress tracking tool. As each column that contains a date related value (for example, a year value, a MM/DD/YY value, or a Julian date value) is identified, converted, and certified for year 2000 compliance, you check off the appropriate columns. Management loves to see this type of organization.

Internal data sources

When you're searching for sources of data, don't overlook internal sources. One example is data that comes from another division in the company. If the other division is only slightly associated with yours, the relationship may be more like dealing with an external source than an internal one.

Examining the application

After you find fields that appear to be dates, you need to decide how to handle them. By this point, you know several important pieces of information regarding your external date sources. You know which sources are used by which applications, which sources include apparent date fields, and which positions (columns) those dates are in. Now you need to switch your focus to the application.

Digging into an application is a lot like rooting around in the dirt in your garden. You know you'll come away with dirty hands, but you never know what you'll run into. When you examine an application, you essentially read the source code, looking for fields that appear to be a date or date oriented. When you find date fields, you need to examine the logic to determine whether the application can handle years greater than 1999.

Obvious date fields

Look at two places in an application. Your first stop is the easiest: It's the variable declaration area of the program header. A well-written program contains a nice neat, well-lit area (much like an interstate rest stop) where the variables are declared and documented.

If the program adheres to this Norman Rockwell style of documentation, you're all set. All date-oriented variables will be clearly named and documented as such. Keep a list of these date-oriented variables after you're fortunate enough to locate them.

The second place to look is in the body of the code. You need to search for all instances of words that have anything to do with dates. Here's a preliminary list:

```
begin
dat
date
day
ddmmyy
dow
dy
end
mmddyy
month
mon
year
yr
yyddmm
yymmdd
```

Investigate each "hit" on the words that you're searching for. If it turns out to be a date related variable or date-oriented processing, document it. You can modify it later. Right now, focus on finding all such instances.

After you've found all date-oriented variables and processing, examine them more closely. Determine whether the variables need to be expanded from their current size (such as 6 characters) to a larger one (such as 8 characters).

Hidden date fields

You need to examine incoming data and applications also for hidden date fields. In this case, *hidden* means a type of usage that doesn't come out and declare that a date is involved.

Prime examples of hidden dates are invoice numbers, order numbers, and record numbers that begin with the year or the full date. Figures 3-5 and 3-6 show examples of this type of usage of date fields.

In Figure 3-5, the date is hidden in a matter (case) number. The matter number contains the date embedded in the format YYMMDD. Following the date field is a sequence number field that differentiates between different matters that have been created on the same day. This sequence field restarts at 1 every day. The first matter created on June 2, 1997, is assigned the number OM9706020001 by the applications. The second matter that day is assigned the number OM9706020002. The first matter generated on the next day becomes OM9706030001. In this way, multiple matters can be generated and uniquely identified.

Figure 3-6 shows invoice numbers generated by an application. These invoice numbers also contain a hidden date field. The first invoice generated on October 1, 1997, is assigned the number 09710010001. The second invoice on that day becomes 09710010002. On the next business day, the date portion of the invoice number changes and the sequence portion of the invoice number restarts at 1. The first invoice generated on the next day becomes 09710020001.

Matter Number	Matter Name	Attorney In Charge	Description
OM9706020001	Smith vs. U.S. Government	WTH	Lawsuit filed by L. A. Smith against the U.S. Government
OM9706020002	Hogshead vs. Whiffie	LAB	Lawsuit filed by I. M. Hogshead against Mr. Whiffie
OM9706020003	Jones vs. The Board of Education	REL	Litigation filed against local school board
OM9706030001	Hendrickson vs. Acme, Inc.	RTR	Improper employment termination litigation
OM9706030002	Anderson vs. Tawdry Books, Inc.	TWP	Illustrator suing publisher for modifying figures submitted

In this system the matter (case) number includes an embedded date in the format YYMMDD. Each new matter (case) created on a given day is assigned the next sequential number.

Figure 3-5: Examples of a date hidden in a legal application.

Invoice Number	Customer ID	Open Date	Total Value
09710010001	46801	1-Oct-97	4500
09710010002	51325	1-Oct-97	56.79
09710020001	63124	2-Oct-97	876.45
09710020002	93425	2-Oct-97	1,000.00
09710020003	53184	2-Oct-97	574.32
09710030001	23	3-Oct-97	741.89

The invoice number is automatically generated in this system. Its format is YYMMDDxxxx where xxxx ascends for each invoice every day.

Figure 3-6: Examples of a hidden date field in an invoice system.

How will your systems handle these values? Specifically, how will the system handle records if the number begins with a 00 sequence?

✔ Will a 00 prefix affect how records are ordered or sorted on screens or in reports?

✔ Will users recognize and accept a situation where the most-recent data appears at the end of screens or reports?

✔ Will a 00 prefix cause problems with an application's search capabilities?

Talking to Other Administrators

After you've identified the data sources coming into your system, you need to talk to the people at the organizations that generate these data sources. Specifically, you need to know what their plans are regarding the year 2000 problem and the data they produce. The questions you can ask them include the following:

✔ Have you identified all date-oriented values?

✔ Which date values will be changed?

✔ How will they be modified?

✔ When will this change permanently go into effect?

✔ May I obtain examples of changed data in advance?

✔ Will all your data sources be changed simultaneously?

✔ If problems develop, what are your contingency plans?

Perhaps the foremost question is how will date values be modified. If the date currently includes a two-digit year value, will it be expanded to four digits? If the year is expanded, will any other aspects of the date (such as the order) be altered?

Dealing with resistant sources

You may have to deal with groups that have no intention of modifying their data. They may not see the year 2000 as a problem, or they may be taking a different approach than yours. Whatever their rationale, their needs and yours differ.

If this happens, it sounds to me like it's time for a conversion program. A program could be written that reads in data as it is currently received and then modifies it to your standard year 2000 format. At that point, the existing application would have access to the data. With a conversion program, you don't have to rely on the data source making changes.

Another avenue to consider is the use of a third-party conversion package. A number of packages claim to convert data from virtually any format to any other format. If their claims are accurate, a conversion effort, such as converting data from a six-digit date value to an eight-digit value, shouldn't be difficult.

Dealing with data sources that won't be made year 2000 compliant involves additional work for your organization. This includes designing, writing, and testing a new program, as well as modifying the existing application. If you communicate with the data source as early as possible (and learn their intentions), you'll have the maximum possible lead time for your extra work.

Data source schedule

You'll probably be communicating with each data source organization regularly for a long time, so you should develop a feel for the accuracy of their schedule projections.

Many organizations will claim that all their conversion projects are right on schedule. I hate to sow seeds of doubt, but you need to have an attitude of "trust, but verify." Be wary of glib assurances that everything is going fine. Don't be convinced until you have concrete examples of their progress.

By requesting — and obtaining — examples of their data in the new format, you can track their progress. If they continuously dodge or put off your requests for test data, suspect trouble! They're probably behind on their conversion schedule.

Another excellent reason for requesting (or demanding) test data as early as possible is that you can use it to verify that modifications made to your programs were implemented correctly. Running your modified applications with test data in parallel with your production applications should produce identical results. Any digressions should raise a big red flag.

What can you do if you relied on an external data source's promises to convert data by a certain date but it doesn't deliver? I'm not in favor of frivolous litigation, but you might have a legitimate claim against them. Contact competent legal representation to determine your options. Working together from the beginning, however, is a better solution than a court battle.

Ensuring that your system recognizes and handles bad dates

You need to be prepared for the worst-case scenario when dealing with data from an external source. Surprisingly, the worst case might not be an unconverted data source. Rather, it might turn out to be a data source that's converted but contains errors.

How will your system handle erroneous data? If an invalid date slips through, will your applications be capable of recognizing and handling it? The only way to be certain is to examine your code meticulously, add logic checks where necessary, and test it thoroughly!

Your control over the quality of incoming data is significantly lower than when the data is generated in-house. Because you have less control, assume that the quality is correspondingly more suspect. You would be wise to keep this in mind while inspecting and modifying your application code. Add checks for bad data where appropriate.

Chapter 4

Checking Outgoing Data for Year 2000 Compliance

. . . .

In This Chapter

▶ Determining what data you export

▶ Figuring out how to change your exported data

▶ Checking your system's output

▶ Exporting test data to other systems

▶ Being on schedule — or not

▶ Handling the unexpected

▶ Covering your exposure

. . . .

1 think deep down all of us want to be good citizens. When it comes to MIS and the year 2000 problem, being a good citizen entails certain obligations. These boil down to the Golden Rule: "Do unto others as you would have others do unto you." This chapter outlines these obligations (as I see them).

If you don't produce output for other organizations, this chapter doesn't apply to you. Look closely at your systems, though, because they could be generating data you're not aware of.

You might have overlooked these data exports for a number of reasons, such as the following:

✔ This activity has been in place for a long time and fulfilling it has become routine. It never encounters problems to raise its visibility.

✔ The data is provided to another department of the organization. It isn't provided to a paying customer and therefore generates no invoices, billings, or revenue.

✔ The export takes places infrequently, perhaps quarterly or yearly. Because of this, it falls under the "out of sight, out of mind" phenomena.

✔ The export media are diskettes. This could be easily overlooked because they require no special equipment.

✔ The data might be exported to an industry group that produces statistics about the industry as a whole. The lack of revenue could help explain why it is overlooked.

✔ The export might be to a government entity, such as OSHA, the EPA, or the EEOC. Local government bodies might also require data exports.

✔ The export process might have been created without MIS being informed about it. The department in question might have hired a contractor to develop and install this application.

Locating Data Sent to Others

Finding data exported to other organizations involves some detective work. Your first clues should be instances of generated output in the system documentation (if you can find it).

If no data exports are listed in the documentation, you're not necessarily in the clear. Incomplete documentation has plagued the MIS field since its inception. References to data exports in the documentation may have been overlooked, not completed, or conveniently ignored.

Many times, you can't find data exports in the documentation because they weren't included in the original specifications. If data exports were added as the system evolved over the years (or decades), the odds are even slimmer that the data exports were documented. Maintaining the documentation generally has an even lower priority than producing the original documentation.

If your search through the documentation comes up dry, you'll have to explore other avenues for finding this information. Appeal directly to the user community. Send out a memo or e-mail asking for assistance in locating data exports. Describe what you're looking for and ask for any information that users can contribute.

As you identify data exports, you need to maintain information on each of them. Figure 4-1 is an example of a spreadsheet you could use for this task.

System	Application	Name of Destination	Transfer Media	Freq-uency	Volume	Description
Production2	Accts/Payable	Southwest	9-track tape	1,000	weekly	Accounts Payable records for Southwest region
Production2	Accts/Payable	Southeast	1/4" cartridge	2,000	weekly	Accounts Payable records for Southwest region
Production2	Accts/Payable	Northeast	CD-ROM	2,500	weekly	Accounts Payable records for Northesat region
Production2	Accts/Payable	Northwest	9-track tape	1,500	weekly	Accounts Payable records for Northwest region
Production2	Accts/Payable	Midwest	diskettes	500	weekly	Accounts Payable records for Midwest region
Production2	Accts/Payable	Alaska	electronic upload	50	daily	Accounts Payable records for Alaska region

Figure 4-1:
A spread-sheet for tracking data exports.

Identifying date-oriented data in your output

After you identify data exports, you need to check whether they contain date values. This task can be initiated from either of two directions. The first is to carefully examine the data itself. The second way to detect dates is to examine the application that generates the data being exported.

The variety of date values in the business environment is amazing. Following are some of the more common date values that appear in data records:

- Birth date
- Hire date
- Rehire date
- Most recent review date
- Date of grievance filing
- Date of grievance resolution
- Transfer date
- Promotion date
- Date of disciplinary action
- Birth dates of dependents
- Birth date of spouse

✔ Date health insurance becomes effective

✔ Date health insurance ends

✔ Date life insurance becomes effective

✔ Date disability insurance becomes effective

✔ Date of first contribution to payroll savings

✔ Vesting date

✔ Resignation date

✔ Retirement date

✔ Date of first educational assistance

✔ Date of undergraduate degree

✔ Date of training activities

✔ Certification dates (such as CPA, actuarial exams, bar exam, or broker's license)

This list is a good start, but your systems could include other types of data values. If you discover any new uses, add them to this list so that you (and others) can identify instances of them later.

Date values tend to be like ants: If you find one, many more are in the vicinity. For example, a single data record in a personnel system might include many of the date fields in the previous list. Each date that's identified must be examined to determine how it will be handled.

Modifying date values

After you locate all date-oriented values, you need to determine which will be modified and how. These modifications need to be made in accordance with your overall year 2000 project plan.

You can modify dates to handle the year 2000 problem in a number of ways. These methods are introduced here and are more fully explained in Chapter 6.

Date expansion

The first method of handling dates is to expand all two-digit year references to four digits. If a date value contains only the year, it would be expanded from two digits (98) to four digits (1998). If the date value is currently six digits (123198) it would be expanded to eight digits (12311998). Both expansions allow the full four-digit year value to be stored.

Fixed window

Another technique for handling dates is called a fixed window. When implementing this method, you identify a 100-year interval (such as 1930–2029). All dates that your system references will be in this time period. A two-digit year value of 98 in a data file is interpreted as the year 1998. A two-digit year value of 28 is interpreted as 2028. Using this technique avoids having to physically expand date fields in data files and programs.

Sliding window

Similar to the fixed window technique is the sliding window approach. This method also requires you to identify a 100-year window. Again, the dates your applications can access must be within this period. The difference is that the 100-year period slides forward every year. If the period is originally 1930–2029, for example, the next year the window will be 1931–2030. The following year it will be 1932–2031.

Using the fixed year window, the number of years into the future you can reference decreases every year. If the window is defined to be 1930–2029 and the current year is 1998, you can reference 31 years into the future (1999 through 2029). If the current year is 2002, the number of future years that can be referenced is only 27 (2003 through 2029). For many organizations, this will cause problems. The sliding window methodology solves this problem by continually moving the window forward. You are always able to reference the same number of years into the future.

Date compression

Date compression, or date encoding, is one more technique for handling the date problem. This methodology requires that you compress a four-digit year value in the space previously used to hold a two-digit value. This is accomplished by storing the value in a number system other than decimal. One possible number system is hexadecimal. This system allows 16 values to be stored in a single digit (0–9, A, B, C, D, E, F). In a hexadecimal system you can store 256 values in a two-digit field (00 through FF). This is a significant increase over the 100 values the decimal system can store in the same space.

Encapsulation

The Gregorian calendar repeats itself every 28 years. If January 1st is on a Monday this year and it's a leap year, the calendar will be the same 28 years from now (and 28 years in the past). January 1st will be a Monday in that year and it will also be a leap year.

Implementing an encapsulation solution requires that an application subtract 28 from the year value before storing it and adding this value back before the year value is shown to the user. A data record created on 1/1/2000 will be internally stored as 1/1/1972. Before being shown to the user, the 28 years will be added back.

By internally storing years this way, date calculations that span the millennium will be delayed for 28 years.

Changing date fields affects data export files

The method your organization chooses to deal with the problem dictates what changes you must make to dates in the export file.

Date expansion

Assume that your project plan calls for all dates to be expanded to an eight-character field. This modification would be reflected in the dates in your export files. Date values that looked like 112098 will now be 11201998.

This seemingly simple change will affect a surprising number of things. First, you might need to enlarge variables in the source code that hold a date value. Many date fields are declared to be six characters in length (to hold MMDDYY or some variation). It's likely that the declaration statements for these variables will need to be altered to eight characters. The new declaration statement would instruct the compiler that this variable is now a character string that is eight characters long. This larger version of the variable would be able to hold either character date field.

Changing the length of date fields has a ripple effect on other aspects of an application. Suppose a data record is currently 100 characters in length and contains five date fields. Enlarging these date fields from six characters to eight will increase the size of each record by ten (5 × 2) characters. You might need to also change the declaration statements for any program variables or arrays that hold the record. This is necessary because now the data record is ten characters larger. The previous declaration statement isn't large enough to handle the larger data record.

Frequently, data files include a header as the first record. Header records often contain a value denoting the length of the entire file. If each record has been expanded, this needs to be reflected in the header record. The logic that calculates the size of the file will likely need to be updated as well.

The ripple effect can extend even further, as shown in Figure 4-2. Including larger date fields increases the amount of data being transferred. If the number of date fields or the record count is extremely high, the size of the export file can be affected substantially. In extreme cases, the physical transfer media could be affected. For instance, you may need large tapes or more of them to handle the same export.

Fixed and sliding windows

If the method chosen was to use either a fixed or a sliding window, no changes would be made to the data files. But the recipients of the data would need to know what you have defined to be the 100-year window. There will be problems, if they think the window is 1950–2049 and you have defined it to be 1930–2029. They would incorrectly interpret all dates from 1930–1949 and 2031–2049.

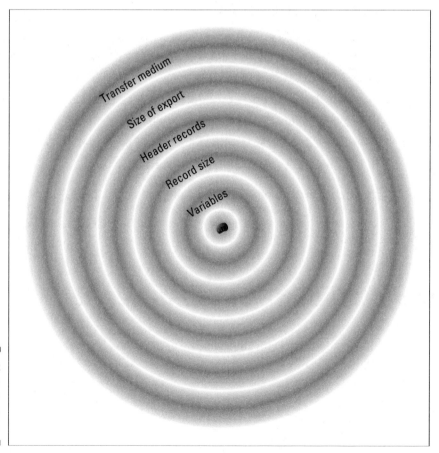

Figure 4-2:
Ripple effect of an expanded date field.

Date compression

If you choose to encode date values, the recipients of your data will be in for a very big surprise! When they encounter digits that aren't numeric, their applications will very likely abort.

Encapsulation

Encapsulation will also cause problems for data recipients. If they aren't informed of this change, all their dates will be off by 28 years. This might be even worse than encoding. At least with encoding they would find out about the problem right away, when their first application aborts. With encapsulation, their applications would function but the results would be very questionable.

Contacting the Recipients

After you determine how your organization will handle the year 2000 situation, you need to inform the recipients of your data exports. You must provide them with a number of details, including:

- Which data exports are affected
- Which fields in these exports will be modified and how
- When data exports with test data will be available
- When the exports will be permanently changed

Your changes will require the recipients to make changes to their own systems. They will appreciate being given as much notice as possible. The more time you give them, the easier it will be for each recipient to plan and implement their own modifications.

Implementing Your Changes

Before you can export data, you must correct all the year 2000 problems you have identified. Only after your own house has been cleaned can you export data to an external recipient.

Testing the changes

Changes made to computer systems must be thoroughly tested before they can be made in a production environment. The cost of taking down a production system or damaging its data is too great to allow any lesser level of vigilance. Users, management, and clients won't (and shouldn't) stand for people taking chances with live systems.

The testing part of the project has multiple phases. The first testing phase, called unit testing, tests only modified modules. Later phases, called integration and system testing, verify that the entire system works together to function the way the users expect it to.

Testing can be performed without interfering with a production system. If the system isn't used 24 hours a day, you can perform testing during off hours. This will probably include testing over the weekend. If the system must be operational 24 hours a day and seven days a week, testing must be performed on a dedicated test system. Chapter 15 is devoted to the topic of testing the changes.

This principle is even more important when the data is going to an external recipient because the risks and costs are much higher. Releasing bad data to a client or a customer exposes your company to a tremendous liability. Besides the possibility of litigation, you could lose the clients' business. External clients most likely won't tolerate flawed data feeds. If they have alternative sources for the data, they may well explore them.

When external clients are involved, the costs of correcting bad data (or correcting programming errors for that matter) escalate quickly. In the best of circumstances, you would need to re-export their most recent data transmission. In the next worse situation, you would need to re-export a number of data transmissions. Is this feasible under your current production environment? How long is data of this type retained online? How much effort and money will it take to go through these corrective actions?

An aggressive testing program can significantly decrease the likelihood of these problems. Export data generated after program changes should be examined in greater-than-normal detail. Testing should include events such as month-end, quarter-closing, and year-end scenarios.

Exporting test data to other systems

Giving data recipients access to test data as early as possible has a number of advantages. It enables them to run their own test suites against the data. If they uncover problems, they'll probably inform you immediately. This is essentially an extension to your own testing efforts at little or no extra effort.

Errors in the data aren't the only problem that the early delivery of test data can uncover. If you change the sizes of date fields, there will be corresponding changes to the data record sizes, header records, file sizes, and so on. When you deliver test data, you are implicitly testing all these aspects of the test data. If problems created by different sizes of records, headers, and files exist, they will very likely be discovered when you transmit test data. Finding problems during testing is much better than uncovering them on the day you are obligated to deliver year 2000 compliant, error-free data.

By providing recipients with test data earlier instead of later, you enable them to test their own programming changes. If they have internal errors, the recipients can detect them earlier than otherwise. Although this doesn't directly improve your operations, it certainly contributes to their goodwill towards you. These days, no one can have enough of this valuable commodity, especially on the part of clients.

Being on Time

Will you be able to deliver the modified data on schedule? This could be the $64,000 question.

Setting up a delivery schedule

The first step toward meeting a delivery date is to set up a realistic schedule for identifying, modifying, testing, and delivering data. Heed the use of the word *realistic.* An overly optimistic schedule is of no use here. We've all been on projects with ludicrous schedules. They serve no positive purpose and are disheartening to the troops in the trenches.

A number of factors affect how long your tasks will take. The schedule you publish must take all factors into account. Some of the factors to consider are presented here:

- Estimated amount of effort for converting export data
- Quality and quantity of system documentation
- Number of data exports that must be examined
- The task's priority
- The relative priority of each specific data export
- Available staff for these tasks, including contractors and new hires scheduled to be included on the project

 ✔ Vacation and holiday schedules of your team

 ✔ Availability of test systems, test data, and network connections

 ✔ Tools that will be used for the effort

 ✔ Training time to get your team up to speed

Notifying recipients if you won't make the schedule

If you can't make a schedule commitment, first notify the affected recipients as soon as possible. The earlier you inform them, the sooner they can react to this new situation. Although it's never easy to convey this type of information, you would expect and appreciate the same consideration if the roles were reversed, wouldn't you?

Schedule estimates can prove to be wrong for many reasons. You may have simply underestimated the amount of work. People may not have been able to begin working on the effort when originally planned. Tools or procedures may not have been as efficient as anticipated. The list of explanations or excuses can be endless.

After examining reasons for the current schedule inaccuracies, revise your schedule accordingly. Make sure the newly developed schedule is as accurate as you can make it. Inform all affected data export recipients of the new schedule.

Developing contingency plans

What if you come to the realization that there is no way you'll be finished by 1/1/2000? What will you do if errors in the data are exposed at the last minute? Have you developed contingency plans for the worst-case scenario?

To some it might sound like a defeatist attitude to even consider failure. I feel it's a prudent idea to give at least some thought to this possibility. The bleak reality is that a significant percentage of software projects end up failing.

One possible plan is to revert to the original, unmodified data export. You would continue to export the original data while trying to correct the problems. If this is your decision, some advanced planning at this point might make this process easier and faster. You'll want to make sure that original copies of the programs are always available. (If the originals are deleted or modified, you may not be able to revert to them.)

Another alternative is to continue sending the flawed data while working like crazy to correct it. To choose this alternative, you should get the concurrence of the data's recipient. If they can function with bad data for a short time, this alternative might be viable.

Any alternative plan you enact has its own pros and cons. What's most important is that you have some plan in place before you reach this point. You also need to ensure that everyone affected knows what the contingency course of action will be. That way, if the worst case does occur, you can minimize confusion and the amount of time lost.

Your Organization's Liability Exposure

If your year 2000 efforts include data exports, you probably have an additional liability exposure. Consult competent, experienced legal counsel early in this project so that you're aware of any liability before you need this knowledge.

Exporting bad data to a client probably constitutes a breach of your contract with them. If the contract includes provisions for damages, they could be assessed against you. Even if there is no explicit damages clause, the client could initiate litigation against you. Potential damages a client might attempt to collect include loss of income, business interruption, and negligence.

Above and beyond litigation, exporting bad data has other risks. Additional potential costs are a loss of clients and the resulting loss of market share. Your organization's reputation could also be severely affected. Losing your clients or your reputation could have both short-term and long-term effects on your organization.

Part II
Developing a Year 2000 Plan

" IT'S CHAOS — BUT IT'S CHAOS THAT WORKS."

In this part . . .

To accomplish just about anything in life, you need a plan. If you don't take the time and effort to plot out where you're headed and what route you're going to take, you probably won't be successful.

Year 2000 projects are no exception — and actually deserve more planning than most software projects. The next few chapters are devoted to planning this project. They outline possible approaches to the year 2000 problem, what you should change, and how to determine when the initial changes should be put into place. You find out how to put your project plan together. Finally, I describe the different calendars used throughout the world and how they can affect both your business and your project.

My father has a lot of sayings. When I was a kid, they sounded pretty corny, but now I know they contain a lifetime of wisdom. One of his favorites is "You're going at it like you're killing snakes." He meant I was doing something without planning or forethought. The results usually reflected my lack of planning. My advice to anyone who is participating in a year 2000 project is to have a plan. Take the time to develop your plan in adequate detail. After you start the project, do your best to stick to the plan. Otherwise, if my Dad runs into you, he'll say. . . .

Chapter 5

The Person with the Plan

. . . .

. . . .

*E*very successful project requires both a leader and a plan. Studies indicate that the single most reliable indicator of a project's success is the success rate of the project leader's previous projects.

This chapter provides an overview of both the year 2000 project leader and some factors that must be considered to develop an effective and comprehensive year 2000 project plan.

Staffing

Staffing a year 2000 effort is one of the first actions an organization must undertake. It also has a huge impact on the project. This task must be accomplished early and correctly.

Finding the project team leader

A project of this scope and importance requires a dedicated leader. Selecting the project leader for your organization's year 2000 effort is one of the most important decisions that will be made. To a large degree, the project plan and project team will be influenced by how the leader approaches the situation.

The qualities required by a project leader are qualities all of us would love to have but can't honestly claim in abundance. Due to the imperative nature of this effort, the attributes of the project leader are all the more important. Some of the qualities this individual should possess are listed next:

✔ **Integrity.** The project can be crippled if the leader is bullied around. If a project leader knows that something is right or wrong, he or she must do the right thing without being swayed by short-term reactions.

✔ **Great communication skills.** The leader acts as an information interchange between management, users, clients, and the project troops. When time is short, the ability to communicate effectively is critical.

✔ **Technical proficiency.** The ability to understand and choose between a number of technical approaches is crucial. Someone without an intuitive grasp of the technical issues is likely to get off track.

✔ **Perseverance.** There will be times when the light at the end of the tunnel will be a mere pinpoint, if it's visible at all. A leader with sufficient perseverance won't become discouraged.

✔ **Ability to set and achieve objectives.** The project leader is instrumental in both setting and achieving objectives that are realistic and aggressive. Unrealistic objectives quickly disillusion the project team, and simplistic ones provide no challenge or exuberance. It takes experience and intuition to properly balance these requirements.

✔ **Innovative.** The year 2000 problem has never occurred before, so it's bound to bring both unforeseen problems and opportunities. New situations require someone who's thinking is innovative, not tied to conventional methods.

✔ **Ability to instill inspiration.** Face it, this project will be a long haul. At times, things won't go as expected, and it will look like you won't be successful. A project leader who can serve as an inspiration to team members and users will be invaluable.

✔ **Gatekeeper.** The year 2000 project will be surrounded by an immense amount of tension, especially when it appears that the work won't be completed on time. I'm thinking about Old Faithful geyser-type of pressure here folks. The team leader needs to be a gatekeeper who can protect the team from pressures it shouldn't have to deal with.

Locating a person with all these skills will be difficult. Sometimes you have to make due with the best individual you can obtain — but you might be surprised at how a person can grow into the role.

Assembling the team

After you choose the project leader, it's time to select the remainder of the team. Because the deadline for this particular project truly is cast in stone, you want team members who are experienced, productive, and willing to do whatever it takes to complete the job.

The professional experience you'll want depends on the environment in which you'll be working. Some shops consist primarily of mainframe computers and COBOL code; others might have C, FORTRAN, PL/1, or RPG as their primary language. Don't overlook including someone on your team who has experience with PC-based software packages.

Outsourcing

Outsourcing has become a significant factor in MIS shops in the last few years. Many organizations will be utilizing outsourcing for their year 2000 efforts. This section details a number of reasons for making — or not making — this decision.

Advantages

The most pressing reason for outsourcing is when the size of the task exceeds what your staff can handle. This situation is more prevalent in companies that must convert extremely large code libraries — some have more than 100 million lines of code.

By outsourcing the bulk of the work, you can avoid certain staffing problems. You don't have to find and hire experienced people to build up your staff. You also avoid the issue of what to do with newly hired people after the project is completed — you may no longer need as many MIS people.

An outsourcing decision can also take advantage of economies of scale and experience. A consulting group specializing in year 2000 conversions will certainly have acquired or built tools to automate the process. You could reproduce both the tools and the experience, but it would cost money and take time.

Disadvantages

Choosing the outsourcing route isn't without its own perils. One of the primary dangers is choosing the wrong firm. This crisis wouldn't be the first opportunity in which people have claimed to have experience that they didn't possess. You don't want to be a guinea pig for someone who is trying to make it big in the year 2000 outsourcing business.

Going with a larger, more established consulting firm would appear to be safer. The larger consulting firms, however, are likely to be more expensive. Even worse, many of them are completely booked and are refusing to take on additional clients.

A general drawback of using consultants or outsourcing is that the skill level and experience of your own people isn't improved. Consultants come in, do the work, and leave. Unless your people are tenacious and aggressive, they probably won't acquire the skills to duplicate the consultants' accomplishments.

Before contracting with an outsourcer, ask some pointed questions. Depending on the responses, your comfort level may rise or fall. The following represents just a starting point of what you should be asking outsourcers:

- ✔ What experience do they have on your hardware platforms?

- ✔ What experience do they have with your languages or software packages?

- ✔ Do they guarantee their work? What is this guarantee worth?

- ✔ What experience do the individuals assigned to your project have? Can you interview them?

- ✔ Will the individuals you meet and talk to be permanently assigned to your project? You want to avoid a bait-and-switch operation.

- ✔ Are you able to unilaterally demand that a team member be removed from the project?

- ✔ Is this outsourcer doing work for any of your competitors? If so, are you comfortable with this situation?

- ✔ Will they have access to confidential data or systems? If the answer is yes, require that all individuals sign nondisclosure statements.

- ✔ Is there a ceiling on what this contract can cost you?

Other individuals or groups in your organization, such as legal, accounting, and auditing, might have questions as well. Get them involved with choosing an outsourcer up-front instead of regretting it afterwards.

Hiring contract personnel

Another potential source for year 2000 team members is to hire contract personnel. These individuals can be hired through a consulting firm or directly.

Hiring contractors and outsourcing the work have a number of similarities. The primary difference between them is that when you outsource the project, the supervisory functions are outsourced as well. The outsource firm has management personnel as well as programmers who will be doing the work. When you hire contract personnel, the management function is performed by someone in your firm.

Advantages

The biggest advantage of hiring contractors is that they can be terminated quickly if necessary. Examples of when you might want to terminate contract personnel follow:

- ✔ The project is completed.
- ✔ Efforts on the project are put on hold.
- ✔ The contractor isn't as productive as you expected.
- ✔ A full-time employee has been hired to replace the contractor.

Another advantage of using contractors is that they don't receive any benefits. You don't need to schedule training for them. If they are sick or on vacation, they don't bill during that time. They aren't entitled to participate in payroll savings or your pension plan.

Disadvantages

Hiring contractors has some disadvantages as well. Some of the drawbacks follow:

- ✔ The hourly rate of a contractor is higher than the fully loaded (that is, including benefits) rate of a full-time employee.
- ✔ There is always the worry that contractors will violate your trade secrets. They may be required to sign a nondisclosure agreement, but that doesn't guarantee that they will abide by it.
- ✔ When you hire contractors, you're taking a chance. Although you can terminate them if they don't work out, you will have wasted time and money before determining how productive they are.

Planning

On the weekends, I like to start projects around the house. (Notice that I didn't say I ever finish any of these projects.) To avoid wasting wood, I repeat an old carpenter's saying to myself while I work: Measure twice and cut once.

What does this have to do with a year 2000 project? Measuring twice is simply a way to make myself plan what I'm going to do before I rush in and do it. The more expensive the materials and the more delicate the work, the louder I talk to myself.

Your year 2000 project is a task that has two absolute restrictions. First, it has to be completed on time. Second, it has to be performed right the first time. If these two requirements don't justify adequate planning, I don't know what does. Plan ahead to avoid making a costly mistake.

Getting upper management on board early

Management isn't likely to be very enthused about this project without your efforts. Management will probably view the project in one of two ways:

✔ This is much ado about nothing. Management's position might be that two missing digits can't possibly cause so much trouble. Just stick them in, and everything will be all right.

✔ This project has no return on investment. A successful year 2000 project just assures management that things will be business as usual on January 1, 2000.

The project leader or project champion has the responsibility of educating management and stressing that this crisis could bankrupt the organization. If this project is successful, the company will be able to send out invoices, respond to customer queries, update inventory, and process bills into the next century.

The alternative isn't a pretty sight. What if your computer systems can't process incoming orders after the first of the year? How will the public, your clients, and government regulatory agencies react if you aren't able to accomplish basic business functions? How would the stock market react? Would your creditors, bank, or utilities respond kindly if they were informed that your organization can't pay bills for the next 60 days?

You must make upper management fully aware of these worst-case scenarios. Otherwise, management may not be sufficiently motivated to back this project.

If you have to ask how much it costs . . .

Don't kid yourself. Year 2000 corrections will be expensive, as shown in Figure 5-1. Estimates of what it will cost the U.S. range from $100 to $600 billion. Estimates of what it will cost the average Fortune 500 company to correct their code are $50 to $100 million.

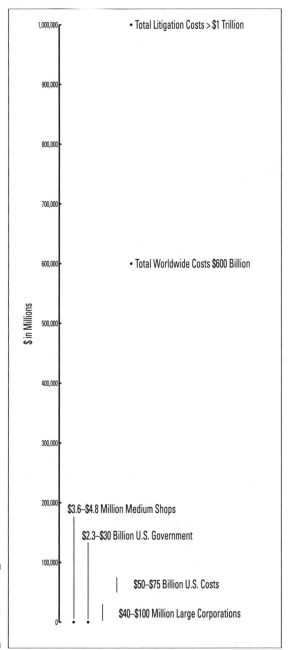

Figure 5-1:
Estimated
year 2000
costs.

Following are the estimates that back up the amounts in Figure 5-1, from the bottom to the top:

- ✔ The Gartner Group estimates that a medium shop with approximately 8,000 programs, each averaging 100 LOC and a date reference to an LOC ratio of 1:50, will spend in the range of $3.6 to $4.8 million.

- ✔ The Office of Management and Budget estimates it will cost the government $2.3 billion. Other experts estimate it will be $30 billion.

- ✔ Most major corporations are expected to spend $40 to $100 million.

- ✔ The ITAA Year 2000 Task Group members report estimate costs in the United States at $50 to $75 billion.

- ✔ The February 5, 1996, issue of *Information Week* estimates worldwide costs at $600 billion.

- ✔ In the June 2, 1997, issue of *Newsweek,* Dean Morehouse is quoted as saying that litigation costs could be over $1 trillion.

Even if the costs turn out to be on the low end of these estimates, we're still talking about a lot of money. As U.S. Senator Everett Dirksen said, "A billion here, a billion there, and pretty soon you're talking about real money."

The MIS industry as a whole dug itself into this hole over a long period of time. Don't expect that getting out of such a situation will be quick, cheap, or easy.

Getting out of this pit will cost more than just money. Some of the non-monetary costs include the following:

- ✔ Time
- ✔ Opportunity costs
- ✔ Political capital

People throughout the organization will spend a great deal of time on this problem. Those involved will include your board of directors, the highest levels of management, the legal staff, the public relations department, and the MIS department.

Opportunity costs are another expenditure. Time and money spent resolving year 2000 problems represent resources that can't be invested elsewhere, such as on enhancements to current computer systems or participation in new systems and ventures.

Some of the reasons I list may explain why your upper management seems to be resisting the idea of implementing a year 2000 project. Management may be afraid to commit resources and money to a project that doesn't seem to provide any sort of return.

Perhaps you can use some of the following facts to overcome this resistance:

- ✔ The costs will never decrease. On the contrary, most experts feel that the cost of year 2000 experienced personnel will skyrocket as the deadline approaches.

- ✔ Failing to act now increases the likelihood that qualified, experienced consulting firms will be completely booked.

- ✔ If you don't act in a prudent manner to address this problem, directors and officers could be setting themselves up for a lawsuit.

- ✔ If this problem isn't adequately addressed, your firm may not be able to conduct business after 1/1/2000 due to nonfunctioning computer systems.

- ✔ Many of your competitors are already addressing this problem. They will be able to conduct business after 1/1/2000. Will you?

The project leader will also be expending political capital, fighting to accomplish something that not everyone completely understands or appreciates. If others don't fully understand it, you have to convince them that it deserves the priority you're pushing for. Each battle will use up political capital.

Determining how much software your organization has

When I was a kid, a local TV channel started the 10 p.m. news every night with a policeman asking "Parents, it's 10 o'clock. Do you know where your children are?" I'll ask you a similar question: "It's almost the year 2000, do you know where your software is and how much you have?"

If your answers to these questions are no, you should feel guilty but not alone. One poll of Fortune 1000 sized firms found that only 20 percent knew how much code was in their software inventory.

Until you know how much software you have, you can't realistically predict how long it will take to correct it. One of the first tasks in the year 2000 effort is to develop an accurate inventory of the software your organization possesses.

You need to examine each of your mainframes, servers, and PCs. Following are some of the questions you need to answer:

- ✔ What software is running on each?
- ✔ Were these applications developed in-house or purchased?
- ✔ Is the source code available?

✔ Are you sure that the source code matches the executables?

✔ How many machines does the software execute on?

✔ Where is the data stored that this machine accesses?

✔ Is there backup or historical data? If so, what format is the data backed up in?

It would be very useful during the project if this inventory included additional information on each software application. The information gathered on each software system should include the following:

✔ System name.

✔ Abbreviation or acronym by which the system is known.

✔ Description of the system's usage (for example, is it an online-processing decision-support system?).

✔ Primary user group.

✔ Lead user or "owner."

✔ Whether it was developed internally, custom developed, or off the shelf.

✔ Who the maintainer is and whether the maintainer is internal or external.

✔ What language it was written in.

✔ Whether the source code is available.

✔ What hardware platforms it runs on.

✔ How many instances of this system exist throughout the organization and where are they located.

✔ Where its input data comes from (manually entered, imported, online, and so on).

✔ What other systems it exports data to?

✔ How its data is stored (flat files, relational database, both).

✔ Where its data is stored (that is, on what machine and where is that machine located).

✔ Whether this system utilizes dates.

Converting applications

After you identify all your applications, where they run, what language they were written in, and where the source code is, then what do you do? This situation reminds me of when my wife and I brought our first child home from the hospital. We had a beautiful new baby, but what were we supposed to do now? The answer for us was "raise him." The answer to you is "convert them."

The first question regarding converting an application is "Does it process dates?" For the overwhelming majority of applications, the answer will be a resounding "Yes." The Gartner Group estimates that between 70 percent and 90 percent of all programs handle dates.

For programs that do handle dates, you need to plan how each will be converted. The areas that must be covered for each application include the following:

✔ Which conversion technique (date expansion, fixed window, sliding window, compression, encapsulation) will be used for this program?

✔ What data does it access?

✔ Who will perform the conversion?

✔ When will it be converted?

✔ Will any temporary (bridge) programs be needed?

✔ What testing is required?

✔ On what hardware platform will testing be performed?

Many of the items listed in this section are covered in later chapters. The first item in the preceding list, for example, is covered in Chapter 6. The third item, which refers to personnel, is covered in Chapter 10. Testing is covered in Chapter 15.

Implementing

A good project team and a well-laid-out project plan are absolutely required for this project to be successful. The implementation phase, however, is where the rubber meets the road. During implementation, people have to put forth time, effort, and craftsmanship to make sure that the project is a success.

Repairing and replacing hardware

Most hardware repaired or replaced during the year 2000 efforts will consist of PCs (although I have heard that some very old mainframes will need to be replaced). Acquiring and paying for a single PC isn't difficult, but doing so for dozens or hundreds of machines will be an effort.

Your best strategy is to identify any PCs that will have a year 2000 problem and concentrate on them first. Compile a list of computers that need to be replaced and those that need to be upgraded.

For PCs being upgraded, you might group them by the type of BIOS they have. Then contact manufacturers of the largest number of PCs first. This will enable you to focus on the group that returns the biggest impact for your effort.

Don't forget to actually replace those PCs that need to be replaced. It would be easy to get distracted by other year 2000 activities and forget this task. Also make sure that any PCs you buy are 2000 compatible! Chapter 2 covers identifying PCs that aren't year 2000 compatible and how you should handle them.

Casting call for converting all data

Depending on the solution you choose for addressing the year 2000 problem, you may be required to convert existing data. If you chose to expand date fields, all existing data will need to be modified so that the new applications can access it.

Converting data to an expanded date field involves reading the data in, expanding it, and writing it back out to storage. This requires that you write a data conversion program or buy a third-party tool specifically designed for data conversion. Data Junction (from Data Junction Corporation), for example, claims to have more than ten functions specifically designed to address year 2000 data problems.

Don't forget to convert all backup and archived data to the new format! Otherwise, you won't be able to access it with new versions of the applications. If you needed to access this data to recover after an emergency, you'd be out of luck. An alternative to converting archived data is to retain a copy of the original version of the programs. I wouldn't recommend this approach, though, because it puts you on the slippery slope toward not moving your entire shop to the new system.

The amount of data that a large corporation has accumulated can be staggering. Just as many corporations have no idea how much software they have, many (or most) have no idea how much data they have stored over the years. All this data must be examined, and a significant percentage of it will need to be converted to make it year 2000 compliant. One estimate is that for every dollar spent on converting the software, it will cost an additional dollar to convert the data.

In his white paper "The Global Impact of the Year 2000 Software Problem," Capers Jones provides estimates of how much data large corporations have. This amount can be only estimated due to the lack of available metrics. Mr. Jones has estimated that the average large corporation has more than 1,000 pages of data per employee. What percentage of this data will require year 2000 conversion is currently unknown.

Testing, testing, testing

You probably wouldn't feel comfortable flying in an untested airplane. Why would your system users be any different? They have a right to expect that any changes you make to their systems to handle the year 2000 will be well tested before they use them.

Your project plan for the year 2000 must adequately address testing requirements. Testing must be built into the plan from the beginning. I address the topic of testing in Chapter 15. The time, tools, and people for testing can't be an afterthought if you want to do a satisfactory job.

Cutting over without cutting off users

A great deal of wisdom can be found on T-shirts these days. One T-shirt I saw recently read "You'll never get to second base without taking your foot off first." In a similar fashion, during your year 2000 conversion, you have to leave the safety of your current operations to implement changes. You need to develop a plan that allows migration from existing programs and data to the year 2000 compatible versions without leaving your users stranded.

Two essential ways exist to move from here to there. One is to take a number of incremental steps. Before and after these steps, users have complete access to the system. Each step in this process might involve the conversion of several additional applications. Gradually, applications are converted until everything is complete. Bridge programs (which I cover in Chapter 6) would be used to allow both converted and unconverted programs to access the data.

The alternative to a gradual process is to do it all at once. Think of this as the "big bang" approach to the year 2000. One day, users are using the old system. The next day, everything has been converted to the new version.

Each approach has advantages and disadvantages. The gradual transition has the advantage that fewer elements are modified at any given time. If something goes wrong, it will be easier to isolate and identify what caused the problem.

One downside to a gradual approach is that it generally involves more effort because each transitional step has to be tested before it is released. The incremental approach also requires more "scaffolding." You'll need a number of bridge programs to allow all the applications access to all the data at all times. After the project is finished, the bridge programs can be deleted.

Going with the incremental approach extends the discomfort over a longer period of time. You will need to be in constant communication with the user community, informing users each time an incremental change will be made. The big bang approach performs all the conversions in a single event.

The big bang approach is the riskier of the two methods. It is essentially an all-or-nothing implementation. If everything works as planned, wonderful. If things don't quite work out, you must either revert to the old system or leave the new system in place and work like crazy until it's fixed.

Testing is just as important under the big bang approach. You will almost certainly need additional hardware for test platforms. All applications being converted will need to be tested before the cutover.

The technique you take depends on many things. If your applications can be divided into distinct groups, an incremental approach might be best. If all applications are tightly tied together, the big bang approach might be preferable.

The size of your software and data inventory can also affect your decision. If the volume is extremely large, it might make sense to break it down into manageable pieces. Using the big bang approach for a more modest installation might be achievable.

Another determining factor in which approach you take is your combination of nerves and confidence. If you have a high level of confidence in your team, you might be more willing to take the all-or-nothing approach. Less confidence and nerves might sway you to take the safer but slower approach.

I hate to be an alarmist, but I've heard that a Mr. Murphy is working on your year 2000 problem during the off shift. No matter how you approach cutover, you'll need to develop contingency plans in case something bad happens. You must be able to revert to a working system quickly. Your users won't be happy campers if they can't do their jobs for an extended period of time, and management isn't likely to be tolerant of this situation, either.

Chapter 6

Approaches to the Year 2000 Problem

*T*here's more than one way to skin a cat. Who hasn't heard that old saying? It applies also to your year 2000 project — you can deal with it using a variety of approaches. This chapter highlights some major year 2000 techniques, noting the advantages and disadvantages of each.

Expanding Date Fields

One approach involves expanding dates in the system to a four-digit year format. When you specify a four-digit year, no ambiguity exists about the century or millennium that the year belongs to, as shown in Figure 6-1. The date expansion solution is considered by many to be the only one that is both permanent and easily understood.

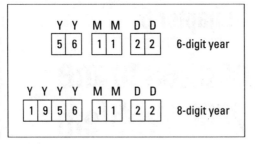

Figure 6-1:
Illustrating
the concept
of date
expansion.

A date expansion approach requires that you make significant changes to your systems:

- ✔ **Program changes.** You must examine — and possibly expand — any variables that hold date fields in your source code.

- ✔ **Data changes.** You must convert data — and the layout of data records — from the old format to the new, larger format. (Expanding the year segment of date fields from two digits to four lengthens the size of data records.) The amount of effort depends on the number of data files and the amount of data. Converting the data also requires a lot of planning and testing.

- ✔ **Screen changes.** Users will need to enter the two high-order digits of year values in their input screens (also called *forms* or *windows*). The amount of effort to change individual fields and screens depends heavily on the tools used to build the applications.

- ✔ **Report changes.** In many reports, year values are limited to two digits so that more data can be printed on a given line or page. These fields should be expanded if using the two high-order digits of the year value (that is, 19).

Don't underestimate the effect on programs, data files, screens, and reports under this approach. You need to examine the source code of every program to determine what changes are required. If you don't have access to the source code, you have to obtain it or create it using a process of reverse engineering. The process of *reverse engineering* is studying a completed product to determine how it was created. This can enable you to copy or improve the product.

You don't need to modify some date fields, such as those that users only read. You should, however, present these fields in a context that is absolutely clear. An example of a cosmetic field is the one that lists the current time and date. The user understands which century is being referenced even when the date has only two digits.

When deciding which date fields require expansion, it's best to err on the side of caution. If you have any doubt about whether a date should be considered cosmetic or not, put it into the noncosmetic category.

Advantages of this approach:

✔ Provides a permanent and complete correction to the year 2000 predicament. No other date related changes are required for the next 8,000 years. By then, you will have retired, expired, or both.

✔ Conceptually, this approach is straightforward.

✔ Sorted data will always be what users expect. For example, the year 2000 will follow 1999 in a sorted list.

Disadvantages of this approach:

✔ You need to examine — and possibly expand by two digits — all program variables that contain dates.

✔ You must scrutinize subroutines, functions, library calls, and so on that accept date and year values as inputs.

✔ The size of data records is increased. You must examine and possibly adjust data record layouts, variables, and any other references to these records.

✔ You must convert all existing date data from a two-digit to a four-digit format. This conversion effort is significant all by itself.

✔ Larger records require additional storage resources, including disk space and tape backup requirements, where applicable.

✔ Processing time might be slightly slower due to the necessity for the program to access larger data records.

✔ Users must enter four-digit year values in applications. They can no longer assume that the two high-order digits are 19. Applications could be modified to supply the two high-order year digits, but this approach requires you to develop more code or change the code. In addition, the application's assumptions regarding the values to be supplied might be incorrect. The user should always be allowed to override default values and supply all four year digits.

✔ A date expansion solution affects a significant amount of source code. Many experts feel that if you didn't begin addressing your year 2000 problems by mid-1997, it is too late to implement a date expansion solution.

Using a Fixed Window

The first step of the fixed window technique requires you to identify a static 100-year period. These dates will be the only ones accessible to your applications. The system continues to express year values as two digits. All two-digit year values represent a date in this time window.

For example, suppose that your company determines it needs to access the dates between January 1, 1970, and December 31, 2069. This 100-year period represents the fixed window your company can reference. This means that any year value in the system must be within this 100-year interval. A data record with a year value of 32 would be referring to 2032. The year 71 in the system would mean 1971. Years before 1970 and after 2069 could not be referenced. Figure 6-2 provides a graphic example of how a fixed window is implemented.

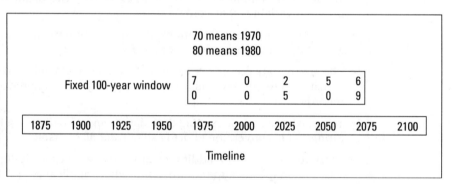

Figure 6-2:
The fixed window solution.

Advantages of this approach:

- ✔ Users continue to enter two-digit year values in their data entry screens.

- ✔ The cost can be considerably less than date expansion. This can be especially attractive if you intend to replace the software soon.

- ✔ You aren't required to expand date fields in programs, data records, screens, or reports.

- ✔ You can obtain four-digit year values by referencing a subroutine, a function, or an array of four-digit year values.

Disadvantages of this approach:

✔ It requires that *all* dates in the system be within a 100-year period. Although this might not appear to be a significant restriction, it could turn out to be. People today live longer, and if date information related to individuals is contained in your system, it will almost certainly exceed this limitation. In addition, computer systems retain expanding types and volumes of data; someday your system might be required to retain information spanning more than 100 years.

✔ Some applications might need to reference different 100-year periods. If so, your company would need to maintain different fixed windows. Multiple fixed windows can easily confuse users, programmers, management, and customers. Data between applications can't be shared, summarized, compared, and so on without the dates undergoing conversion.

✔ Each year, the future horizon becomes shorter and shorter. Eventually, you will be forced to adjust the window. Doing this entails additional effort, and will result in the oldest date values in the system being dropped.

✔ Processing time might be slightly slower due to the references to the function or array that translates two-digit years to four digits.

✔ The sorting sequence of two-digit year values in some instances won't meet user expectations. For example, the year (20)00 would precede (19)99 in a sort.

Using a Sliding Window

The sliding window technique also references a period of 100 years. Two-digit year values in the system refer to a specific year within this time period. The difference between the fixed and the sliding window techniques is that the sliding window always maintains a consistent number of years in the past and the future.

Assume that business practices require an application to access the previous 60 years and the upcoming 39 years. During calendar year 1999, the sliding window would allow the application to reference the years 1939 (1999 - 60) through 2038 (1999 + 39). In the application, a two-digit year value of 30 refers to 2030. A two-digit year of 41 is the year 1941.

During calendar year 2005, the sliding window would allow applications to reference years 1945 (2005 - 60) through 2044 (2005 + 39). At this point, a two-digit year value of 41 would refer to the year 2041. (See Figure 6-3.)

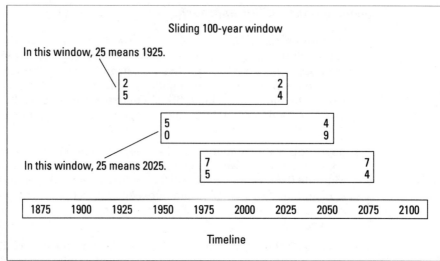

Figure 6-3:
The sliding
window
solution.

Advantages of this approach:

- ✔ The 100-year window advances automatically. This eliminates the need for manual intervention because the future horizon of the window doesn't become too small.
- ✔ The cost can be considerably less than date expansion. This can be especially attractive if you intend to replace the software in the near future.
- ✔ Users can continue to enter two-digit year values.
- ✔ You aren't required to expand date fields in programs, data records, screens, and reports.
- ✔ Four-digit years can be obtained by referencing a subroutine, a function, or an array of four-digit year values.
- ✔ Applications can reference their own customized sliding windows.

Disadvantages of this approach:

- ✔ It requires that *all* dates in the system be within a 100-year period. Although this might not appear to be a significant restriction, it could turn out to be. People today live longer, and if date information related to individuals is contained in your system, it will almost certainly exceed this limitation. In addition, computer systems retain expanding types and volumes of data; someday your system might be required to retain information spanning more than one hundred years.

✔ Some applications might need to reference different 100-year periods. If
so, your company would need to maintain different sliding windows.
Multiple sliding windows could easily confuse users, programmers,
management, and customers. Data between applications couldn't be
shared, summarized, compared, and so on without the dates undergoing conversion.

✔ Different companies will undoubtedly define their windows differently.
Company A might say that all years greater than or equal to 70 are 19*xx*
and years less than 70 are 20*xx*. Company B might choose 50 as its
breakpoint. When data moves between companies, what standards will
be agreed upon?

✔ Sorts based on year values will not always meet user expectations. For
example, the year (20)00 will precede the year 19(99) in a sort. You could
write specialized logic to handle this, but it requires additional work.

Compressing Dates

The date compression solution represents the equivalent of four-digit
decimal values in existing two-digit fields. This technique requires two parts.
The first is that you must establish a base year. The values in existing two-
digit year fields represent offsets from this base year.

The second part of this solution is that the values in two-digit year fields
contain hexadecimal values. The hexadecimal numbering system contains
16 values represented by the digits 0 through 9 and the characters *A*
through *F*. A single digit in the hexadecimal, or hex, number system can
represent the decimal values 0 through 15.

Following is a comparison of values in the decimal and hexadecimal
systems:

Decimal	Hexadecimal
00	0
01	1
02	2
03	3
04	4
05	5
06	6
07	7
08	8
09	9

(continued)

Decimal	Hexadecimal
10	A
11	B
12	C
13	D
14	E
15	F
16	10
17	11
18	12
...	
25	19
26	1A
27	1B
...	
31	1F
32	20
33	21
...	

The possible values represented by a two-digit hex field range from 00 to FF. Expressed in the decimal number system, the values are 0 to 255. This range represents the number of years (255) available to your applications.

The base value you select represents the earliest year that your applications can reference.

When a date is referenced, a calculation is performed first. The two-digit hex value in the date field is converted to a decimal value, and then the decimal year value is added to the base year. The result is the requested year value.

Figure 6-4: Calculations used to create an effective year by adding an offset to the base year.

Base Year Value	1900	1900	1900	1900	1900
Hex Offset in Date Fields	46	4F	64	6A	FF
Decimal Equivalent of Hex Offset	70	79	100	106	255
Effective Year	1970	1979	2000	2006	2155

This calculation is demonstrated in Figure 6-4.

You would most likely write a set of subroutines or functions to perform these calculations. A calling program (that is, a program that calls a subroutine) can pass the two-digit hex year value. The value returned would be a four-digit, decimal year value.

There is nothing magical about using the hexadecimal number system for the two-digit year values. You could use all ten digits (0–9) and all 26 alphabetic characters (*a–z*). This would effectively be a base 36 (10 + 26) system. The largest number represented by two digits of a base 36 system is 1295. This widened range would allow the window of dates to stretch from 1000 to 2295, with a base year of 1000.

Stretching credibility even farther, you can utilize all ten digits (0–9), lowercase alphabetic characters (*a–z*), and uppercase alphabetic characters (*A–Z*). This would effectively be using a base 62 (10 + 26 + 26) system. The largest number represented in two digits of a base 62 system is 3843. With such a range, you could reference dates from 0 to 3843, with a base year of 0. This would most likely handle any date related needs.

Figure 6-5 demonstrates the use of base 36 and base 62 offsets.

Base Year Value	1900	1900	1900	1900	1900	1900	1900
Base 36 Offset In Date Field	0K	11	2d	2s	3g	a2	zz
Decimal Equivalent of Base 36 Offset	20	37	85	100	124	362	1295
Effective Year	1920	1937	1985	2000	2024	2262	3195
Base Year Value	1900	1900	1900	1900	1900	1900	1900
Base 62 Offset In Date Field	0A	11	1C	1Z	20	30	ZZ
Decimal Equivalent of Base 62 Offset	37	63	100	123	124	186	3843
Effective Year	1937	1963	2000	2023	2024	2086	5743

Figure 6-5: Compressed date calculations using base 36 and 62.

Advantages of this approach:

- No additional disk storage space is required because the date fields in current data records aren't expanded.

- The range of dates that can be referenced in applications is 255 years (at a minimum). This is probably sufficient for most applications. Using larger number systems (base 36 or base 62) can extend this range considerably with no additional programming.

- If you handle all computer systems in your organization this way, all dates can be compared, counted, summed, and so on.

Disadvantages of this approach:

- This approach is not intuitive to users, programmers, management, or anyone else. Future modifications to code will likely result in errors when programmers don't intuitively understand how the date values are represented. Code for this technique needs to be very well documented!

- You must modify date values in all existing data files to conform to this format. This entails a significant conversion effort. Don't underestimate the amount of time, effort, and testing required.

- You must synchronize the conversion of dates to the new format and programs that include new logic. Neither aspect can be installed without the other half.

- The execution time of programs will be somewhat slower due to the additional required calculations.

- Dates exported outside your organization will be in this encoded format. Recipients must be aware of the technique used and must perform their own conversions before they can use your data.

- Encoded dates will be difficult to recognize and understand at first sight in their "raw" state. This will probably affect the amount of time analysts and programmers take to resolve future problems with your system.

Encapsulating Dates

The encapsulation technique takes advantage of the repetitive nature of the Gregorian calendar — every 28 years, the calendar repeats itself. Thus, the days of the week and the first day of each month are the same in 1990 as they will be in 2018, 2046, and so on. By subtracting 28 from the current year value, you can refer to identical calendar years.

The code that must be changed is limited to areas where dates are read from and written to data files. Each time a date is read, 28 is added to the year portion. When a date is stored, 28 is subtracted before it's saved.

For example, if a user enters a date of January 1, 2000, the value stored in the data file is 010172. If the user enters a value of January 1, 1972, 010144 is stored in the database. This allows years before and beyond 2000 to be stored and accurately handled. Figure 6-6 illustrates this activity.

Figure 6-6:
A demonstration of how date encapsulation works.

	Y Y MM D D			
Date stored in database	3 2 0 1 0 1	5 0 0 9 1 5	7 2 0 1 0 1	8 8 0 5 3 1
Adding 28 years	1932+28=1960	1950+28=1978	1972+28=2000	1988+28=2016
Effective date	Jan. 1, 1960	Sept. 9, 1978	Jan. 1, 2000	May 31, 2016

Advantages of this approach:

✔ Changes are isolated to code that reads and writes dates to storage.

✔ The performance impact is minimal because the modifications are fairly simple.

✔ Users can continue to enter two-digit year fields.

Disadvantages of this approach:

✔ All dates in the system must be consistent, that is, all must have this modification.

✔ Data coming into your system from external sources must be modified before it can be written to data files. This may require bridge programs capable of handling other techniques used to deal with the year 2000 problem.

✔ Data exported from your system would be considered misleading or incorrect. Data recipients must be told early (and often) that this approach was used.

Using Bridge Programs

A *bridge program* is a method of moving data between differing formats by converting the data from one format to another. Bridge programs aren't limited to year 2000 situations. Many projects require conversion efforts to migrate data from an old system or format to a newer one.

Situations that benefit from using a bridge

One reason for requiring a bridge is that your organization may not employ the same year 2000 technique for all its systems and applications. You may have decided to convert most, but not all, date fields to four digits. You can use a bridge so that any application has access to all data in the organization.

Bridges don't need to be permanent. In many situations, a short-term conversion is required. For example, suppose that applications X and Y share a large amount of data. Your year 2000 project plan has scheduled the conversion of application X in January of 1998 and application Y in June of that year. A bridge program would allow application Y to reference the data it needs until it is converted in June. After that point, the bridge is superfluous.

This use of a bridge demonstrates how you can convert your applications gradually. The applications that have not yet been converted can continue to access dates that are already converted. As additional applications are converted, the use of bridge programs diminishes and gradually vanishes.

A bridge can prove beneficial when a problem exists for only a short time. Suppose that an application deals with data for just the most recent seven days. This program will function flawlessly up until 1/1/2000. It will also work fine after the calendar flips over to 1/8/2000. The only time it will have logic errors is during the window of time from 1/1/2000 until 1/7/2000. It seems excessive to modify the program for such a small time period. Instead, you could develop a bridge program to allow the program to function during that week.

When dealing with bridges, make sure that they don't become permanent. Suppose that you've put a temporary bridge in place until a certain application is converted, but various crises erupt and the application never gets converted. Now the temporary bridge has become a permanent fixture of your MIS landscape, and it's one additional processing task that can develop errors or become misplaced. If you use temporary bridges, make sure that they are in fact temporary.

Using a bridge to handle incoming data

You also might need a bridge if your organization receives data from an external source. If the external source uses a different technique for handling the year 2000 than you did, the data might not be compatible. A bridge could be required to convert data from their format to yours. Most likely, the burden is upon you to develop such a bridge.

If, for example, the external source uses a sliding window but your organization expands dates to four-digit year values, their dates will be two digits wheras yours are stored in four digits. You will need to determine how they have defined the 100-year window, that is, which years in the window are past and which are future. Using this information, your bridge program can convert incoming data to your internal format.

If you have multiple sources of data, you may need to develop multiple bridge programs. Ideally, all your bridge programs will be based on a standard design and customized for each distinct source.

Deciding Which Technique to Use

It isn't possible for someone unfamiliar with an organization to provide recommendations on how to handle the year 2000 decision. A great deal of knowledge about your systems, requirements, staffing, and operations must be taken into consideration. The only recommendation I can offer is to consider this decision long and hard before making it, because it will fundamentally drive your efforts.

Table 6-1 summarizes the advantages and disadvantages of each approach for correcting the year 2000 problem. You can use this table to help determine which solution is best for your situation.

Table 6-1	Comparison of Year 2000 Solutions	
Method	*Advantages*	*Disadvantages*
Date Expansion	Permanent solution	Requires extensive modifications to code
	Straightforward	Date record size is increased
	Data sorts correctly	Existing data must be converted

(continued)

Table 6-1 *(continued)*

Method	Advantages	Disadvantages
Fixed Window	Less extensive code changes	All dates in system must be within a 100-year window
	Users continue to enter two-digit year values	Multiple windows can be confusing
	Data record size isn't increased	Data sorts aren't correct
		Future horizon shortens every year
		Different companies can have different windows, which can cause problems on data transfers
Sliding Window	Less extensive code changes	All dates in system must be within a 100-year window
	Users continue to enter two-digit year values	Multiple windows can be confusing
	Data record size isn't increased	Data sorts aren't correct
	Future horizon stays the same	Different companies can have different windows, which can cause problems on data transfers
Data Compression	Data record size isn't increased	The data stored isn't intuitive to anyone who accesses it directly
	The range of available years can be from 255 to 3843	Existing data must be modified
	Comparisons between dates is possible if all dates have been compressed	Companies to which data is exported must be aware of the compression used
Encapsulation	Changes are isolated to code that reads and writes dates to storage	Existing date must be converted
	Users can continue to enter two-digit year values	Data being imported must be converted
	Impact on performance is minimal	Companies to which data is exported must be aware of the compression used
		The data stored isn't intuitive to anyone who accesses it directly

Going the date expansion route is very simple and provides a permanent solution. Unfortunately, it also involves the most work. Depending on the amount of code your system has, it might be impossible to complete this effort before 1/1/2000.

The sliding window solution requires less effort than date expansion. The drawback of this solution is that your applications are limited to accessing dates within a 100-year window.

It is feasible to mix-and-match your solutions. Some applications can be corrected with a date expansion. Others can be handled using one of the other techniques.

One fairly common approach is to expand only the date fields used in keys. A key is the field in a data record or database table that is used to access records. Normally the values in the key must be unique; that is, two records can't have the same key value. In an invoice table, the key is the invoice number. In a personnel data file, the key is the employee ID number. A two-digit year value can be expanded to four characters. For all other date fields, you can use a windowing approach. This mixture of approaches can considerably reduce the amount of code that needs modification.

If you choose to apply a mix of year 2000 solutions, thoroughly document which applications have been corrected with which technique and why. Programmers of the next century will forever be in your debt.

Chapter 7

Event Horizons

• •

• •

*I*n the business world, an *event horizon* refers to how far into the future a system or program "sees." Just as the horizon is the farthest point you can see in the distance, a program's event horizon is the farthest date into the future that it encounters.

For example, a computer system that deals with home mortgages must "see" a great distance into the future. If you apply for a 30-year home mortgage in 1998, your dealings with the mortgage company won't conclude until the year 2028. The program must account for your payments, equity, outstanding balance, and so on until this date. The program's event horizon is the length of your loan.

Compare the mortgage with a car loan, which is paid off usually in two to five years. Consequently, the program that processes car loans has a much shorter period that it "sees." Event horizons vary considerably between business situations and the programs that support them. (See Figure 7-1.)

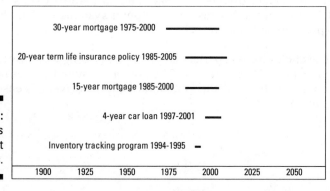

Figure 7-1:
Examples
of event
horizons.

The year 2000 and black holes

Before writing this chapter, I thought the only meaning of the term "event horizon" was the business-oriented one. While researching this chapter, I discovered that physicists have their own meaning for this phrase. In their world, an event horizon is the area around a black hole at which light can no longer escape the black hole's gravitational pull.

Oddly enough, I think the two definitions can be related. Both are inescapable. Just as light can't escape the black hole, society won't be able to escape the year 2000 computing crisis.

Real-Life Event Horizon Snafus

Examples of event horizons encountered by other organizations can help clarify what an event horizon is. Each of these examples has been reported by the press.

Some insurance companies found that they could no longer sell five-year annuities in the year 1995. The final pay-out date occurs in the year 2000, but the software system for some companies can't accept a date past 1999.

A five-year budgeting system of a major federal government agency failed recently. The fifth and final year being processed was 2000. That wasn't even the worst of it — the COBOL compiler used to compile the system was no longer being supported.

A number of credit card holders have had their credit cards rejected by merchants. The expiration date on their cards is the year 2000. Card readers used by merchants can't handle expiration dates beyond 99. The short-term solution has been to reissue cards that expire in 1999 instead of 2000. The long-term solution will be to replace the verification equipment at all merchant locations.

In several states, truck drivers have had their interstate driver's licenses canceled. This occurred because the computer systems couldn't handle renewals past the millennium.

Car rental agencies have experienced problems dealing with driver's licenses that expire in the year 2000. The holders of such licenses have been refused rental cars because the system thought the driver's licenses had already expired.

A car insurance program was designed to keep track of the driving records of policyholders. The number of traffic violations directly affects the premium. After a traffic ticket is five years old, however, it no longer affects the premium. Therefore, a violation that occurred in January of 1995 will be dropped in January of 2000. When the system compares this expiration date (00) with the current date (97, 98, and so on), it appears that the violation has expired so it isn't included in the premium calculation. It's a good deal for the driver, but not for the insurance company.

Perishable products (such as food and drugs) are marked with an expiration date. After this date, the product can no longer be sold. As the millennium approaches, the expiration dates of more products are in the next century. Some stock management systems reject products with expiration dates of 00 because the systems' logic determines that the product is almost 100 years old.

Programs were written to solve business needs. The majority of these business requirements involve dates, and many will have event horizons. When these dates and event horizons extend into the year 2000, your programs may begin to experience problems. If your systems have stored the year portion of date values in two digits (99) instead of four digits (1999), you can expect trouble — the code that compares dates won't produce the expected answers.

These potential errors must be corrected before you reach the event horizon in question. You don't have the luxury of waiting until December 31, 1999, to correct them. If a program has an event horizon of one year, for example, it will start encountering problems on January 1, 1999.

Programs also deal with a variety of event horizons, some long and some very short. Your project plan should identify and correct programs with longer event horizons before those with short horizons. A program with a long event horizon will encounter problems first and therefore need to be corrected sooner. You have more breathing room for addressing problems with shorter horizons.

Identifying Event Horizons in Your Organization

The Gartner Group projects that, if all applications are not corrected, up to 60 percent of all applications will fail or return incorrect results *before* the year 2000 arrives. Do you want your organization to be in this distinguished group? Your management and stockholders certainly don't want to be in the majority here.

There's no easy way to identify event horizons in your organization. The task requires knowledge about your systems and some hard work.

Two groups that should be familiar with your organization's event horizons consist of your systems analysts and programmers. They are aware of programs and how each interacts with data and future dates. Perhaps they've already been called upon to correct problems. Discuss the event horizon situation with all of your technical personnel — they should be able to identify some of the programs that could cause problems.

Another way to find event horizons is to enlist the help of users. In a memo or e-mail, spell out the concept of event horizons and why these dates and programs must be identified and corrected. Explain that with their assistance in locating these types of systems, you can help assure that their applications will function correctly as the year 2000 approaches.

As responses filter back, you need to document them. Some of the details that must be maintained include the name of the system, what department is affected, and when the event horizon will occur. A spreadsheet such as the one in Figure 7-2 should be sufficient for tracking event horizons as you identify them.

Handling Event Horizons

After you've identified and gathered the necessary details for each program in your organization that has an event horizon, you've completed the investigation part of your effort. Now you need to act on this knowledge.

You need to factor into your year 2000 project plan the order in which you expect to encounter these problems. In general, the first event horizons that you correct should be the ones that will cause problems the earliest (that is, the longest event horizons).

System Name	Application Name	Identified By	Horizon Interval	Must Be Fixed By
Financials	Loan Aging	KCB	5 years	12/31/94
Financials	Bad debt prediction	LAG	3 years	12/31/96
Human Resources	Employee Vesting Calculation	JHW	5 years	12/31/94
Human Resources	Sabbatical Projection	HJH	6 years	12/31/93
Legal Systems	Archive old matters	RRL	7 years	12/31/92

Figure 7-2: A spreadsheet for tracking event horizons.

Has your organization already encountered event horizon problems? How many times has this happened? How were the problems resolved? Was the solution to modify the code to handle all future dates and foreseeable situations, or was a quick-and-dirty patch applied to get the program back up and running?

If the solution was a quick patch, you should verify two things. First, make sure that this solution won't cause additional problems in the future. Specifically, will this patch work until and after January 1, 2000? Second, all patch corrections should be well documented and as consistent as possible. If all patches are similar, it will be easier to locate and correct them if necessary.

Chapter 8
Calendars and Clocks

● ●

In This Chapter

▶ Understanding the major calendars of the world

▶ Predicting the effect of different calendar systems on your year 2000 efforts

▶ Supporting a multinational corporation through the year 2000 situation

▶ Finding out how 1999 and 2000 can occur at the same time

● ●

*A*lthough one calendar reigns supreme in the Western Hemisphere, the rest of the world runs on a number of calendar systems. If your organization has branches or dealings around the world, you might have felt the effects of other calendar systems. Oil companies with operations in the Middle East need to convert Western dates into the Hejra calendar system.

The most serious reason for being familiar with a local calendar system might be because it's mandated by law. The local government may require that all dates in contracts and paperwork use the local calendar system.

Another reason for this is that local holidays and religious festivals are usually identified on the local calendar system and are then transferred to the Western calendar. Failure to convert accurately will lead to lost work days and productivity. It could also severely affect you relationship with citizens of the local country.

The arrival of the new millennium

The night of December 31, 1999, will be alive with parties and ablaze with fireworks. Times Square in New York City will be jammed with people waiting for the lighted ball to descend. Other cities around the world will be equally as festive. Everyone will want to celebrate the start of the new millennium with style. It raises an interesting question: When does the next millennium actually begin?

Most people assume that the 21st century and the new millennium both begin at midnight on January 1, 2000. The calendar no longer starts with 19; it now starts with 20. Surely this must prove that the new millennium has arrived, doesn't it?

Actually January 1, 2000, isn't the first day of the new millennium. That event doesn't arrive until January 1, 2001. Who says so? The National Institute of Standards and Technology. Their explanation is that the first century consisted of the years 1 through 100, the second century was years 101 through 200, and so on. Following this logic, the twenty-first century (and the next millennium) doesn't occur until the year 2001.

A word of warning is appropriate here. If you choose to discuss this technicality with others, you will probably encounter people who are convinced that the new millennium begins on 1/1/2000. They won't listen to your calm and logical explanations. Some of them might even become belligerent. I wouldn't waste my time or energy arguing with anyone about it. You and I know that you are right and they are wrong.

The World's Major Calendars

The Western, or Gregorian, calendar is recognized around the world. Other calendar systems, however, play important roles in specific countries or regions. In this section, I describe some of the more significant calendar systems.

Islamic calendar

The Moslem world uses the Islamic calendar to mark the passage of time. This calendar is based solely on the lunar calendar. It has 12 months — 6 months have 29 days and 6 have 30 days. The number of days in a year is 354.

A lunar calendar system is based strictly on rotations of the moon. Each month begins when a new moon is sighted and ends when the next new moon occurs. A lunar month is approximately $29^1/2$ days. A year in a lunar calendar consists of a set number of lunar months — usually 12.

Solar calendars, in contrast, are based on the Earth's rotation around the sun. A solar year is the time it takes for the Earth to travel around the sun once. This is approximately 365.25 days. A lunar calendar system with 12 months per year is approximately 354 days long. This is about 11 days shorter than a solar year.

The word *hejra* (also spelled hegira, hejira, and hijra) means emigration, or flight, in Arabic. The first day of the Islamic calendar marks the date that the Prophet Muhammad was forced to flee Mecca. This date corresponds with July 16, 622, of the Julian calendar. Dates in the Islamic calendar are followed with the letters *AH,* for *annus hejra,* or *the year of the hejra.* January 1, 1998, of the Gregorian calendar translates to the second day of the month of Ramadhan 1418AH.

Because of differences between the lunar and solar calendars, the Hejra months cycle backward through the solar year. For example, the first day of the month Muharram 1418AH coincides with May 8, 1997, with April 28, 1998, and then with April 17, 1999. The two calendars synchronize every 32^1/$_2$ years.

The Muslim world uses the Hejra calendar to schedule religious feast days and the Western calendar to schedule nonreligious events.

Julian dates aren't in the Julian calendar

Many computer systems and languages make a Julian date format available. Julian dates refer to the number of days that have passed since January 1, 4713 B.C. Many computer systems base their Julian dates on other reference dates — January 1, 1900, is a popular date to start counting from.

Julian dates make it very easy to determine the number of days between two dates by simply subtracting one date from the other. For example, suppose you want to find out the number of days between January 2, 1998, and March 28, 1998. These dates expressed as Julian dates are 35796 and 35881. Subtract them and you get the answer, 85 days.

You might think that the Julian date system was named after Julius Caesar. That's a logical, but incorrect, assumption. The system was invented in 1582 by Joseph Scaliger, who named it in honor of his father, Julius Caesar Scaliger.

I wanted to mention Julian dates to clear up any confusion. The Julian calendar and Julian dates are two different and unrelated things. The Julian calendar was created in 45 B.C. by the Roman Emperor Julius Caesar. The Julian date system was invented over 1600 years later and is used as way of easily comparing dates. The only thing they have is common is the word *Julian*. The inventor of the Julian date system, Joseph Scaliger, will never know how much confusion he has caused by reusing this particular name.

Chinese calendar

The People's Republic of China uses the Chinese calendar to determine when festivals and other domestic events occur and the Gregorian calendar for administrative purposes. The Chinese calendar has twelve months of either 29 or 30 days. Each month begins on a day when the new moon arrives. An extra month is added every two or three years to keep the calendar in synch with the solar year.

The year 2000 will correspond to the year of the dragon in the Chinese calendar.

No worldwide calendar standard?

People have made attempts to create a World calendar. Such a proposal was considered in 1954 but (obviously) not adopted by the United Nations. This calendar was based on a 52-week, 364-day year. A 365th day was added at the end of every year. This day, called Year-End Day, wasn't part of the 12th month or the 52nd week. Every fourth year, a second extra day, called Leap-Year Day, was added between June 28 and July 1.

In 1955, Henry Cabot Lodge, Jr., U.S. Representative to the United Nations, gave an impassioned speech opposing this change to the existing calendar system. One of his points was that it is inappropriate for the United Nations to sponsor a calendar that would conflict with the principles of religious faiths around the world.

Another proposed calendar system was the International Fixed Calendar. It was composed of 13 months of 28 days each. The thirteenth month, called Sol, was placed between June and July. A 365th day (Year Day) was added at the end of every year. Year Day doesn't belong to any specific month or week. Every fourth year, a Leap Day was added after June 28.

A third proposal was the Perpetual Calendar. It had four quarters composed of three months each. A Year-End Day was added to every year, and a Leap-Year Day was added every fourth year. Monday was the first day of every week, and all quarters began on Mondays. This arrangement made certain business calculations easier.

All these proposals were rejected for a number of reasons. Two specific points of resistance were the impact on religious calendars — the Sabbath would not always be every seventh day — and on nonreligious ones — some national holidays would need to be relocated.

It would be easier if everyone in the world operated on the same calendar because conversions between calendar systems would be unnecessary. We could all be like Star Trek, running on the same date throughout the galaxy. Unfortunately, this isn't likely to happen due to the tight link calendars have on the religious, national, and cultural aspects of a nation.

Japanese calendar

The Japanese calendar marks the year of the reign of the current emperor. Each year in this calendar contains 12 months. Japan uses the Western calendar and the Japanese calendar interchangeably.

Japan experienced a calendar crisis recently. In 1989, Emperor Hirohito died, so the 64-year Showa period ended. Computer systems in Japan had to change their Japanese calendar system from year 64 of the Showa reign to year 1 of the Heisei period. This event marked the first change in emperors since computers were invented.

Hebrew calendar

The Hebrew calendar is both the official calendar of Israel and the liturgical calendar of the Jewish faith. The Hebrew year is made up of 12 lunar months. Each month is made up of 29 or 30 days. Days are added or subtracted to two months (Heshvan and Kislev) to maintain consistency with the solar year.

The first date of the Hebrew calendar corresponds to when they believe the world was created. This year is equivalent to 3760 B.C.E. (before the common era).

Millennium may cause strange behavior

The advent of a new millennium is likely to bring out some strange behavior. A number of people are predicting that the new millennium is the dawn of a new era. Others predict that it will be the end of the world.

Predictions for what will happen toward the end of this millennium aren't new. One prediction from Nostradamus refers to a "king of terror" descending from the sky in mid-1999. Some interpret this to foretell a nuclear attack. The predictions of Nostradamus were written to be deliberately vague to avoid his being persecuted by the church.

Another shrouded prediction was made at Fatima, Portugal. On May 13, 1917, three children saw a vision of a woman while they were tending sheep. The woman told them to come to the same place on the 13th of every month until October 13th. On October 13th she appeared and made a number of predictions, one of which has been supposedly kept secret. This prediction is supposed to come to pass around the year 2000, but its details have never been revealed by the Vatican.

Our only example of a new millennium is when the calendar flipped over from the year 999 to 1000. According to reports, the population of Europe became wild with fear as the year 1000 approached. People supposedly abandoned their crops, sold their belongings, and forgave all their debts in preparation for the end of the world. I hope the managements of Visa and MasterCard follow this example.

Converting Other Calendars

Multinational companies must be aware of regional calendar systems. Local holidays and religious festivals would be defined on the local calendar system. For example, in Saudi Arabia, the religious holidays occur on the Islamic calendar. One particular religious holiday might be on the first day of the month of Shawwal. This date would need to be converted to the Western calendar each year. In 1998, the first day of Shawwal will occur on January 30. In 1999, it will be January 19. If this translation is performed incorrectly, it will certainly cause problems and confusion.

To fully understand the implications, imagine how you would react if someone was ignorant of your national holidays. Assuming you live in the United States, how many people would attend an important meeting scheduled for July 4? What if your kickoff sales meeting was scheduled for December 25 or the last Thursday in November? Likewise, ignorance of local holidays and religious dates of another country won't endear you to its citizens.

None of the other major calendar systems will undergo the rollover that the Gregorian calendar will on 12/31/99. Their year values won't need to be expanded to four digits any time soon. That's the good news.

The bad news is that programs that convert or translate between multiple calendars may be affected. If these programs can't properly handle the year 2000, the conversions will be incorrect. For example, if a PC thinks the day after December 31, 1999, is January 1, 1980, and converts 1/1/2000 into another calendar system, will the result be correct? Not likely.

A second example deals with a mainframe computer. Assume that a record is created on January 1, 2000, and stored in a six-digit date field as 010100. If the system hasn't been made year 2000 compliant, the first time the record is referenced, the program will assume that the date is 1/1/1900. If this date is converted to another calendar system (Islamic, for example), the result will certainly be incorrect.

The local or religious holidays placed on reports or computer screens won't be accurate.

Experiencing 1999 and 2000 Simultaneously

A brief but potentially disastrous interval exists for multinational companies at the end of 1999. Due to differences in time zones around the world, multinational companies will be in the years 1999 and 2000 simultaneously. During this period, one group in an organization could be entering data on December 31, 1999, while another is entering data on January 1, 2000.

This situation will begin when it becomes January 1, 2000, in Auckland, New Zealand. The condition doesn't end until it becomes January 1, 2000, in Tonga and the Midway Islands (just across the International Date Line) 24 hours later. Figure 8-1 should help illustrate this point.

Will this cause additional problems for your system? It's hard to predict the impact of this wrinkle on the year 2000 problem. As you examine your systems and code, keep this possibility in the back of your mind.

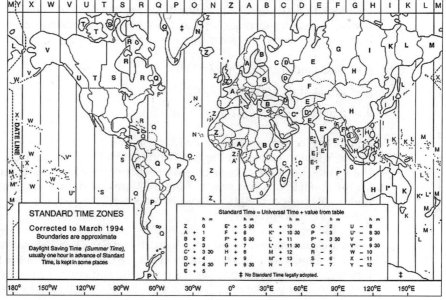

Figure 8-1:
The effect
of time
zones
on the
year 2000.

Networks will be especially affected

One area in particular that you should consider is how your network will react to different nodes on the system being in different millennium. Suppose you have sites in Auckland, New Zealand, Munich, Germany, and San Francisco, California. The first site to experience the year 2000 will be Auckland. When the date rolls over there, it will be 1 P.M. on 12/31/1999 in Munich and 4 A.M. on 12/31/99 in San Francisco.

Messages that travel throughout a network include a time stamp field. The value in this field will be different for messages coming from Auckland than for messages coming from Munich and San Francisco. Specifically, the year might be expressed as 00 in the time stamp field from Auckland but 99 in the time stamp field from Munich and San Francisco. Figure 8-2 shows a map of these three locations and a chart illustrating how the dates and times differ between them.

Will this impact the capability of the network to correctly handle network traffic when time stamp fields from different locations have different year values? To find out, you will need to create test cases that specifically test this scenario. Include test cases on network hardware simulating different locations that straddle time zones. Your test equipment could include three nodes, one each representing Auckland, Munich, and San Francisco. One test scenario would be to set the times to the following:

- ✔ Auckland: 12/31/1999 23:00:00
- ✔ Munich: 12/31/1999 13:00:00
- ✔ San Francisco: 12/31/1999 04:00:00

Initiate test scripts on each node that will exercise programs for many hours. When the clock on the Auckland node advances to 1/1/2000, observe the results. Does the network handle it correctly or have problems surfaced? Do the applications continue to function? Are the Munich and San Francisco nodes able to access data entered in Auckland? Are records with year 2000 dates processed properly?

Continue running tests until both Munich and San Francisco advance into the next millennium. Have problems occurred at any point in the test case? If problems have occurred, you must identify and correct them. Rerun the test again after you install a fix. Does the problem still exist? If so, the fix wasn't sufficient. Continue the cycle of testing and correcting until all tests run without errors.

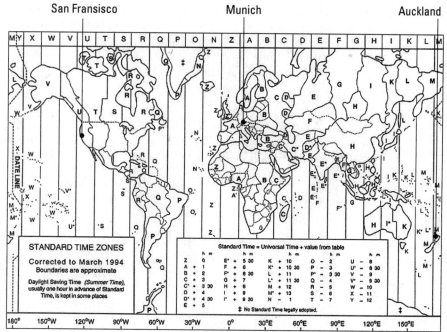

Figure 8-2:
Time zones
in three
locations.

Auckland		Munich		San Fransisco	
23:00	12/31/1999	13:00	12/31/1999	04:00	12/31/1999
00:01	01/01/2000	14:01	12/31/1999	05:01	12/31/1999
09:00	01/01/2000	23:00	12/31/1999	14:00	12/31/1999
10:01	01/01/2000	00:01	01/01/2000	15:01	12/31/1999
19:00	01/01/2000	08:00	01/01/2000	23:00	12/31/1999
20:01	01/02/2000	09:00	01/01/2000	00:01	01/01/2000

Embedded dates

Dates embedded in other fields such as invoice number and account number fields also present possible problems for multinational organizations.
Data records in both data files and relational databases rely on keys to
access the correct data. A key is a unique number that identifies one specific
record. An example of a key is an employee ID number, an invoice number,
or an account number. Frequently, keys, such as invoice numbers, contain
an embedded date value. For example, the first invoice generated on
January 1, 1998 might be 9801010001.

How will the act of moving from one millennium to another affect the generation of the keys? Can records with an embedded date of 00 or 2000 be created at one location while other locations generate records containing embedded dates such as 99 or 1999? Will this present problems for the applications? You need to test this scenario to find out.

For many international companies, this final concern may not be a problem. New Year's Day is a holiday in many places in the world. If an organization isn't planning on being open on New Year's Day, this last problem may not be a concern. When companies open up for business in the next millennium, all their branches will be in the same year.

Chapter 9

Deciding How Much Software Will Be Changed

To solve the year 2000 problem, you need to replace or modify software. The differences between replacing or modifying software will dictate how much of your systems will be affected and to what degree. The topic of how deep your changes should go embraces many schools of thought, from doing the minimum feasible changes to replacing both the baby *and* the bathwater. This chapter helps you choose the approach most appropriate for you.

One of the first steps in a year 2000 project is to understand how much software your organization has. To produce this information, you must inventory all of your computer systems to see what software runs on each of them. This includes all mainframe computers, PCs, file servers, database servers, e-mail servers, and network servers. The list of software compiled after examining these locations is your inventory of software. This inventory will be used during the actions described in this chapter as well as other steps during your year 2000 project.

Retiring Programs

In a survey of 100 IS managers (April 21, 1997, issue of *Information Week* magazine), 43 percent said that their year 2000 projects helped them identify unneeded or obsolete systems. During your year 2000 efforts, you too may discover obsolete programs or multiple applications performing essentially the same functions. Perhaps reports or data that were once highly valued have been superseded by another system. Maybe changes in the way business is handled or legislative changes have made certain systems obsolete.

Many times, changes in the outside world aren't communicated to the people in the back room. If MIS isn't told that a particular report, data file, or other output is unnecessary, they'll continue to churn it out. The year 2000 effort may be the first time MIS is made aware that some programs can be dropped.

When you identify a system that is no longer needed, back it up completely before deleting it from the system. That way, you'll be prepared if the system needs to be resurrected. At the least this will save you time; at best it could save your job.

What do you need to archive? Following are some elements to archive — you'll probably add to this list:

- Source code
- Compilers
- Libraries
- Executables
- Associated utilities
- Test programs and *scaffolding,* which consists of the programs, test scripts, and test data used to support testing activity
- JCL (Job Control Language)
- Data
- Data record layouts
- All documentation — user, programmer, and operational

Who backs up this information? That depends on how your organization divides responsibility. Perhaps software librarians are responsible; if so, provide them with a list of what needs to be backed up. If network personnel perform periodic tape backups, they may perform a permanent backup of these objects.

No matter who performs the backup, I recommend that you take two preliminary steps. First, place everything that needs to be backed up into a single location (area, volume, disk, and so on). This will make it easier to recover these objects should it ever be necessary.

Second, back up the program being retired onto a special tape rather than onto the normal rotation of tapes. Writing it to a separate tape will make the retired program easier to restore and less likely to be overwritten. If writing to a special tape isn't possible, try to back up onto a month-end, quarter-end, or year-end tape. Tapes saved at these intervals are frequently stored indefinitely instead of being recycled.

Consolidating Programs

When you performed your software inventory, did you notice anything unexpected? Did you find any duplicate systems? It's not uncommon for different departments in a large organization to acquire systems that fulfill the same function. Over time, the number of systems can accumulate.

Budget Rent-A-Car Corporation, for example, found that their organization had 14 distinct accounts receivable applications that had accumulated over a 20-year period. Their plan is to replace all of them with a single package.

Another source of duplication is when a company purchases or merges with another company. It's very likely that both companies have software performing the same functions. Both organizations will have a payroll system, an inventory control system, an accounts receivable system, and so on. This duplication presents an opportunity to consolidate software.

If your organization replaces numerous overlapping software packages with a single package, you can gain a number of advantages:

- ✔ **Reduced maintenance expenditures.** If you are paying maintenance on all the packages and delete all but one, there will be an immediate savings.

- ✔ **Reduction in hardware**. By removing overlapping software packages, you'll likely reduce the amount of disk space used for both executables and data storage. You may be able to consolidate all systems to a single server machine, thus trimming the need for computer hardware.

- ✔ **Single, consistent approach to business situations**. If each department handles their accounts receivables, for example, in the same manner, the data will be more accurate and widely available and training costs will be reduced.

And you thought *your* deadlines were tough

Almost everyone in the software development field has been on a project that had a tight deadline. Did you ever stop to think where the word *deadline* came from? The word originated in military prisons. The deadline was a line around the boundaries of the prison. Guards would shoot at any prisoner who stepped beyond this line.

As I said, almost all software projects have deadlines. Year 2000 projects have much more serious consequences than most software projects if their deadlines are missed. No matter how serious the year 2000 problem becomes, though, the consequences for team members aren't as severe as for the prisoners who faced the first deadlines.

Correcting Only Year 2000 Problems

One leading school of thought is that a year 2000 project should be tightly focused and identify and correct only year 2000-specific problems. The rationale is that this situation is critical enough to warrant being handled on its own. Making other changes at the same time would only muddy the waters. In addition, it's easier for most people to focus on a single objective at a time. The more objectives your team must deal with, the more likely it is that none of them will be met completely.

Another reason for correcting only year 2000 problems is that the process will almost certainly require the use of automated software tools. These tools are built specifically for year 2000 related problems and aren't designed to identify other changes. If you were to make non-year 2000 changes, you might need to develop new tools, extensively modify existing tools, or manually examine every line of code. None of these alternatives is conducive to meeting your schedule.

In addition, many experts predict that testing will occupy 50–60 percent of the time and effort spent on the year 2000 problem. If you were to extend the scope of the project, you'd also be extending the scope of the required testing. Instead of similar, consistent testing of every piece of software, each system would have unique testing requirements. This patchwork of testing objectives and requirements could also result in critical tests being overlooked.

As you know, the time frame for completing year 2000 efforts is already tight. Additional requirements increase the likelihood of failing to meet this deadline. Is it worth risking failure of a critical project by adding a wish list of noncritical items?

A side benefit of a year 2000 project

A year 2000 project generates side benefits that make system maintenance easier. You might want to mention some of the following benefits in your proposal to management:

✔ By deleting applications or systems, less software will need to be maintained or modified later.

✔ You'll have a ready-made inventory of software for later projects.

✔ Missing source code will be identified and recreated.

✔ Test data and test scripts will form a baseline for long-term testing requirements.

The foremost drawback to addressing only year 2000 problems is that it might be difficult to sell this project to management because it has no visible improvements. Completing the project simply enables operations to continue as before. Combining this project with other, more visible improvements might make it more acceptable to management.

Addressing Other Software Problems

The logic behind addressing other software problems as well as the year 2000 problem is pretty simple. Because you're already going to get your hands dirty, why not fix some other problems at the same time? All your software is scheduled to be examined and tested. Addressing additional problems or enhancements adds only an incremental amount of extra work.

The argument that you'll save time by not having to come back later to correct other (that is, non-year 2000) problems can be persuasive. This situation, however, has implications more important than simply saving time.

The overwhelming downside to making additional changes is that you won't be finished when you need to be. Instead of completing 100 percent of the year 2000 changes, you might complete only 50 percent of your expanded change list. This means that on 1/1/2000, your systems may not be functional. Explaining this situation to upper management wouldn't be easy.

You risk losing focus if you attempt to correct other problems as well as year 2000 changes. When dealing with many changes, it's easy to overlook important details. In addition, many people have difficulty dealing with multiple tasks at the same time. A single objective is easier to complete.

I don't recommend that you make additional changes. If your organization started its efforts in 1995, it might be able to successfully complete multiple objectives. If you're beginning your project later than that, focus exclusively on the year 2000 changes. Doing anything else is too risky.

Replacing the Entire System

Suppose that the legacy systems your organization has are old, cranky, and inflexible and need to be replaced. You've decided that the year 2000 is the perfect justification for retiring the old system and replacing it with a new one. Why pour additional money, time, and effort into the old system? Why not junk it and apply the upgrade costs towards replacing it?

The concept that a computer system has an expected lifetime is reasonable. Technology, both hardware and software, changes over time. What was effective in the past may no longer be acceptable today.

In addition, you may no longer be able to obtain hardware and software support for your aging systems. Without support, you're in a precarious position should the worst happen.

Your existing system may use software products (such as compilers and operating systems) that are no longer available. If this is the case, you may be forced to replace the system instead of modifying it.

A plan that scraps the old system and replaces it before January 1, 2000, seems to kill two birds with one stone and might be easier to sell to management than the alternatives.

What could be wrong with this approach? It depends on how complicated the system is and how much time you have to accomplish the installation of a replacement system.

The biggest risk is that you're putting all your eggs in one basket with this approach. By not addressing year 2000 problems in the old system, you're gambling that you'll have the new system ready in time. If you don't complete it on schedule, you won't have a year 2000 compliant system when you enter the next millennium.

You can replace a legacy system in several ways. Each has its pros and cons, which I discuss next.

Rewriting applications from scratch

Suppose that you've decided to replace a legacy system with a new system built from the ground up. The new system will do everything your users have always wanted it to do. It will incorporate the latest technology advocated by the developers. Year 2000 compliance will be designed into it from the outset.

Sounds like a great idea. What could go wrong with this solution? Plenty! The biggest danger of this approach is that you may not complete it in time. There might not be enough time to design, program, test, and install a new system as well as train people before the millennium arrives. If the new system isn't functional by January 1, 2000, the old, existing system may not be able to continue functioning.

Installing a third-party software package

Another way to replace a legacy system is to acquire and install a third-party package. Some software packages claim to do just about everything under the sun. They will address your human resource needs, maintain your inventory, run your financials, and more. Packaged applications are available that run on just about every hardware platform on the market.

This approach avoids the problem of dealing with year 2000 problems in the existing system. There's no need to search through decades-old code for date references that must then be corrected and tested.

Another advantage to this method is that it gives management something "visible" for their investment. They'll be able to point to new features and capabilities when they justify this investment.

If you intend to replace your current system with a year 2000 compliant system, make sure the replacement system is year 2000 compliant. The phrase "year 2000 compliant" means different things to different people, so get specifics on what it means to the vendor. What guarantees do they provide that their software will function after 1/1/2000?

Even if you intend to purchase an off-the-shelf package, it will still take a significant amount of time to develop specifications, request proposals, and receive and evaluate bids. Additional time will be required to acquire, install, and test the new system.

You need to install the replacement system well before January 1, 2000, so that you can run parallel testing and shake out any last-minute problems. Year 2000 experts recommend that all year 2000 changes be completed before the end of 1998. You should follow this guideline when installing a new system as well.

What delivery schedule will the vendor commit to? Does the vendor have enough human resources to install your system when promised? How much confidence do you (and should you) have in their promises?

When you install a new system, you'll need to convert and verify data from the existing system. This conversion will likely require that you deal with the year 2000 problem. If existing data is stored as two-year digits, you may have to expand the values to four digits.

In short, installing a new system to replace an existing one isn't a picnic. Replacement projects are just as prone to running over budget and being late as other software projects. It isn't safe or prudent to assume that you can install a replacement system in time to meet the year 2000 deadline. You might be taking a significant risk to assume that everything will go perfectly on such a project. On January 1, 2000, you might end up with two systems: one that hasn't been converted and one that hasn't been installed. Happy New Year!

Migrating to client/server

The year 2000 situation may justify a desire to move away from a mainframe or minicomputer legacy system entirely. Why not replace it with a shiny new client/server system? You'll be able to show management that they're getting something for their investment.

Client/server systems are frequently based on a relational database management system (RDBMS). RDBMS products don't store dates in YYMMDD format. Their internal date format includes the full four-digit year value. The specific format depends on the software vendor, but all major products store a complete year and time value. Because they store a complete year value, no inherent problem exists with the way the year is stored.

That's not to say that a brand new client/server system can't have year 2000 problems. For the year value to be properly stored, it must be correctly entered into the client/server system. Problems with client/server systems can occur when data is entered into the system. The two primary methods for entering data into a client/server system are

✔ By users into client/server applications

✔ From another computer system via a data feed

If the application wasn't designed properly, problems can occur when users enter data. Date fields on screens might be text fields that are then converted to date values. One potential problem is if the date fields don't have room for a four-digit year value and can fit only a two-digit date. If the date value coming in contains only two year digits, either the programmer or the RDBMS system will convert it to a four-digit value. What will the extra two digits be? I don't know, and neither do you! Only by looking at the code or reading the RDBMS specifications can the extra two digits be determined.

Data feeds into a client/server system can be accomplished by using disk files, tapes, modems, or CD-ROMs. The client/server system would include a program or utility that takes data from the file and inputs it into the relational database. What if the year values in the input feed are expressed in two digits? What century will the program convert these dates to? Again, I don't know, and neither do you. You must examine the RDBMS documentation or the program to determine this.

I admit I'm an advocate of client/server systems based on GUI front-ends and relational database back-ends. I think that when set up correctly, they provide users with significantly more productivity than applications that run on a monochrome, character-only terminal. By "set up correctly," I mean the following:

- ✔ The database must be properly designed. It must include all the data fields needed to support the user. Tables in the database should be designed to minimize the complexity of database operations. If the database isn't properly designed, the system's performance will probably be too slow.

- ✔ Navigation within the application must allow users to perform their jobs with a minimal amount of time and effort. If this isn't properly planned and executed, users will spend excessive time getting from one screen to another. Their perception of the system will be that it is too complicated and doesn't mesh with the way they do their jobs.

- ✔ The performance needs to be fast enough to allow users to accomplish their jobs without long, annoying pauses. If users have to wait for 5 to 10 seconds each time a screen is requested, they will be extremely dissatisfied with the system.

- ✔ The system must help the users! It must enable users to accomplish their work without becoming contortionists. Using the system must be logical, convenient, and easy.

Client/server systems allow a degree of flexibility that isn't possible on legacy systems. A client/server GUI system allows users to see data in a way that has never before been possible. Many client/server systems display data on spreadsheets, pie charts, bar graphs, and scatter plots. Many of these graphical representations of the data can be displayed in three dimensions. Users can use a mouse to highlight certain areas of data on the screen and "drill down" into them. This enables them to see the details behind a chart and understand how the big number or summary value is being calculated. Data can be combined with geographic information systems (GIS) to show on a map where the best clients are located. If a picture is worth a thousand words, how many reports is a map worth? These are the benefits of a client/server system.

To balance the positives, it's only fair that I also present some of the negatives. One of the biggest problems with client/server is that it's trivial to build a demo system with GUI development tools, but deceptively difficult to build a production-sized system. Decisionmakers could easily misjudge the time it will take to develop a client/server system.

Some of the other negatives associated with a client/server project include the following:

- ✔ Schedule estimates are no more accurate than traditional software projects.

- ✔ Testing is more difficult than with a traditional system. This is due largely to the more complex user interface.

- ✔ Obtaining experienced personnel is difficult. There isn't yet a large pool of experienced developers.

- ✔ New hardware, including both servers and client machines, is frequently required. If PCs currently in use aren't powerful enough, the response is too slow. Underpowered servers and a local area network (LAN) that is overburdened also contribute to a system being too slow. New hardware adds to the cost of the project.

- ✔ An organization that does not have experience with networking software or hardware will need to hire network administrators to support the system.

- ✔ Installations at remote sites can be troublesome and time-consuming. This is mostly due to the large number of components that are required to put a client/server system into operation. The needed components include both hardware and software requirements.

- ✔ Training costs are often underestimated. These costs include training both developers and users.

Deciding Which Approach Is Best for You

Your choices in the year 2000 crisis will be determined largely by how much time and money you have. The year 2000 deadline is immovable, so it wouldn't be wise to take an approach that you aren't likely to complete in time. Therefore, this could eliminate a decision to rewrite a large existing system or convert it to a client/server system. Smaller systems might be rewritten or converted in time, but you had better start soon.

For me, the time factor is justification for focusing attention strictly on year 2000 changes. For corporations with a large amount of software, you will be fortunate if you succeed in making your systems year 2000 compliant in time. Doing anything more (such as making other changes, rewriting the system, or converting to client/server) involves a bigger risk than I would be willing to take.

Repairing a system that will be replaced later

When you have a system that's scheduled to be replaced before the year 2000, should you spend time and effort to repair the system? The answer depends heavily on how confident you are in the schedule. If you have absolute confidence that the project will be completed on schedule, repairing the system is a waste of time. If you have less confidence, you might want to at least perform an analysis of the software in question.

Moving targets

Whether your plan is to repair or replace the existing system, you have to know what the result will look like. Will the completed system provide the same functionality as the existing system provides, or are users requesting changes?

Is your system stable or are changes constantly being put into place? If the system is changing, can you quantify the number of changes being made? Are the changes significant or fairly trivial? Can you document how many changes are made to the system on an annual basis?

Hitting a moving target is difficult whether you're making repairs to a system or replacing it. Your year 2000 project will go more smoothly if you can freeze the existing system. How much political capital will it take to freeze the system for this period? If it can't be frozen, be prepared to redo a lot of your changes. If enhancements are made to the current system at the same time year 2000 related changes are made, will the two sets of changes overlap? The only way to answer this question is to examine each module to see whether multiple changes are being made to it.

Relying on the system's original design information

The system's original design information will be invaluable if you choose to replace the system. Although the information certainly can't be used as is, it can provide a foundation for future specifications and requirements, saving a significant amount of time in the early stages of a replacement effort.

Beware of feature creep

Feature creep is the reason many projects don't make their deadlines. It begins innocently enough. Users ask for something that isn't in the original design. It's a fairly small request and would make the system more usable. Including one small change can't possibly affect the schedule, can it? Developers want to be helpful, so the request is added.

The second request comes right on the heels of the first. It asks for a slightly bigger change. Although it also would make the system more useful, it won't be as easy to implement as the first request. Later changes take more time to make. If you're not careful, the time devoted to change requests will outweigh the time spent on the original design.

Requests submitted by users toward the end of a project might be very valuable because they reflect experience and insight that was unavailable earlier. My argument against requests is simply this: A project plan is an agreement to build a defined system in a specified amount of time for a certain cost. If additional features are added, the project schedule and cost estimates are no longer valid. You can't have it both ways. Either the specifications must remain unchanged or the cost and schedule must be expanded.

How can you stop feature creep from occurring? It isn't easy! Someone in authority has to make it clear that this project can't lose its focus. Requests for enhancements or modifications are a distraction that aren't allowed.

Obviously, there will be exceptions to this rule. If legislation is passed that has a direct impact on your organization, it will have to be addressed. If you find a software error, you must address it immediately. Requests for new or modified reports, however, hardly fit into these categories.

At the beginning of the project, you should provide an explanation for taking a hard line against feature creep. You might try having all involved parties sign an agreement to not ask for undocumented changes. Knowing in advance that the project won't be expanded might make people think twice about asking for changes.

Part III
Implementing Your Plan

The 5th Wave   **By Rich Tennant**

" 'MORNING, MR. DREXEL. I HEARD YOU SAY YOUR COMPUTERS ALL HAD BUGS; WELL, I FIGURE THEY'RE CRAWLING IN THROUGH THOSE SLOTS THEY HAVE, SO I JAMMED A COUPLE OF ROACH-DISKS IN EACH ONE. LET ME KNOW IF YOU HAVE ANY MORE PROBLEMS."

In this part . . .

You've developed your year 2000 project plan. What's next? Now you need to put into practice everything you have laid out on paper and implement the plan. You must make several significant decisions during this phase of the project. Choosing the project team is certainly an important consideration. The order in which programs will be examined and corrected is another important matter.

Your year 2000 efforts will likely require the purchase of additional equipment and software. The equipment you require may include new PCs, additional disk drives, replacement computers, and computers that will be used as test platforms. Software expenses may include additional licenses of products you already use, software tools geared toward the year 2000 problem, and general software tools. You should have a handle on what you will need before you start purchasing these items. If you don't build these costs into the schedule from the very beginning, you may easily go over your budget.

Chapter 10
Who Does the Work?

A year 2000 project can't be accomplished without someone sitting down and actually doing the work. For a large organization with decades worth of code, a number of somebodies may be doing the work. A unique aspect of the year 2000 deadline is that companies all over the world are striving to meet it. This means the competition for qualified individuals will be fierce.

Your Year 2000 Project Team Members

To accomplish the objectives of your organization's year 2000 project, you need to recruit a team. The workload will be simply too big for only one person to perform (except in the case of fairly small organizations).

Identifying potential team members

The core members of your team will likely come from the existing computer staff. They may be people who have expressed an interest in this project. Maybe they were enlisted because they know the systems that will be modified. Or they may be on the project because the organization is using everyone it can find for this effort.

When building your year 2000 project team, consider the languages and systems that will be converted. For example, suppose that 80 percent of the programs being converted are written in COBOL, 10 percent in PL/1, and 10 percent in assembly language. Team members should have a significant amount of experience in COBOL, and at least some should have experience with PL/1 and assembly language.

The inventory of software to be converted should include the language each program was written in. Use the information available in your software inventory to predict which languages you'll need the most experience in. If you don't have people with the necessary experience, plan on hiring or contracting.

Increasing user involvement

Year 2000 projects are going to be "big tent" events. By this I mean that everyone in your organization needs to be included. Opportunities will exist for people of all skill levels and backgrounds.

One source for team members that may be easily overlooked is your user community. The experience and background of users can prove useful in a number of ways. Following are some areas of experience that could be valuable:

✔ Experience with large projects

✔ A background in testing software

✔ Time spent using the applications that are being modified

Users might also offer suggestions on which applications should be converted first and which can safely be delayed. And a very important way that users can help is by having them identify less visible, easily overlooked, components. Some examples of these include the following:

✔ Data coming into or leaving your organization

✔ Software that runs on only one or two PCs

✔ PCs that require testing for year 2000 compliance

The most valuable role for users may be participating in the testing phase of the project. After systems or subsystems have been converted, they must be tested. Users who are already familiar with the system will not need time to become adept in the environment. If the system is being replaced with a new one, users can participate in testing the replacement system as well.

Users acting in the role of testers should be provided with guidance on what constitutes an error or a problem. They may be looking for dates that are still expressed with two-digit years. Negative ages are another indication of an error. By showing the testers the types of errors to look for, you'll encounter fewer false alarms.

Testing can be performed either manually or with tools. A new breed of test tool is coming of age. Many of these tools run on PCs and use *graphical user interfaces* (GUI) to interact with users. With the availability of such test tools, it's easier for non-programmers to make contributions during the testing process.

Not all users will be interested in participating in this project. Some might be considered too valuable to leave their current position for any amount of time. Others might be reluctant to become involved in something new. Even if you must work out some aspects, such as which users will be involved, the idea of including users in this project should be considered.

Shielding team members

While your year 2000 project is in progress, normal business activities must continue. Reports still need to be printed and distributed. Month-end closings must be performed on the third business day of the month. Checks must be cut and mailed. Invoices must be sent from or entered into the system. Backups of your data need to be written to tape and sent off-site on schedule.

Even in a well-organized shop, problems have a habit of cropping up, and someone has to handle them. Problems of this type include an application that hangs up a PC, a new column requested on a report, a user needing access to a database table, or the need to recover yesterday's data from backup tapes and insert them into the database. If employees who previously put out these little fires have been reassigned to the year 2000 project, there will be pressure for them to continue to fulfill their old functions. In addition, most programmers and developers want to maintain good relations with the users, so they don't want to turn down user requests that seem reasonable.

It won't be easy, but these pressures must be resisted! If team members have their time consumed by daily firefighting, eventually they will have little time to devote to their year 2000 project duties.

Upper management should issue explicit orders stating that members of the year 2000 team must be left alone unless there is a true emergency. Day-to-day problems must be dealt with by someone else or put on hold until the year 2000 project concludes.

Training your team

Team members on the year 2000 project will be presented with many new concepts and situations. For example, most year 2000 projects will include the use of new software tools. Team members must be trained on when and how to use these software products. The better trained they are, the more quickly they will become productive. Skimping on training will likely result in frustration, missed deadlines, and lower-quality work.

Training yields an additional advantage. If a bunch of programmers are given a new tool but no training, they will all use the tool differently. Team members who receive training will tend to use the tool the way it was designed to be used. Consistent use of tools will allow team members to work together better and to fill in for each other when necessary. The output from the tool is also more likely to be correct if the tool is used consistently by the entire team.

Motivating your team

After the team has been selected and trained, you can set them loose on the project. Later, if team members become disillusioned, it's the responsibility of the team leader to provide motivation.

In *The Psychology of Computer Programming* (published by Van Nostrand Reinhold), Gerald M. Weinberg described his search to identify what motivates computer programmers. From a survey at one large programming shop, he identified the following top four motivators (actually numbers three and four tied for third place):

- Salary increase, bonus, or both
- Personnel involvement in planning tasks
- Promotion
- More time to give work a personal touch of quality

Good team leaders know their team well enough to recognize what motivates each individual. Salary increases and promotions are beyond the immediate control of the leader. Therefore, the leader needs to develop alternative (that is, non-compensation-based) means to motivate his or her team. For some people, a few well-timed words of public praise do wonders. Others respond to a challenge.

One of the most effective ways of killing motivation is to set unrealistic schedules and deadlines. Worse yet, each time an unachievable deadline is missed, create another that can't be met. Nothing will drain your team's enthusiasm faster. Schedules need to be challenging but also reachable.

When objectives are surrounded by doubt or ambiguity, they are less likely to be accomplished. Individual assignments and objectives must be crystal clear — with no uncertainty about who is responsible for each task in this project.

Retaining People until the New Millennium

Building a year 2000 team isn't your final personnel-oriented issue. You'll want the team to stay in place until the project is complete. If you lose team members, you'll lose time while you recruit, train, and integrate replacements. This is time you can't afford to lose.

What could cause members of your team to leave? They may decide to retire. Another opportunity may present itself. They might yearn for a career change. The biggest reason for leaving, though, might turn out to be intense competition for programmers qualified for year 2000 projects.

Repulsing raiders!

I can state without reservation that your year 2000 team members will be recruited by other organizations! As the deadline draws closer, other organizations will realize that they are behind in their year 2000 efforts. Many will panic and try to enlarge their staff. If no new programmers are coming into the workforce, these raiders will look to programmers who are already employed.

Loyalty

Loyalty is heightened when an employee has a feeling of belonging to an organization. Loyalty can be improved by encouraging a team atmosphere on a specific project. In this case, an individual's loyalty toward the team may be greater than his or her loyalty toward the organization.

If people feel loyalty toward an organization, they will think long and hard before leaving it. This is especially true if their departure could jeopardize the success of an important project. Loyalty is no guarantee against team members leaving, but its effectiveness shouldn't be ignored.

Before counting on employee loyalty to protect you from team attrition, ask yourself whether your company deserves their loyalty. How has your organization been loyal to its employees? How many of the following questions can be answered in the affirmative?

- ✔ Does your company provide competitive compensation and benefits?
- ✔ Is your company flexible when an employee has a justifiable but unusual request?
- ✔ Has it been company policy to promote from within?
- ✔ Do employees really matter to the organization?
- ✔ Are employees retrained when they are no longer useful or are they cast aside?

Your answers to these questions might provide insight into the level of loyalty your employees feel toward the organization. If a significant number of your answers were no, don't count on much of a loyalty factor.

Employment contracts

Another way to retain employees through the life of your project is to require them to sign an employment contract for this period. However, those who are already working for the company (as opposed to new hires) might not be very excited about signing such a contract.

If you are thinking about taking this route, consider its effect on employee loyalty. Employees may feel that being asked to sign an employment contract — that is, being compelled to stay — isn't a sign of loyalty on the part of the organization.

Employment contracts aren't foolproof. Even after signing one, an employee may still leave. Courts frequently throw out employment contracts that they judge too restrictive. Make sure that your legal advisors approve any contract before asking employees to sign it.

Can you say bonus?

When organizations are in a panic, they may be willing to pay a lot of money to acquire the right people. Before another company flashes an open checkbook at your people, consider increasing their pay.

Management might find it difficult to adjust pay rates. Existing policies probably dictate pay rates for various job descriptions, and those rates are probably modified only after a great deal of time and research.

However, management will need to recognize that this is an exceptional situation where haste is of the essence. If it takes a year to adjust pay rates, during this interim you will lose employees and have difficulty replacing them because your pay rates won't be competitive.

Instead of a pay raise, consider a bonus. This approach has an advantage: Paying a bonus doesn't increase an employee's base pay. And because base pay is the basis for benefits and future raises, bonuses can save you money in the long term.

The list of bonuses that can be offered is limited only by your imagination. A few examples of bonuses and what must be accomplished to qualify for them are listed here:

- ✔ **Performance bonus.** A performance bonus could increase the compensation enough to retain or attract high performing programmers. Defining what constitutes high performance, however, is difficult and must be clearly described in advance and easily measured.

- ✔ **Completion bonus.** A completion bonus is easier to define than a performance bonus. As soon as the project, including installation and testing, is finished, bonuses are paid. Such a bonus encourages people to stay through the end of the project.

   Think twice before offering a completion bonus that is paid up-front. If the employee or contractor leaves before the completion date, repayment may be difficult or impossible to collect.

- ✔ **Stock options.** Existing stock option plans could be extended to include employees or new hires on the year 2000 project. This would encourage team members to complete the year 2000 effort because an incomplete project would have a big impact on the price of the stock. Self-interest in increasing the value of stock holdings can motivate people to successfully complete the project.

- ✔ **Early retirement.** Some legacy systems have been in place for years or decades. Programmers familiar with the system might be approaching retirement age. Suppose that some programmers will reach retirement age in 2005. Offering them early retirement in the year 2000 may entice them to stay for the remainder of the project. It would be difficult for other companies to hire them away with an offer of a higher salary for only two or three years.

- ✔ **Enhanced retirement package.** With this alternative to an early retirement package, your organization agrees to make additional contributions to an employee's retirement plan in return for a promise to complete the year 2000 project. Again, this inducement would be difficult for another company to match.

The legal implications of offering special compensation can be complex. Before offering early or enhanced retirement packages, you must be certain that the package doesn't violate any legal or tax restrictions. Have a competent compensation expert participate in the development of any special package.

Post-year-2000 career paths

Assuring people that they have a long-term career path might help to retain some. Management should sit down with each individual and lay out a realistic professional development plan. Employees may think twice about jumping to a new position if they've discussed a plan for their long-term career with management.

Unfortunately, if a headhunter calls with a lucrative offer, there's no guarantee that any of the actions described here will keep your employee. You're apt to lose productive people before you finish your project. One way to lessen the loss is to insist that everyone document their progress. If documentation is up-to-date, it will be easier to recover after someone's departure.

Outside Help

You may determine that your existing staff isn't large enough to complete the year 2000 efforts. Adding to your permanent staff may not be acceptable for a number of reasons. A primary reason for not adding staff is that they will not be needed after the project is finished.

Many companies are planning to add temporary personnel for year 2000 projects. Following are some of the decisions you need to make:

- ✔ How many additional people are required?
- ✔ When will they be brought on board?
- ✔ What functions they will perform?
- ✔ To whom will they report?

The decision to hire extra personnel should be made as soon as possible. The year 2000 situation is affecting companies around the world, so the competition for available people will heat up quickly. If you delay in making this decision, it might be too late to acquire competent people.

Consultants

Suppose that you've developed your project plan and identified each task, when it needs to be accomplished, and which tools will be used. You don't, however, have enough personnel to complete the task list, so you plan to hire consultants or contract programmers to perform the work. When the work is complete or your contract with them expires, they will leave.

Articles in the computer trade press are predicting that contractor rates will rise as we approach the year 2000. So, the sooner you sign contracts, the lower the rates are likely to be.

Consulting companies

Your organization might not have developed a year 2000 project plan yet. Perhaps the required leadership skills and experience in this area aren't available. Maybe your expertise is tied up with other projects that can't be held up. In this case, consider dealing with a large consulting company. These organizations can offer a lot of flexibility in the tasks they can provide, from supplying programmers and management personnel to analyzing your situation and writing the project plan for you.

One topic you will want to explore with them is what experience they have. Some questions you might ask include the following:

- ✔ How many similar projects have you been involved with?
- ✔ How many of those projects are finished?
- ✔ How many large projects have you been involved with?
- ✔ Can you provide references?
- ✔ What tools do you have experience with?
- ✔ What environments (hardware and software) are you experienced with?
- ✔ How many people are available for new projects?

Tool vendors

If you've written the project plan and now it needs to be implemented, you might consider getting assistance from a firm that develops tools.

You would want to contact a tool vendor who provides a tool compatible with your method of solving the problem. If you're expanding date fields from two digits to four, for example, but a given vendor's tools don't support this method, you should be talking to other vendors.

The vendor may have personnel that will come on site and perform the work. Or they may require that you send your source code to them. You may want to limit a vendor's involvement to training your personnel in how to use their tools.

Caveat emptor

Before contracting with consultants or vendors, you should consider some points that have to do with getting your money's worth as well as protecting your assets.

Conflict of interest

Guard against a conflict of interest. If a contractor, consulting company, or vendor has strong ties with a competitor, it would be understandable to have legitimate concerns about the relationship. For example, a vendor might be a fully-owned subsidiary of your biggest rival. This might lead you to question their intentions.

Ask all potential outside parties questions regarding their relationships in your geographic area and industry. If the answers make you uncomfortable, consider an alternative source for the assistance.

Nondisclosure agreements

In many organizations, computer systems represent a competitive advantage. These systems may have been developed at great expense by the organization. Outsiders should be allowed to access them only after careful consideration. If possible, you should structure assignments such that no one individual or organization has access to the entire system. That is, no one sees the big picture except trusted employees.

All groups and individuals should be required to sign a nondisclosure agreement drawn up by your legal department. It should include any computer systems they will be working on as well as any other areas they might come in contact with.

It isn't uncommon for a vendor or consulting company to have staff turnover during a project. If new people come onto the project, make sure they sign the nondisclosure statements before they are given access to the system. It would be very easy to overlook this detail, thereby risking your organization's trade secrets.

No-hire agreements

When outside people are brought in to assist on a project, there will be a mixing of internal and external people. Your people and their people will begin to swap old programming war stories. It's human nature for your employees to compare their present positions to the consultants working next to them.

It isn't uncommon for employees of either organization to start thinking that the grass is greener on the other side of the fence. This is especially true if your employees ever get a glance at the rates on invoices submitted by the contractors. Pretty soon people may be sending out feelers for potential employment. If you're not careful, the act of bringing in a consulting agency might result in the loss of your best employees.

You probably can't completely eliminate this problem. You can minimize it, however, if you obtain an agreement with the agency not to hire each other's employees. An employee who wants to leave will likely do so, but losses can be reduced if the consulting agency isn't actively recruiting your people.

Security concerns

For many organizations, their data is an extremely valuable asset. Security of your data has to be one of your utmost concerns. Some information that needs protection follows:

- ✔ Employee salaries
- ✔ Marketing plans
- ✔ Client lists
- ✔ Production costs
- ✔ Rates paid to attorneys, consultants, accountants, and so on
- ✔ Costs of raw materials and subassemblies
- ✔ Leasing rates
- ✔ Litigation settlements
- ✔ Personal information on employees
- ✔ Executive compensation plans
- ✔ Labor negotiations
- ✔ Accounts-receivable information
- ✔ Negotiations with cities and landowners for new sites

Make sure that access to data is limited to a need-to-know basis. Even if people have signed every agreement you've asked, they shouldn't be allowed unlimited access to all data. People should have access to only the data they are currently working on.

Data is eminently portable. A single $3^1/_2$-inch floppy diskette holds almost 1.5 megabytes of data. When the data is compressed, it can hold up to 10 times that amount. A few diskettes carried out in a shirt pocket can contain enough sensitive information to devastate an organization.

Some project plans require that your code and data be sent off site to be converted. If so, make sure that the consulting company or vendor treats this material with the utmost care. Loss of tapes, diskettes, and so on, as well as the information they contain, could represent a significant blow to your company. It could result in the loss of income and clients, as well as a lawsuit from your clients.

Warranty

Does the consulting company or vendor offer a warranty covering their work? If so, what exactly does it cover? When does it begin and end? Details of this nature should be determined before signing a contract.

If they don't offer a warranty, why not? Does this indicate a lack of confidence in their own work? Determine why they offer no legal assurances of their work before moving forward with them.

The existence of a warranty represents merely a promise. If the promise is broken, it should be backed up with cash or other assets. If the entity providing the promise has no attachable assets, what good is it? Does your vendor or consulting company possess enough capital to compensate your for potential damages? If not, their warranty isn't worth much.

These questions regarding a vendor's potential conflict of interest, nondisclosure agreements, no-hire agreements, security, and warranty could be critical to the success of your year 2000 project and ongoing viability. Getting legal advice from a qualified attorney is highly recommended before contracting with a vendor.

Chapter 11

Triage

• •

In This Chapter

▶ Understanding triage

▶ Applying triage to the year 2000 situation

• •

*I*f you've ever gone into a hospital emergency room, you were probably evaluated on the basis of a triage system. If your injury was relatively minor, you may have noticed that patients who arrived after you were treated before you. Victims of a serious car accident or illness will be treated immediately no matter how long you and your sprained ankle have been waiting. This is because the staff determines which injuries are more serious and need to be treated first. Your condition, though uncomfortable, isn't life threatening. It may be frustrating to wait, but how would you feel if the situations were reversed?

If your year 2000 project is like most, you need to correct a large number of programs but have a limited number of programmers to perform this work. Therefore, you're able to correct only a limited number at one time. How do you decide which programs should be converted first?

When time or resources — or both — are scarce, you need to prioritize. For the year 2000 project, this means separating your work into groups based on how quickly they must be corrected.

Survival-Based Grouping

Each organization will have slightly different criteria for ranking, or prioritizing, systems. The following is a generic start:

✔ Systems that do not require any modifications to be year 2000 compliant

✔ Systems that require moderate revisions to be year 2000 compliant

✔ Systems that require extraordinary efforts to be year 2000 compliant

Already compliant systems

The first group — systems that do not require modifications — includes systems that contain no dates. Don't expect to find many systems that meet this criterion. One industry guru estimates that 85 percent of all systems process date values.

This compliant category includes systems designed from their inception to handle four-digit dates. Many systems built on relational databases, which retain a full date value, are already compliant and therefore in this category. Other systems may be compliant because they don't deal with dates.

In addition, many PC applications are in this group. Current releases of PC software such as spreadsheets, personal databases, and word processors may have been designed and coded with the year 2000 in mind and therefore won't require revisions.

Many personal relational database systems and spreadsheets as well as other PC-oriented software are year 2000 compliant. However, this does not guarantee that they all are. Year 2000 compliance can be threatened by the way an application has been designed or coded. In relational databases, for example, you can write programs that store date values as character fields rather than use the date type. This opens up the possibility of year values being stored in two digits instead of four. I think the best position you can take is to be skeptical of all PC software. Until it has been tested and proven to be year 2000 compliant, assume that it isn't compliant.

Somewhat compliant systems

The second category contains systems that need revision but the expected changes aren't extensive. Programs in this category perform some date processing but it isn't intensive. Plan to concentrate your efforts here because making this group compliant is an achievable goal.

Noncompliant systems

The third category contains the most difficult systems or applications — those that contain an extensive amount of date-processing logic. These systems typically store date values with two-digit year values and have many calculations based on date values. Many, many lines of code are involved in correcting these systems.

Making this third category of systems compliant will be time consuming, difficult, and — depending on when you begin your year 2000 efforts — perhaps impossible. Therefore, address these systems only after the second category of systems has been made compliant. Otherwise, you'll complete neither.

Grouping Systems by Need

Another approach to categorizing software is to group systems and programs by how critical they are to the organization. This technique might yield categories such as the following:

- ✔ Systems that must be made year 2000 compliant for the organization to survive
- ✔ Systems that it would be nice to make year 2000 compliant sooner rather than later
- ✔ Systems that can wait indefinitely before being made year 2000 compliant

Users or management may claim that all systems in the organization are required. The year 2000 situation, however, requires that you view the computer system in a new perspective. You must be able and willing to decide which systems are absolutely necessary and which aren't.

Necessary systems

A particular system or program may be on the "must be completed" list for a number of reasons. Perhaps it's the system that generates income for the organization. A catalog sales company, for example, lives or dies by its order entry system. If this system isn't converted before the end of 1999, the company can't sell its products and will quickly go bankrupt.

A system that could endanger lives must be made compliant as soon as possible. The systems that run a nuclear power plant, for example, must operate without polluting the environment with radioactivity.

Another justification for being on the top list is a system required by law. The nuclear power plant already referenced is required to file reports with the Nuclear Regulatory Commission (NRC). If these reporting requirements aren't met, the NRC can shut the plant down.

The Internal Revenue Service (IRS) is another example of a government agency that requires businesses to report information to them. If an employer doesn't properly calculate and forward payroll taxes, the IRS will certainly take action. The resulting penalties and potential jail terms can close a company.

Important systems

Other systems are important but not critical. Many management information systems are in this category. They provide information that enables management to efficiently run the company and make long-range planning decisions.

Although such systems are important, you can operate without them for awhile. Other means of acquiring this data can be developed for the short term. Resulting decisions may be less optimal than they are with the computer system, but there isn't the danger that the organization will collapse, be shut down, or be slapped with fines.

Noncritical systems

The lowest level of priority are systems that the organization can live without for an extended period of time. An example of such a program is a report that runs infrequently. Its results may not be requested (or missed) until quite awhile after January 1, 2000.

Some programs may be identified as no longer needed, perhaps because the business environment has changed. But the program may still be chugging along simply because of inertia — it requires effort on someone's part to remove a program from the job cycle. Systems of this nature can be archived and never made year 2000 compliant.

Dealing with a Project That's Behind Schedule

When drawing up your year 2000 project schedule, you should assign resources to the top-priority group first. After systems in this category have been converted, or are well on their way, you can address the second category. The third category must be deferred until the two higher priority groups have been completed.

What if the first group can't be completed in time? You have only a few options. The first option is to reassess whether or not all programs in this group should truly be there. After closer examination, some may be lowered to the second priority level.

What if all programs in the top group really do belong there? If this is your situation, you may be in trouble. This section details two ways to handle this predicament, but neither is guaranteed to solve your problem.

Adding people

One solution is to acquire additional resources for the project. If more people are added to the project, the team may be able to perform more work in a given period of time.

Adding people to a late project can have unexpected results. Instead of helping to get the project back on schedule, it can make the project even later. Why? Current productive team members must interrupt what they're doing to assist new team members. You experience a net loss in productivity until the new people become productive. More members on the team also means more communication between individuals. A higher percentage of team members' time will be spent on this activity, so they will be less productive than before.

Partially converting priority systems

A second alternative is to examine each system in the top-priority group and ask whether the entire program's functionality needs to be converted right away. For example, you may have a system that processes invoices and cuts checks for your suppliers. It includes complicated logic to perform this operation as efficiently as possible. For example, it attempts to minimize the number of checks cut by holding invoices until the amount owed to a supplier reaches a certain dollar level (thereby saving postage and keeping money in your bank account longer).

Although this processing is an asset to the organization, is it absolutely necessary? Would it be possible to turn off the more complicated logic for the short term? If this is possible, a significant portion of the program may not need to be converted and tested right away. This will allow the team to finish the program more quickly and move on to converting other high-priority programs.

Factored into your assessment must be the cost or complexity of converting the program. Suppose that two programs of equal importance need to be made year 2000 compliant. One is a large and complex system while the other is fairly simple. It makes sense to convert the easier one first. If they are converted in the reverse order, you may find that neither is completed in time. Figure 11-1 shows programs separated into these three groups.

Setting up a method of prioritizing programs may not be easy. At first it may seem that absolutely all programs are necessary and have a high priority. Assigning some of them to a lower-priority group may seem to be an admission that they aren't important. You may also be afraid that this could lead to questions such as, "If they aren't important, why were they written in the first place?" Worrying is unnecessary. It's a fact that some programs are more important than others.

System	Module Name	Triage Level	Related Programs	Explanation of why it requires this level
Accounts Payable	ap_main	1	all ap programs	Required to cut A/P checks
Accounts Payable	ap_open	1	all ap programs	Required to cut A/P checks
Accounts Payable	ap_read	1	all ap programs	Required to cut A/P checks
Accounts Payable	ap_validate	1	all ap programs	Required to cut A/P checks
Accounts Payable	ap_calculate	1	all ap programs	Required to cut A/P checks
Accounts Payable	ap_consolidate	2	all ap programs	Not required to cut A/P checks
Accounts Payable	ap_print	1	all ap programs	Required to cut A/P checks
Accounts Payable	ap_update	1	all ap programs	Required to cut A/P checks

Figure 11-1:
A spreadsheet to detail year 2000 prioritizing.

Defining these groups may be difficult for another reason. It may seem to be an admission of failure to admit that you won't convert all systems before the year 2000. Don't look at it this way. Instead, view it as a method of focusing on programs in their order of importance. You plan to get to all of them before the deadline, but this ensures that you will complete the critical programs first.

Chapter 12

Weekends Are an Important Resource

*H*ow many weekends are between today and January 1, 2000? That question is intended to open your eyes to a resource you might not have recognized — weekends. In this chapter, I hope to instill in you just how precious and limited this valuable resource is.

Obviously, the number of weekends between the current date and January 1, 2000, depends on when you're reading this book. If your digital wristwatch (you are wearing one, aren't you?) or your daily planner (the brown, faux leather one on your desk) reads 1/1/98, you have 104 weekends until the magic date. If you've put off reading this insightful book (and filling my coffers) beyond that date, shame on you. As a punishment, the number of weekends will be correspondingly fewer.

In time, you will probably wish that you had some of those weekends back. A wise man, or maybe it was just somebody I worked with, said that the foolish man wastes time, the prudent man uses it, and the wise man invests it. Pretty soon, you'll find out which category you and your company belong to.

Counting the Number of Weekends

Your first response to the question "How many weekends are between today and January 1, 2000?" is probably "Who knows, and who cares." Your understanding and appreciation of what a valuable commodity weekends are is about to be increased. The number of weekends available to you will make your year 2000 project difficult or outright impossible. Why? In most companies, weekends are the best (or perhaps the only) time for testing software changes.

It would be wonderful if the world could stand still while you addressed your year 2000 problems. What a luxury it would be to test whenever you wanted without worrying about reality interfering with your efforts. Life in the business world rumbles on, however. Users still expect to log on and use their applications every Monday through Friday. Orders still need to be entered into the system. Invoices must be mailed out to customers. The mail still brings the daily quota of bills. All of this means that during normal business hours, your computer systems must support the company in the customary manner. Their functions cannot go on hiatus while you modify them.

Weekend Testing

If systems must be up during normal business hours, when will you and your project team be able to test changes? Weekends will probably provide the bulk of year 2000 testing time. They'll provide the largest block of time available for installing changes, testing them, and getting things restored in time for users on Monday morning.

Weekends represent the last oasis of tranquility for many software workers. Many of you arrive at the office early and stay late. Leisure lunches were last seen about the same time as leisure suits. Evenings and night times are frequently interrupted by phone calls or a hyperactive beeper. It's an unfortunate possibility that your precious weekends may be devoted to testing year 2000 changes.

Weeknights after working hours can provide a certain amount of time for testing. The problem is that you may not know when all users have logged out of the system. In fact, they may not log off at all! Someone in accounting may be staying late tonight hoping to finish that quarterly report. A person in auditing may have begun printing a sizable report just before leaving for the day. Perhaps someone in purchasing has a tendency to kick off a monster query at the end of the day. Each of these user activities limits the amount of time available for testing on a typical weekday night.

If your organization supports users in multiple time zones, your testing window is smaller. Suppose that the organization has its headquarters in Omaha, Nebraska. (Don't laugh; stranger things have happened.) Having users located on both the East and West coasts wouldn't be unusual. The typical business day would extend from 7:00 A.M. Eastern time (6:00 A.M. Central time) until 7:00 P.M. Pacific time (9:00 P.M. Central time). This means that the system must be operational for a minimum of 15 hours each day.

Things get worse. If any of your users are located in Hawaii, Alaska, or foreign countries, the testing window is smaller still. Toss in users located in Europe or the Pacific Rim, and your testing window shrinks by six hours at least. All of this explains why nights may not constitute sufficient testing time for many organizations.

You might propose that a memo be distributed informing users that the systems are reserved for testing during certain hours. This proposal will have all the flight performance characteristics of a lead balloon. Users aren't likely to welcome restriction to their access to the system, especially if the restriction is in place until the year 2000.

Testing 7 x 24 Systems

Any computer system that is operational 24 hours a day, 7 days a week is referred to as a 7 x 24 (pronounced as "7 by 24") system. Similarly, any computer professional who works 7 days a week and 24 hours a day is referred to as "average." Seriously, a great many organizations and computer systems operate continuously, such as a credit card processing center, a hospital, utilities, railroads, and 911 emergency call systems.

These organizations don't have the luxury of taking down their systems at night or over the weekends. In fact, their systems may never come down. These systems are required to be operational 24 hours a day, 7 days a week. Consider an airline reservation system. When an application like this is down, the company can't book new flight ticketing requests. No new ticket reservations means no income. It also means that the airline can't respond to customer requests for information about the arrival and departure times of flights.

If any of your systems must be operational at all times, this necessity needs to be considered when developing the project plan. Organizations with systems that are operational at all times frequently have backup systems for support purposes. The backup system is used in the event that the main system crashes. It is also used to test software changes or version upgrades.

If a backup system exists, it can be used to test year 2000 related changes. The software on the backup system can be modified with year 2000 changes. Then data that is year 2000 compliant can be loaded onto the backup system. The system running on the backup machine can be executed to verify that the changes generate the expected results. In a way, this makes testing 7 x 24 systems easier than non-7 x 24 systems that don't have existing backup systems.

The real complications for a 7 x 24 system will come during the cutover phase of the project. *Cutover* is the act of making a transition from the old and functional but flawed system to the new and improved but unproven system. It requires a great deal of planning and timing. This joyful moment will be the climax of your efforts — if not your career.

Weekends May Not Be Enough

The time afforded by weekends may not be sufficient to accommodate all necessary testing. A pragmatic project manager must take this possibility into account.

If there simply isn't enough time to do the job, what's a project manager to do? An old but fairly accurate saying in the software development field states that every project has three axes. Not axes like Paul Bunyan carried, but axes like the X, Y, and Z ones from your high school geometry class. These axes are

- ✔ The project can be on schedule.
- ✔ The project can meet the budget.
- ✔ The project will have an acceptable level of quality.

Figure 12-1 illustrates this concept. The project manager is allowed to choose his or her favorite two of the three. Conventional wisdom dictates that achieving all three objectives on a given project isn't possible.

If this old programmer's tale is accurate, it has unusual implications for year 2000 projects. First, this is perhaps the only project in the (short) history of this fair industry that has an absolutely unchangeable deadline. You don't have the option of pushing back the deadline simply because you aren't ready. So your first choice in axes is forced upon you.

There's not a lot of room for maneuvering on the quality axis, either. If you want your company's computer systems to work properly in the twenty-first century, you must correct the code to handle the year 2000. This entails changing both the software and the dates and thoroughly testing these changes. Sounds like the second axis has been chosen for you as well.

Because you have no flexibility on the schedule or quality axes, that leaves the cost axis as the one that fluctuates. The implication is that the costs for the project aren't easily predictable or controllable. They will be driven up in the effort to achieve the mandatory quality within an unyielding time constraint. Talk about being between the proverbial rock and a hard spot! I guess this is what you're getting paid the proverbial big bucks for.

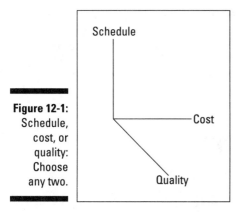

If Time Grows Short

One solution to a lack of time is to use the available time more effectively. How can you use time more effectively? The two immediate answers are to divide the work between more people or make the existing people more efficient.

Adding people

Most organizations have limited budgets, so the prospects of adding an unlimited number of people are rather slim. Besides busting your budget, the act of quickly increasing the size of a project team introduces its own problems. Some problems have to do with increased communications, training, coordination, and supervisory matters. For both management and budgetary considerations, it isn't always reasonable or possible to substantially increase the staff size.

Using testing tools

The only remaining alternative is to use the existing time more effectively. How can this be achieved? The solution is to use tools. The extensive use of tools is one of the skills that separate humans from lower species, such as mollusks and cephalopods.

The Industrial Revolution was fundamentally an improvement in the tools that were used. Better tools and better techniques of production allow fewer workers to produce more goods of better quality. Software development and testing are no different than building widgets in this regard. Better tools can allow fewer developers to produce higher-quality computer systems in less time. These tools can be used also when making changes to existing software to correct the year 2000 problem.

The tools employed might help your staff find references to date fields in source code. They might enable you to re-create lost source code. A tool might allow you to execute an application, feed data into it, and capture its results. This allows tests to run unattended all night, every night. Just try to get your staff to work all night and every night without complaining! Chapter 14 provides an overview of tools that are available to assist in your project.

Weekends and Wee Hours

No matter which tools you use, the year 2000 project will almost certainly require that you and others work off-hours and extra hours. You know it. Upper management knows it (or maybe they don't). Users know it. Project team members most certainly know it! If you're not up front regarding this "minor little inconvenience," you'll diminish your credibility in the eyes of the project team. You can't afford to take this kind of hit to your integrity, especially at the beginning of the project. You need to save credibility for the conclusion of the project when you exhort your project team to work even harder!

As I previously mention, between now and the year 2000, all current systems must continue to function. It's a fact of life in MIS that systems need a certain amount of support. Errors surface in even the most stable of systems. Users require ongoing training and hand-holding. Someone has to be available for this type of duty.

I've never worked on a computer system where changes weren't always being requested. As the jobs of system users evolve, they want the system to follow suit. New screens, new reports, new calculations, and alterations to access rights are an ongoing theme for modern computer systems. To maximize your project's chance of success, changes to the current systems should be reduced to the absolute minimum. Otherwise, your year 2000 project will be like trying to hit a moving target with a catapult.

Unfortunately, even if modifications are held to an absolute minimum, some changes are unavoidable. Try turning down a request from the CEO for a new report. You also can't avoid changes mandated by the government — OSHA and the FDA have voracious appetites for data. Changes of this nature must be addressed even when they adversely impact your project's schedule.

The result? Your existing systems will need to be supported during the year 2000 project. Unless you've hired staff specifically for the year 2000 project, there will be attempts to force your project team to pull double duty — supporting both the current applications as well as the project to make those applications year 2000 compliant. This double duty may occur occasionally but should be held to an absolute minimum. The only exceptions should be true emergencies. Allowing double duty to become commonplace will jeopardize the success of your year 2000 project.

Management needs to be aware of the combined responsibilities thrust upon its staff, especially when the inevitable crises erupt. Your staff may be capable of pulling double duty for a short time, but asking them to do this for an extended period of time will likely result in burnout, disillusionment, and a change of employment. The last thing you can afford at this stage is to drive off experienced people.

Dedicated Systems for Testing

A dedicated system is a computer (or a system of computers) that is exclusively devoted to a single user, effort, or application. The PC on your desk is dedicated to a single user — you. You don't have to worry about it being busy when you need to use it. You don't have to worry also about its performance being slowed by other users. That machine is dedicated to you, and you alone determine what will run on it.

If the testing time window in which your systems must be completed is small or your project staff wants to see the light of day, acquire additional hardware. A computer system that can be dedicated to testing solves a number of requirements in one shot.

Daylight hours

A dedicated system enables you to perform testing during daylight hours so that your project team can work during normal hours. Your project staff will thank you. Your staff's spouses and children will thank you. (Or they'll at least be glad that their spouse or parent is home more.)

Safety factor

Another advantage to testing on a dedicated system is that it's much, much safer. No matter how careful you are, risks are associated with performing testing on a production system. Files that shouldn't be changed are inadvertently modified. Data that should be restored after the test concludes isn't. Mysterious and inexplicable problems occur and annoy both the production and testing personnel. Each group blames the other, but neither is really at fault. It's simply the problem of trying to have the system serve two masters — which is not a good idea for people or computers.

Greater productivity

Your team will be significantly more productive when a dedicated test system is available. Your team won't have to spend precious time loading and unloading files, executables, and data every shift. This results in less time being spent on administrative minutia and more time spent actually correcting and testing the software. What a concept!

Running Systems in Parallel

Another significant advantage of having dedicated test systems is that it makes it easier to run the new system and old system in parallel. The concept here is to run both systems at the same time with the same data and compare the results. Although getting the same data into both systems can be tricky, the rewards are great. Essentially, knowing that the data in both systems is identical allows you to compare output between the systems, such as reports, screens, and data feeds to other systems. If the resulting outputs match, it's a fairly safe bet that changes to the source code haven't adversely (or perversely) affected the program logic.

Test data

The first requirement for successful parallel testing is to enter data only a single time. You don't want to require users to enter data into both systems for a few show-stopping reasons: It takes too long and therefore cuts productivity, and it results in data entry errors.

If different values are entered into the two systems, it's inevitable that the results will differ. How is a tester to know whether differences are due to data entry errors or programming errors? You'd waste lots of time trying to track down the sources of these errors.

Actually there's another drawback to requiring users to enter data a second time. They'll refuse to do it! They'll claim that it isn't possible for them to do their jobs *and* spoon feed data into the test system — and they're probably right!

You will therefore need an automated method of transferring data from the production system to the test system. The exact way to do this depends on the system. It might be possible to capture data as it's being input and feed it into the test system and the production system simultaneously. Another approach is to copy the production database or data files at the end of the business day and then pump them into the test system. This second approach may seem low-tech, but it's fairly easy to implement and just as effective.

Automated comparisons

The second requirement for a successful parallel implementation is the capability to automatically compare output from the two systems. Log any differences (and only the differences) in a well-documented location and fashion.

Automating comparison activities makes sense for at least two reasons. One, you — unlike computers — are not well designed for the mundane task of comparing line after line of output from two systems. Allowing even a single error to slip through can be disastrous to the project, company, and your job security. Two, your applications can produce data as plentiful as the water going over Niagara Falls. It can take an army of testing personnel to compare the output, and most shops don't have an open checkbook for hiring such a staff. Using computers to compare output, however, is effective and cost efficient.

Acquiring Test Systems

Okay, assume that I've convinced you that dedicated test systems are the way to go. Where are you going to get them? As you might expect, you have several choices:

- ✔ Purchase
- ✔ Lease
- ✔ Borrow
- ✔ Share

Purchasing test systems

The first solution is an outright purchase of the test system. If the computers in question are mid-range, that is, anything smaller than mainframes, you can probably acquire new hardware that is both cheaper and more powerful than your current production systems.

To make this purchase more acceptable to management, you might plan to make the new hardware permanent. After the systems have been converted and tested, the newer test system can completely replace the current system. An additional benefit is that this simplifies the cutover scenario significantly. You end up with a system that properly handles the year 2000 and is also faster. Who could ask for anything more?

Leasing test systems

Hardware and software procured for testing year 2000 changes needn't be a permanent acquisition. If you no longer need the test systems after the project is complete, it might make sense to lease the hardware for the dedicated test systems. This might be the lowest-cost alternative — the corporate bean counters will be your friend for life.

Borrowing test systems

Is it possible to have a dedicated test system without buying or leasing it? Possibly. Many companies contract with third parties for disaster recovery backup systems. For a fee, the organization has access to a backup system in the event of a disaster. Does the year 2000 crisis constitute a disaster? I don't know, but you should check your contract. It might be possible for your organization to utilize this resource for testing year 2000 changes.

If you finagle your way into this position, be aware of a few drawbacks. First, other clients might experience an honest to goodness disaster while you're in your testing effort. If their building burns down, they might bump you out of the picture. They aren't likely to view your protests favorably when they're trying to keep their company afloat and you're simply testing changes. Another problem with this solution is if everyone tries to do it. If this should happen (because they all got the idea from me), the demands on the availability of disaster recovery systems will undoubtedly exceed their availability. All in all, it isn't realistic to expect to do all your testing on systems of this sort.

Sharing test systems

If other departments in your organization are in the same predicament, you might be able to arrange something to reduce overall expenses. Perhaps two or more departments can jointly purchase a test system. This would substantially reduce the costs for all involved parties.

Before embarking on this path, make sure that you can work effectively with the other groups. Each of your hardware needs must be similar — if not identical. The sum of the time each group expects to utilize the test system can't exceed 24 hours a day. There should also be a basic understanding about how the hours will be distributed — who gets the graveyard shift and who gets the first shift. If this isn't resolved beforehand, it will certainly cause hard feelings later.

Chapter 13

Start Writing Those POs

*T*he year 2000 project will cost a lot of money. Some of that money will be in salaries paid to employees. A significant amount, though, will flow out your doors in the form of purchase orders (POs) or invoices. Careful planning will enable you to plan these costs up front. Overlooking them will result in your project going over budget.

Hardware Purchases

You may be required to purchase a variety of computer hardware. I describe potential hardware acquisitions in this section.

New server and mainframe computers

Many year 2000 experts predict that year 2000 compliant code will run more slowly than your original code. This will likely be true for a number of reasons, including the following:

- ✔ If you implement a data expansion solution, you will be reading more data. Each data record will be larger and fewer will be transferred per I/O (input/output) operation.

- ✔ If you implement a windowing technique (fixed window or sliding window), you must add logic to convert a two-digit year value to four digits. This addition will require access to a translation table, and it may require a disk I/O to reference this table.

> ✔ A date encryption year 2000 solution doesn't require additional disk accesses. It merely requires that the two-digit encrypted date be converted to a decimal value. This conversion takes only a few computer instructions. Users shouldn't notice the impact of this technique.
>
> ✔ If you chose the date encapsulation solution, the impact should also be minimal. A value of 28 will be added to the year value, which should take only a single computer instruction.

If your current performance is acceptable, you won't be affected. A system with marginal or outright slow response time, however, might be pushed over the edge if it becomes any slower. To compensate, you might decide to upgrade server or mainframe-level computers. If this is necessary, it will represent a significant expense.

Test platforms

All year 2000 modifications need to be tested extensively. This testing needs to be on a platform similar, if not identical, to the production system. If you can't perform testing on the production system, you must obtain hardware dedicated to testing.

If the hardware being used on the production platform is obsolete, it presents a complication. You can try to contact dealers who handle used equipment. If they aren't able to provide this equipment, you have a problem much more serious than the year 2000. If you are relying on obsolete hardware, have no backup computers, and aren't able to purchase replacements, your company's computer operations are hanging by a thread. You should implement a plan to upgrade hardware immediately.

The outright purchase of hardware dedicated to the testing effort is one option. The test equipment purchased can be a newer (that is, faster) version of the same model of computer. After the year 2000 project is complete, this equipment can replace the existing production system, be used as a backup to the current hardware, or become a permanent development and test platform. Any of these uses would be extremely useful to an organization.

Leasing the hardware needed for testing is another viable option. The primary advantage of this approach is that it represents less of a financial outlay than a purchase. The downside of this approach is that the hardware won't be available for future uses.

Additional disk storage (DASD)

Most year 2000 efforts will require additional amounts of disk space. Depending on your operations, the additional storage space could be substantial. Some of this disk space will be permanently needed, and other portions will be needed only during the conversion project.

Almost all levels in the organization will need additional disk capacity. The server or mainframe level will require a boost in capacity. Other disk drive requirements will be at the individual PC level. Plan carefully to avoid either overbuying or underbuying. Coordinating the purchase of all drives at one time might result in a better purchase price.

Temporary requirements

Additional disk space requirements will be particularly high while the year 2000 effort is in progress. One explanation of this is that up to twice the normal amount of data will need to be stored. During conversion and testing, you'll need to hold data in both the old and new formats. If you're expanding date fields in the data, the test version of the data may be larger than the production version of the data.

Data isn't the only thing that will be stored in duplicate. You'll also need to store two versions of the organization's programs. The current versions are needed to meet business operations. The second copy will consist of programs being converted. As more and more programs are successfully converted, the size of the second set of programs will grow.

It's likely that you'll obtain a number of software tools for this project that will reside on the system for the duration of the project. Some of these tools will be running on the mainframe or a server, but a number will be located on PCs.

Make sure that any PCs being used are up to the task. If they have less than a gigabyte of storage, think about upgrading their internal drives. Failure to do so will result in lost time and frustration later when the local drives become full.

Permanent requirements

Your permanent disk space requirements will be larger for a number of reasons. If your approach to the year 2000 solution is date expansion, you'll be particularly affected. Expanding six-character date fields to eight characters represents a 33 percent increase in the size of that field. To determine the effect of this increase on a given data file, you must know the

- Number of date fields in each record
- Number of data records in the file

Then multiply the number of date fields in each record by two. This gives you the number of extra characters per record. Multiply this by the number of data records in the file. The result is the additional size of the file.

To calculate the overall additional disk space required by data, perform this calculation for every data file and add up these numbers.

For some programs, the source code may not be available to you, making it very difficult to modify the program. In these cases, you'll need to install the latest version of the software package.

Newer versions of software seem larger, perhaps because they contain more features. If you haven't upgraded a package in a while, the amount of additional space may be significant. The more packages you upgrade, the more disk space required.

After the year 2000, you might have to maintain some data in both the old and new formats permanently. Data that comes into your system from outside might have different year 2000 conversion techniques applied to it. For example, suppose that your organization expands all its date fields to a four-digit year, but data coming in from an external source uses a sliding window technique (see Chapter 6). You must have a bridge program to convert between the two formats. During this conversion, both formats reside on your system. Twice as much disk space is required while storing both versions of the data.

New PCs

Your year 2000 project plan may require that you purchase new PCs for several reasons:

- ✔ The current PCs might contain BIOS chips that don't handle the year 2000 and can't be upgraded with a software correction.
- ✔ If you're upgrading software and your PCs are old, they might not be capable of running the latest operating system or might not be fast enough for the new software.
- ✔ If the size of your project team increases, you'll need additional computers.

BIOS upgrades

Some PCs that can't handle the year 2000 can be corrected by upgrading the BIOS software or replacing this chip. Either of these solutions is significantly cheaper than purchasing a new PC.

Many PC manufacturers provide BIOS upgrade software for free — and you might be able to download the upgrade from their Web page. For BIOS upgrades that aren't free, try to negotiate a company-wide license if you have many PCs.

If the software in the BIOS chip can't be upgraded, you may be able to purchase a new chip. Investigate this decision carefully. If the PCs and their components are this inflexible, consider whether you want to invest more money in them — the equipment may be nearing the end of its life expectancy.

If you can make a PC year 2000 compatible by simply upgrading the BIOS chip, that's great. If you have to replace any additional parts, I caution you to be skeptical. I have never been a big fan of upgrading PCs. The primary argument against it is the cost. When you start upgrading a computer, it just seems to go on forever. First it's the CPU chip or the motherboard. Then it's the video card. Next it's new memory, a new disk controller card, a new hard drive, and so on. Pretty soon you've spent what it would have cost to purchase a new PC, and what do you have? You have a mishmash of parts in a box with no warranty and little assurance that it will work together properly. If something goes wrong with it, who do you call?

Embedded systems

Microchips are embedded in a large number of devices, such as elevators, fax machines, copy machines, process control equipment, and security systems. You need to contact the manufacturer to determine whether or not these devices will require replacing. You should also resolve who will be responsible for paying for the replacements.

Project-wide expenses

Some hardware expenses can't be pinned to one particular piece of equipment. They apply to the project as a whole, but they shouldn't be forgotten or overlooked. Omitting them will have a negative effect on your budget and can wreak havoc on your schedule.

Electrical circuits

If you are adding hardware, the overall electrical requirements at your facility will be increased, and existing electrical circuits might be unable to support the higher load. In this case, it may be necessary to install additional electrical circuits.

Determining whether this is necessary shouldn't be too difficult. Determine the electrical load that each piece of equipment draws. Determine the requirements of any equipment you're proposing to buy. Add these figures to obtain the projected requirements. Finally, consult with your organization's engineers to determine the capacity of existing circuits. If there isn't anyone in this position, contact a qualified, licensed electrician. I'd suggest that you contact my father, but he's retired now.

The following table provides a few examples of the load that equipment in my office requires. You need to examine your equipment to obtain the electrical rating stamped on it by the manufacturer. This information is also provided in the technical documentation provided with the equipment:

Equipment	Required amperage
CPU	1.5
External drive pack #1	0.5
External drive pack #2	0.5
Monitor	1.8
Tape backup unit	0.2
External CD-ROM drive	0.2
Laser printer	0.5

If you determine that additional circuits are necessary, act immediately because it can take a long time to schedule the work. Failure to properly plan may cause schedule problems if you have to delay using any new equipment installed during your year 2000 project.

Uninterruptible power supply (UPS)

Pieces of computer equipment that many users rely on — such as servers, routers, and gateways — must always be available, even during a power outage. An uninterruptible power supply (UPS) is an electrical device that assures the availability of a steady supply of power for devices plugged into it. A UPS is essentially a battery that is constantly being charged from the local power source. If the power supply to the building is lost or diminished, the UPS battery provides power for up to several hours, depending on how much equipment it is supporting.

An intelligent UPS recognizes that its internal battery is supplying power in place of the normal power supply. The UPS monitors how much battery capacity it still has. When the battery discharges to a certain level (such as 10 percent), it sends a warning message to the computers plugged into it. This message travels across a communications cable plugged into both the UPS and the computers. A signal from this cable tells the computers to initiate a safe shutdown process. This allows the computers to properly log off users, close files, back up data, and so on. When power becomes available again, the system can start right back up.

Implementing an intelligent UPS takes additional effort, requiring you to install software on the server and write scripts to shut down programs on the server. The scripts to log off users, back up the data, shut down the database, and shut down the server must be thoroughly tested. This work is worth it, however, especially for a mission-critical system.

Although most organizations already have their production equipment on a UPS system, you need to address any new equipment. Is your current UPS capacity able to support any new equipment? If not, you need to expand the capacity of your UPS systems.

Surge protection

The AC power coming into your organization is a dangerous beast. Electronic equipment — including computers, printers, fax machines, modems, and disk drives — are very sensitive to variations in the voltage of power coming across this line. They need to be protected from the danger of being damaged or destroyed by AC power fluctuations.

The best advice I can provide here is to contact an expert! Spending a few dollars on a discount surge protector may provide you with a small degree of psychological comfort, but it doesn't provide your equipment with the protection it needs and deserves. To prevent potentially thousands of dollars worth of damage, you need to install the proper protection. Don't scrimp and try to save money on this particular item.

Getting connected

In many organizations, the staff will be increased to handle the year 2000 problem. This expansion may be temporary or permanent, but everyone will need a place to work. Additional workspace may need to be made available. Each workspace is likely to require a connection to either a local area network (LAN) or a mainframe computer. Include these costs and the time lags while making the connections in your project budget.

If you are adding to your staff, be sure to plan ahead. Have workspaces, PCs, network connections, and network security access available when the new people get there. If any of these items isn't in place when the new people arrive, you'll be paying a lot of money for people to sit around!

Software Purchases

Another significant type of expenditure you will likely make involves software. Quite a few different types of software costs can be incurred during this project. A number of these costs are described in this section.

Additional software licenses

If you add hardware for testing, you may have to purchase additional software licenses. These licenses include additional copies of operating systems, such as Windows 3.11, Windows NT, or UNIX.

Another type of license that you might need is a license for application software. For example, if you are converting a system based on a relational database package (such as Oracle, Ingres, Sybase, or Informix), you can't legally run the database package on test hardware without a license.

The same licensing requirement applies to other software packages, such as GUI development products (PowerBuilder, Visual Basic, C++, and so on) and report writers (for example, Crystal Reports or InfoMaker). Just because your organization has licensed versions on its production platform, that doesn't mean that you can make copies for your test hardware.

Software tools

Many organizations have developed millions of lines of code. You can't possibly correct all this code without using tools. In your project cost estimates, include the expense of purchasing these tools.

The methods of how tools are licensed varies. Some vendors license their products for individual workstation use; others provide a network or enterprise license. Before submitting your project budget, make sure that you are aware of your vendor's licensing methods.

New versions of software

For many systems, the solution to the year 2000 problem will be to upgrade to the latest version of certain software products. Depending on the license agreement of each product, you may be entitled to free upgrades. Before estimating costs, compile a list of each license upgrade and its particular cost.

Application software

Many software applications require an upgrade to become year 2000 compliant. Examples of such packages are

- ✔ Inventory control systems
- ✔ Accounts receivable packages
- ✔ Human resource systems
- ✔ Databases to maintain customer names
- ✔ Payroll packages
- ✔ Timekeeping systems

Depending on your licensing or support agreements, this upgrade might be provided at no cost. On the other hand, if you haven't maintained a maintenance agreement, you might have to pay for upgrades. Purchases of this kind may represent the biggest software expense of your year 2000 project.

Compilers

In many shops, it will be necessary to recompile programs with a compiler that is year 2000 compliant. Include the cost of acquiring such a compiler in project cost estimates.

PC software

Some older versions of PC software, such as spreadsheets and personal database packages, aren't year 2000 compliant. Upgrading this software may turn into a significant expenditure.

An individual license isn't a significant expense. The costs add up quickly, however, if your organization has hundreds or thousands of PCs. If this is your situation, try to negotiate a site license for these products.

Training

Not providing needed training is a case of being penny wise and pound foolish. If you don't provide training for new tools and packages, your employees will be significantly less productive. They will also make more mistakes during their initial use of the product, requiring you to spend time and effort correcting these mistakes.

Although training costs may seem expensive, the alternative will cost you much, much more. Don't fall into the trap of thinking that training is optional or a luxury.

Attending year 2000 conferences

Atending conferences on the year 2000 topic can pay huge dividends. Hearing national speakers can be extremely informative, and discussing your experiences with other attendees can uncover how they solved similar problems. It also instills in people the feeling that the company thinks they are worth an investment.

Classes for tools

Acquiring a new tool brings with it a number of unknowns. Learning to use the tool properly is crucial. Otherwise, any hoped-for productivity gains may be lost.

Training can usually be performed on or off site. Depending on how many people are involved, it might be less expensive to bring a trainer to your site. Paying travel costs and expenses for just the trainer will be less than paying for everyone being trained.

One downside to performing training in-house is that people may be called or paged during training classes. Such interruptions aren't conducive to effective training for either the person involved or the rest of the class. If training is conducted in-house, you might want to consider checking pagers and cell phones at the door.

Training on new hardware

Part of your year 2000 plan may be to install new hardware for testing only or to replace existing equipment. If this equipment is substantially different from existing hardware, training might be advisable. Plan to perform this training before the hardware is installed. You can limit this training to systems support personnel, particularly systems administrators and LAN administrators.

Consulting

Many year 2000 project plans include utilizing consultants. If your plan does, you need to factor these costs into your budget.

Many articles in the trade press predict that consulting rates will increase as January 1, 2000, approaches. No one knows for sure whether this prediction will be accurate. It might be wise to contract with consultants as early as possible to avoid potential higher rates later.

Your project plan may include high-level consulting at the front end of the project. Obtaining guidance at the beginning of your efforts might allow you to start on the correct path from day one. Be forewarned: This level of advice isn't cheap.

Your year 2000 efforts may require that you supplement your team with contract programmers. If so, be sure to include in your project plan all costs for contract personnel, such as projected overtime and the possibility that the personnel will be needed longer than expected.

Chapter 14

An Overview of Year 2000 Tools

● ●

In This Chapter

▶ Understanding why tools are necessary

▶ Discovering the types of tools available

▶ Examining some specific tools

● ●

*T*he only way most organizations will complete their year 2000 project in time is by automating the process by using tools. Tools enable your team to become significantly more productive. One vendor claims that good automated tools can reduce the effort by approximately 50 percent. Other vendors make similar or even higher productivity claims. Whether or not your organization will achieve this level of greater productivity is unknown. As the saying goes, "individual mileage will vary."

Tips on Tools

Using tools isn't something new to year 2000 projects. A variety of software tools have been used by software development projects for years. Many existing tools are being applied to millennium projects. In addition, new types of tools have been specifically developed for year 2000 projects.

Tools applicable to year 2000 projects can be broken down into a number of categories. To some degree, an attempt to classify these tools is subjective. I have divided these tools into the following categories:

- ✔ Project management
- ✔ Configuration management
- ✔ Code manipulation
- ✔ Date utilities
- ✔ Data management
- ✔ Testing

This chapter provides an overview of each category. In many cases, I list specific tools. This doesn't mean that these particular ones are the best.

One final word about tools before plunging into the topic. Using a tool doesn't give you permission to turn your brain off. Neither computers nor sophisticated tools can replace your mind. Tools can help complete the job more quickly, but without a person overseeing the job there's no guarantee that the tools are working correctly. End of lecture.

Project Management Tools

Project management tools enable the project manager to get a grasp of the work that needs to be performed. These tools provide a high-level view of all tasks that must be accomplished to reach the goal.

The silver bullet

If you use the phrase *silver bullet* in casual conversation, your listener may interpret it in a number ways. This term has a surprising number of usages. A quick search on the Internet turned up the following:

- The Lone Ranger used silver bullets in his fight against crime and injustice in the American Old West.

- A popular American beer company advertises its product as "The Silver Bullet."

- A women's baseball team (sponsored by the preceding beverage company) is called the Silver Bullets.

- A rock group is named "Bob Seger and the Silver Bullet Band."

- One make of recreation vehicles is referred to as Silver Bullets.

- A number of small handguns are referred to as Silver Bullets.

In the software business, silver bullet refers to a methodology or tool that claims to be able to solve all your problems. By purchasing this tool or attending a (probably costly) seminar, you are supposed to handle your software problems with a minimum of time, effort, and inconvenience.

I hate to be the one who breaks the news to you, but there's no Lone Ranger in real life and there are no silver bullets in the software field. Both of them are works of fiction! A tool or methodology may have some good points. It may even help simplify your problems. But I can emphatically state that nothing will solve *all* your software problems.

This goes double for products that claim to solve all your year 2000 problems. This problem is simply too diverse to be addressed by a single tool or methodology.

Peter de Jager wrote an excellent article on year 2000 related products that claim to be silver bullets. You can access this article on his Web page at www.year2000.com.

They also enable the project manager to estimate the money, time, and people that the project will require. You can use this information to convince upper management to provide the resources required for the project.

Inventory tools

One of the first steps experts advise you to perform in your year 2000 efforts is to inventory your computer software and hardware. Creating an inventory of your hardware and software is akin to building a sturdy foundation for a building. Without it, your project will either flounder or be very unstable.

Any inventory needs to include details on all software and hardware used in your organization. For example, what language the programs are written in, what hardware they run on, where the source code is located, and what data files exist.

 One very useful by-product of an inventory is that you can identify obsolete programs. The less software that needs to be made year 2000 compliant, the faster the project can be completed.

Duplicate copies of programs can also be detected during an inventory. Removing redundant copies of software programs has many benefits, such as the following:

- ✔ You waste less disk space on duplicated programs.
- ✔ You don't have to back up duplicate copies.
- ✔ You don't waste money on duplicate licenses.
- ✔ You no longer rely on different versions of a program, which can produce confusing and inconsistent results.

A number of tools can assist you in developing a software inventory.

YR2K Management System

Double E Computer Systems has developed a product called YR2K Management System. It performs an inventory of software on PCs. To perform this activity, you load a diskette into every PC in the organization. A utility on the diskette identifies every software package residing on the PC's local drives. After this process has been completed, the diskettes are returned to the vendor. Data from each separate diskette is compiled by the vendor and is returned in summary reports to the client.

One report displays specific information on each individual PC. Figure 14-1 is a sample of this report. The types of details provided on specific computers are listed here:

- Machine ID
- CPU chip
- BIOS manufacturer
- Whether the BIOS is year 2000 compliant
- Operating system
- Amount of memory
- Size and number of hard drives
- Programs loaded on this machine

Files recognized as programs are those with the following extensions:

- .com
- .cpl
- .dll
- .drv
- .exe
- .lan
- .nlm
- .ocx
- .sys
- .vbx
- .vxd
- .wri
- .386

A number of details are provided for each program loaded on each PC. Figure 14-2 is a copy of one page of this report. The details on this particular report follow:

- File path
- File name
- Date
- Size
- Product name
- Version
- Program manufacturer

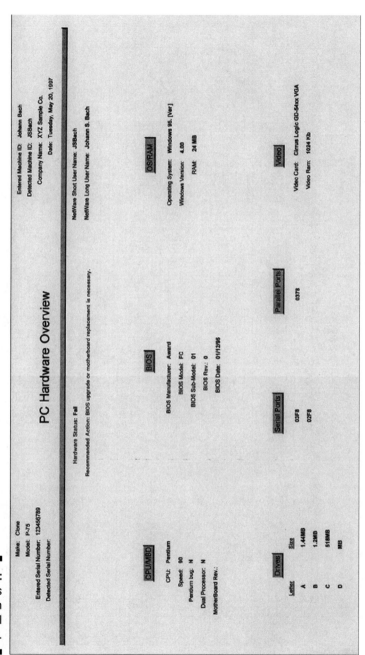

Figure 14-1:
Details
provided on
individual
PCs.

Figure 14-2:
Report details of programs on an individual PC.

Make: Clone
Model: P-75
Entered Serial Number: 123456789
Detected Serial Number:

Entered Machine ID: Johann_S_Bach
Detected Machine ID: JSBach
Company Name: XYZ Sample Co.
Date: Tuesday, May 20, 1997

Local Software Report

P 1

File Path	File Name	Date	Size	Product Name	Version	Manufacturer
C:\	IO.SYS	1995/07/11 09:50:00	223148	MS DOS System File		Microsoft Corporation
C:\	MSDOS.SYS	1997/02/26 13:21:12	1657	MS DOS System File		Microsoft Corporation
C:\	CONFIG.SYS	1997/02/26 13:21:11	0			Unknown
C:\	COMMAND.COM	1995/07/11 09:50:00	92870			Unknown
C:\95ENU	95ENU_N2.EXE	1996/11/08 15:28:12	6834471			Unknown
C:\95ENU\DIAGTOOL	NWDDI.DLL	1996/12/07 13:41:19	32799	Novell Windows Diagnostic Support DLL		Unknown
C:\95ENU\DIAGTOOL	NWDNIOS.DLL	1996/12/21 65:7:11	25904	Novell Windows Diagnostic NIOS Support DLL		Unknown
C:\95ENU\DIAGTOOL	NWDI0S.DLL	1996/12/21 62:0:04	14848			Unknown
C:\95ENU\DIAGTOOL	NWDI2.EXE	1996/12/31 30:7:09	483360			Unknown
C:\95ENU\ENGLISH	NE1000.COM	1996/04/01 13:30:9	21826			Hewlett-Packard
C:\95ENU\ENGLISH	HPISAODI.COM	1996/06/17 15:45:20	24544			IBM Corporation
C:\95ENU\ENGLISH	LANSUP.COM	1996/04/01 13:39:20	23398			IBM Corporation
C:\95ENU\ENGLISH	TOKEN.COM	1996/02/29 14:43:14	30213			Madge Networks
C:\95ENU\ENGLISH	MADGEODI.COM	1996/04/18 16:22:12	42352			
C:\95ENU\ENGLISH	CTL3D32.DLL	1995/09/16 00:00:09	26624	CftD 3D Windows Controls	2.31.000	Microsoft Corporation
C:\95ENU\ENGLISH	CTL3DV2.DLL	1995/09/09 03:15:00	27632	CftD 3D Windows Controls	2.31.000	Microsoft Corporation
C:\95ENU\ENGLISH	NWSHELLX.DLL	1996/07/02 15:40:02	117248	nwshellx	1, 0, 0, 1	Novell Inc.
C:\95ENU\ENGLISH	NWPASSWD.DLL	1996/07/02 15:35:14	29184	nwpasswd	1, 0, 0, 1	Novell Inc.
C:\95ENU\ENGLISH	GWSWITCH.EXE	1996/07/29 12:47:13	149504	Novell IPX/IP Gateway Setting	1, 0, 0, 1	Novell, Inc.
C:\95ENU\ENGLISH	LOCWIN2.DLL	1996/07/01 12:27:28	73728	NetWare| Cross Platform Client Library for Microsoft| Win 5.0.3	5.0.3	Novell, Inc.
C:\95ENU\ENGLISH	CLXWIN2.DLL	1996/07/01 13:33:21	19968	NetWare| Core Protocol Library for Microsoft| Windows 9	5.0.3	Novell, Inc.
C:\95ENU\ENGLISH	CLMWIN2.DLL	1996/07/01 13:02:24	44032	NetWare| Cross Platform Client Library for Microsoft| Win 5.0.3	5.0.3	Novell, Inc.
C:\95ENU\ENGLISH	SETUP.EXE	1996/07/10 16:03:20	311920	Client 32 Setup Application	1.6.2	Novell, Inc.
C:\95ENU\ENGLISH	NWNET.DLL	1996/06/11 00:00:14	225280	Netware Network Calls Library for Microsoft| Windows 95	4.00.93.90	Novell, Inc.
C:\95ENU\ENGLISH	AUDWIN2.DLL	1996/07/01 13:30:13	36352	NetWare| Aud Library for Microsoft| Windows 95	5.0.3	Novell, Inc.
C:\95ENU\ENGLISH	NWGDI.DLL	1996/04/30 11:19:09	108176	NetWare Graphics Device Interface for Microsoft Window	2.01.96.120	Novell, Inc.
C:\95ENU\ENGLISH	NWPOPUP.EXE	1996/05/01 45:7:25	18416	NetWare Broadcast Message Utility for Microsoft Window	3.11.96.121	Novell, Inc.
C:\95ENU\ENGLISH	NWLOCALE.DLL	1996/04/29 08:19:02	43440	Netware Localization Library for Microsoft Windows	4.00.93.90	Novell, Inc.
C:\95ENU\ENGLISH	ODIPAGE.DLL	1996/05/13 11:15:19	26592	Novell ODI property page for Windows 95	v1.00	Novell, Inc.
C:\95ENU\ENGLISH	ODINSUP.SYS	1996/07/09 16:04:10	23552	Novell ODI to NDIS support for Windows 95	v1.02	Novell, Inc.
C:\95ENU\ENGLISH	NOVELLNP.DLL	1996/07/19 16:08:26	125952	Novell NetWare Provider for Windows 95	1.00	Novell, Inc.
C:\95ENU\ENGLISH	NCPWMN2.DLL	1996/07/01 13:04:10	137728	NetWare| Core Protocol Library for Microsoft| Windows N	5.0.3	Novell, Inc.
C:\95ENU\ENGLISH	NETWAPI8.DRV	1996/07/20 14:44:05	170832	Netware Device Driver for Microsoft Windows	3.10.96.201	Novell, Inc.
C:\95ENU\ENGLISH	CALWIN2.DLL	1996/07/01 13:24:24	112128	NetWare| Calls Library for Microsoft| Windows 95	5.0.3	Novell, Inc.
C:\95ENU\ENGLISH	NETWAPER.DRV	1996/05/21 17:24:12	27968	Netware Device Driver for Microsoft Windows	3.10.96.142	Novell, Inc.
C:\95ENU\ENGLISH	NETWIN32.DLL	1996/07/31 07:18:09	99304	NetWare| Net Library for Microsoft| Windows 95	5.0.3	Novell, Inc.
C:\95ENU\ENGLISH	NWCALLS.DLL	1996/02/14 25:9:27	147856	NetWare| Calls Library for Microsoft| Windows NT	4.01	Novell, Inc.
C:\95ENU\ENGLISH	NCVPP32R.DLL	1996/07/02 13:40:12	19456	Novell NetWare Print Provider For Windows 95	1.00	Novell, Inc.

A second report provides a high-level overview of the organization's software. It lists all programs and the number of individual PCs that each program appears on. This allows management to determine which programs are the most widely distributed. It also allows you to quickly identify when different versions of the same program are on different PCs.

Figure 14-3 is an example of a page from this report. Following is the information provided in the report:

✔ Number of PCs each program appears on

✔ Product name

✔ Version

✔ Manufacturer

✔ File name

✔ Date

✔ Size

This tool uses a straightforward method to gather inventory information and doesn't require any expertise to run it. This tool is especially useful when an organization has a large number of PCs or when you need to gather information on a far-flung network of PCs.

GILES

GILES is an automated inventory package from Global Software, Inc., that runs in the IBM/MVS environment. It compiles information by searching through a variety of sources. These sources include the following:

✔ CICS transactions

✔ Copybooks

✔ JCL

✔ Link edit decks

✔ Load modules

✔ Programs

✔ Screens definitions

After the inventory information has been captured, GILES has a robust picture of your systems. This knowledge includes data fields in programs, files, and databases. Most importantly, GILES recognizes how data fields "move" within applications. It recognizes when date values are moved from one variable to another. It also notices when a variable with a date value is compared to other variables. The following code snippet illustrates how values are moved between variables and how variables are compared to date values:

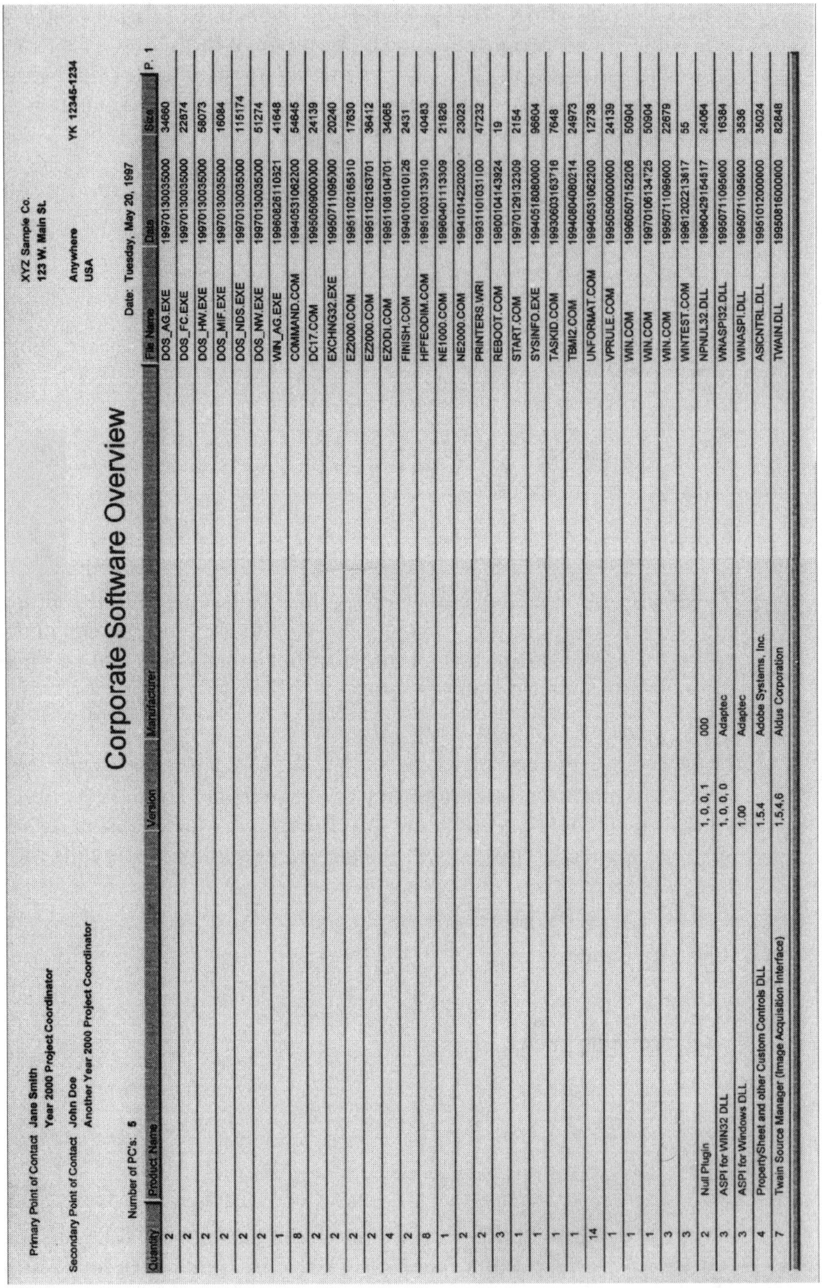

Figure 14-3:
Overview
report of all
programs
on all PCs.

Corporate Software Overview

Primary Point of Contact: Jane Smith
Year 2000 Project Coordinator

Secondary Point of Contact: John Doe
Another Year 2000 Project Coordinator

XYZ Sample Co.
123 W. Main St.

Anywhere
USA

YK 12345-1234

Date: Tuesday, May 20, 1997

Number of PCs: 5

P. 1

Quantity	Product Name	Version	Manufacturer	File Name	Date	Size
2				DOS_AG.EXE	19970130035000	34660
2				DOS_FC.EXE	19970130035000	22674
2				DOS_HW.EXE	19970130035000	58073
2				DOS_MIF.EXE	19970130035000	16084
2				DOS_NDS.EXE	19970130035000	115174
2				DOS_NW.EXE	19970130035000	51274
1				WIN_AG.EXE	19960828110321	41648
8				COMMAND.COM	19940531062200	54645
2				DC17.COM	19950509000000	24139
2				EXCHNG32.EXE	19950711095300	20240
2				EZ000.COM	19951102165310	17630
2				EZ000.COM	19951102163701	36412
4				EZODI.COM	19951108104701	34065
2				FINISH.COM	19940101010126	2431
8				HPFEODIM.COM	19951003133910	40483
2				NE1000.COM	19960401113309	21826
2				NE2000.COM	19941014220200	23023
3				PRINTERS.WRI	19931101031100	47232
1				REBOOT.COM	19800104143924	19
1				START.COM	19970129132309	2154
1				SYSINFO.EXE	19940518080000	96604
1				TASKID.COM	19930603163716	7648
1				TBMI2.COM	19940604060214	24973
14				UNFORMAT.COM	19940531062200	12738
1				VPRULE.COM	19950509000000	24139
1				WIN.COM	19960507152206	50904
1				WIN.COM	19970106134725	50904
3				WIN.COM	19950711095000	22679
3				WINTEST.COM	19961202213617	55
2	Null Plugin	1, 0, 0, 1	000	NPNUL32.DLL	19960429154517	24064
3	ASPI for WIN32 DLL	1, 0, 0, 0	Adaptec	WNASP32.DLL	19950711095000	16384
3	ASPI for Windows DLL	1.00	Adaptec	WINASPI.DLL	19950711095000	3536
4	PropertySheet and other Custom Controls DLL	1.5.4	Adobe Systems, Inc.	ASICNTRL.DLL	19951012000000	35024
7	Twain Source Manager (Image Acquisition Interface)	1.5.4.6	Aldus Corporation	TWAIN.DLL	19950816000000	82848

```
char hire_date = "811018";          /* October 10, 1981 */
char promote_date = "861005";        /* October 5, 1986 */
char resignation_date = "891118"; /* November 18, 1989 */
char vested_date;
char temp_value;

/* Call proc to calculate vested date */
temp_value = add_year_procedure(hire_date, 5)
vested_date = temp_value

/* Was employee vested at time of resignation? */
if (resignation_date > vested_date)
    /* Add pension funds to termination package */

else
    /* Calculate termination package without pension  */
```

In this code example there are three variables that are initialized as dates (hire_date, promote_date, and resignation_date). They should be identified because they have been loaded with values in a recognized date format (YYMMDD). Other variables will be identified as date related because they are directly loaded from a date value (vested_date) or loaded indirectly from a date value (temp_value).

GILES has the capability to recognize data field synonyms, to program calls that reference date fields, and to read/write operations to data files and databases.

GILES supports a number of computer languages. The vendor is willing to develop parsers for nonsupported languages on a consulting basis. Languages that GILES supports as of June 1997 follow:

- Assembler
- CICS
- COBOL
- CSP
- DB2 SQL
- Easytrieve Plus
- JCL
- Mantis
- Model 24
- Natural/Adabas
- PL/1
- System 2000

SoftAudit 2000

SoftAudit 2000 from Isogon is a language-independent inventory tool for the MVS environment. It allows an organization to find source modules that make up in-house applications. It also determines which load modules the applications are related to. Estimates of the lines of code (LOC) for individual applications and for the overall system are generated.

Identifying unused source and load modules is another service SoftAudit 2000 provides. The vendor claims that by identifying unused modules, you can reduce the conversion effort by up to 30 percent. Not all installations are likely to experience this level of unused modules, but every little bit helps.

A number of reports are available from SoftAudit 2000. Each can be filtered by user ID, job name, date, time, and job accounting data. Source reports can be filtered by source library, volume, and source module. Some of the reports available in SoftAudit 2000 include the following:

- ✔ A source report that matches source modules to load modules and vice versa.
- ✔ A source report that shows unused source modules and source modules used only by unused load modules.
- ✔ A source related report that concentrates on lines of code (LOC), reporting the total LOC, unused LOC, and LOC broken down by application.
- ✔ A usage report that provides counts of how frequently a module was used during the monitoring period. Reports can be restricted to either lightly used or heavily used modules.
- ✔ A usage report that provides the number of jobs that have used each application.
- ✔ Installed product reports that list every module in each application in every load library.
- ✔ A load library report that lists applications having modules in each load library on the system.
- ✔ A load module report that lists every load module on the system. Details on the product and library are provided for each load module. Duplicate modules are flagged.

Impact analysis tools

Performing an impact analysis on your systems provides an overview of the risks your system is likely to be subject to. Essentially, performing an impact analysis requires that you examine each system to determine how it will be affected by year 2000 problems. Some of the questions you must ask include the following:

✔ Which systems involve date fields?

✔ Are year values stored in two digits?

✔ Is sorting performed on two-digit year values?

✔ Are input screens limited to two-digit years?

✔ Are values 99 or 00 used to represent anything other than year values?

✔ Do your systems recognize that the year 2000 is a leap year?

✔ Are future dates generated, processed, or stored in your systems?

✔ How are future and past dates created, stored, or reported by this system?

✔ Does data enter the system from other internal or external systems?

✔ Do any systems generate data for other systems, either internal or external?

✔ If a given system were to fail, what would be the affect on your operations?

The answers to questions such as these will help determine how you will approach the year 2000 project. They will help you predict when problems will start occurring and how serious they will be. This information will influence the order in which your systems should be made year 2000 compliant.

Impact analysis tools also help estimate the extent of the needed work by providing the number of affected programs. It also estimates the number of hours each program will require to make it year 2000 compliant. Some tools generate an estimate of programmer costs by multiplying hours by a user-configurable cost factor.

Revolve/2000

Revolve/2000 by Micro Focus is part of their SoftFactory/2000 suite of tools. This suite provides a comprehensive approach to addressing year 2000 problems on MVS COBOL systems.

SoftFactory/2000 operates on desktop PCs. This reduces the competition for mainframe resources. It also allows project teams to operate in a highly productive GUI environment.

Variables and computer programs don't exist in a vacuum. If variables in a COBOL program need to be modified, this will affect other parts of the program. Other variables and data elements may need to be changed. Logic that compares these objects might require rewriting. Fields in data records may need to be modified. To be truly effective, a tool must be able to track these interrelationships.

Revolve/2000 has the capability to trace through COBOL systems to assess the effect of changes. It creates a diagram of how control flows through a program. Figure 14-4 provides an example of a program flow diagram created by Revolve/2000.

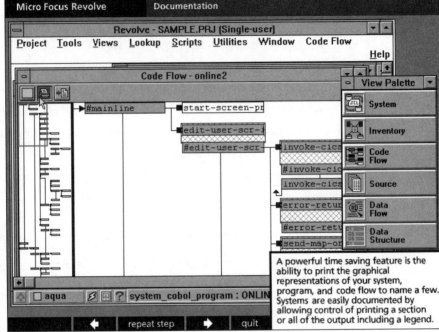

Figure 14-4:
A Revolve/
2000
program
flow
diagram.

Revolve/2000 includes a reporting facility that summarizes the year 2000 effect on a given application. This report provides an estimate of the cost and effort required to convert each application. These estimates are based on the number of date definitions within the program and the program's complexity. User-specified parameters are used to generate cost estimates.

Some of the cross-reference reports available in Revolve/2000 provide the following information:

- Columns in each data file
- All programs that access each data file
- All files accessed by each program
- JCL files that reference each program

ADPAC Inventory

ADPAC Inventory from ADPAC Corporation creates an inventory of executable programs that define a data processing environment. The first step toward defining this inventory is to use the JCL and LOAD libraries to define an initial program member list. Then ADPAC Inventory analyzes each program's CALL statements to compile a complete and accurate application member list.

Mainframe systems frequently contain an extremely large number of programs — in the thousands or tens of thousands. Within the set of programs running on a mainframe, there is likely to be a complex web of which programs are related to or dependent on which others. If one program is being changed, it is almost mandatory that all related programs be changed at the same time.

If a system contains a large number of programs, it can be difficult to know which are dependent on each other. ADPAC Upgrade can identify groupings of related programs by tracing each item's I/O records, COPYLIB structure, and JCL. ADPAC refers to these groupings as upgrade units.

The knowledge of which programs are grouped together in upgrade units is extremely valuable. This allows project management to know what other programs will be affected when a given program is modified. It allows project planners to know which programs must be upgraded and tested as a group.

A report is available that includes estimates of how much it will cost to become year 2000 compliant. It calculates labor and CPU time requirements. It also estimates total costs to change each application based on an organization's cost assumptions and change methods. This report is capable of handling foreign currency exchange rates.

PC-oriented software assessment tools

Although most of the attention on year 2000 projects is on software that runs on mainframe computers, don't ignore software running on PCs. Many PC programs will also encounter year 2000 related problems.

A number of tools deal with PC programs in a specific area. This section describes some of these PC-oriented tools and the environments in which they run.

Spreadsheets

Spreadsheets contain data of all types, including date values. When dates in a spreadsheet are stored in a YY format, you'll have the same problems with date comparisons as you do on a mainframe program.

At least one tool is available that searches through spreadsheets looking for date-associated items, that is, cell data, formulas, charts, or macros. The tool, which assesses Microsoft Excel spreadsheets, is DateSpy from Rigel Desktop Solutions. This tool can examine Excel versions 5 and 7. DateSpy runs under Microsoft Windows 3.1, 3.11, Windows 95, and Windows NT (3.51 & 4.0) on Intel platforms.

When DateSpy is initiated, it displays a control window, shown in Figure 14-5. This window allows you to specify what will be searched, what DateSpy will look for, and how any hits will be handled.

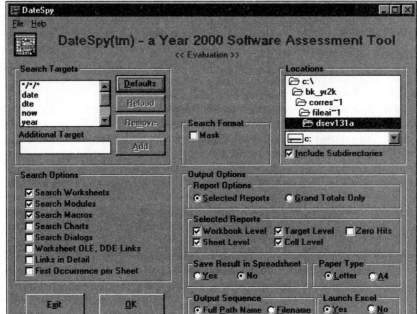

Figure 14-5:
The
DateSpy
entry
window.

When DateSpy completes its processing, it prepares a report, detailing spreadsheet files containing a date related item. You can print this output report, write it to a file, or write it to an Excel spreadsheet. Figure 14-6 is an example of the output from DateSpy.

Visual Basic programs

A large number of programs are written in Microsoft's Visual Basic (VB). At first glance, you may not think that VB programs will be affected by the year 2000 problem because

- ✔ VB programs run on a PC instead of on a mainframe
- ✔ VB programs are new instead of old
- ✔ Many VB programs store data using a relational database instead of flat files

I'm sorry to disappoint you, but VB programs can still have problems. More-recent versions of Visual Basic provide a data type for dates. Unfortunately, this doesn't prevent developers from storing date values in variables that are string data types.

```
DateSpy(tm)
j9 j8            7.0           7.0
```

Search Options	Search Targets		Grand Totals
Do Search Worksheets	*/*/*	3	Workbooks Located
Do Search Modules	date	3	Workbooks With Hits
Do Search Macros	dte	0	Workbooks Zero Hits
Do Not Search For Charts	now	0	Workbooks Skipped
Do Not Search For Dialog Sheets	year	0	Workbooks Unavailable
Do Not Count Worksheet, OLE and DDE Links	yy	0	Sheet Links Found
Do Not Include Each Link	yr	0	OLE/DDE Links Found
Find All Hits On Each Sheet	99?99	6	Worksheets Inspected
Do Not Search For Formats		138	Affected Cells Found
		0	Formatted Cells Found

Reporting Options		
Print Selected Report	5	Module Sheets Inspected
Print Workbook Level Detail	15	VBA Code Lines Found
Print Sheet Level Detail	3	Macro Sheets Inspected
Print Target Level Detail	3	Excel 4.0 Macro Code Cells Found
Print Cell Level Detail	0	Charts Found
Omit Detail For Zero Hits	0	Dialog Sheets Found

Name: Evaluation
Company: Evaluation
Licence No: RDSD05AE80001680001

Run Options
StartDirectory=C:\BK_YR2K\CORRES~1\FILEAI~1\DSEV131A
Do Include Subdirectories
Present Report in PATHNAME order
Set Paper Type To Letter
Do Not Create and Save Lastlook.xls

```
Rigel Desktop Solutions
http://www.rigel.co.nz
sales@rigel.co.nz
support@rigel.co.nz
```

Level	Path	Name	Target	<—Totals—>	Cell	Value	Formula	Format

WorkbookC:\BK_YR2K\CORRES~1\FILEAI~1\DSEV131A\EXAMPLE4.XLS Hits = 56

Level		Name	Target	Totals	Cell	Value	Formula	Format
Sheet		Sheet1		56				
target			*/*/*	10				
cell					B33		Days between 31/12/99 and 1/1/00	General
cell					B36		Days between 31/12/1999 and 1/1/2000	General
cell					B39		Days between 31/12/99 and 1/1/2000	General
cell					B40		Days between 31/12/1999 and 1/1/00	General
cell					B41		Days between 31/12/1900 and 1/1/2000	General
cell					B42		Days between 31/12/00 and 1/1/2000	General
cell					C45	1/1/00		d/mm/yy
cell					C46	1/2/00		d/mm/yy
cell					C47	1/3/00		d/mm/yy
cell					C48	1/4/00		d/mm/yy
target			date	32				
cell					A2		Excel 5.0a Dates in Formulae	General
cell					B13		Date of 29 Feb 1999	General
cell					B1		4Date of 32 July 1996	General
cell					B19		Date of 29 Feb 1900	General
cell					B20		Date of 29 Feb 1995	General
cell					B21		Date of 29 Feb 2000	General
cell					C5		2 =(DATE(1996,6,30)) - (DATE(1996,6,28))	0
cell					C6		3 =(DATE(1996,6,30)) - (DATE(1996,6,28)) + 1	0
cell					C7		3 =(DATE(1996,7,1)) - (DATE(1996,6,28))	0
cell					C8		33 =(DATE(1996,7,31)) - (DATE(1996,6,28))	0

Figure 14-6:
A DateSpy output spreadsheet.

Developers may attempt to avoid date related problems by converting dates to the number of days since a base date. Function CDbl returns the number of days since 12/31/1899. The problem with this solution is that CDbl doesn't know the century portion of a date if it hasn't been provided. The following two VB statements illustrate this problem:

```
MsgBox "Number of days between 12/31/1899 and 1/1/2000 is "
        &
CDbl(DateValue("01/01/2000"))
Number of days between 12/31/1899 and 1/1/2000 is 36526.

MsgBox "Number of days between 12/31/1899 and 1/1/00 is " &
CDbl(DateValue("01/01/00"))
Number of days between 12/31/1899 and 1/1/00 is 2.
```

The first statement specifies a four-digit year value, and the correct result was returned. The second statement didn't provide a four-digit year, and an incorrect value was returned. Problems occur when developers assume Visual Basic always knows what century a two-digit year represents.

Visual DateScope 2000 from Class Solutions Ltd. is a tool that can help identify and correct date problems in Visual Basic programs. This tool works on Windows 3.1, Windows 3.11, Windows 95, and Windows NT platforms. It can scan Visual Basic programs written in versions 3.0, 4.0, and 5.0.

To correct date problems, the tool calls a new function, yr2kDate, that interprets dates within a 100-year sliding window. You define what the upper bounds of the date range will be. For example, suppose that you define the upper date window to be 30. Function yr2kDate interprets a date of 1/1/26 as 1/1/2026. A date of 1/1/31 is converted to 1/1/1930.

When DateScope 2000 scans a Visual Basic application, it automatically includes this function. This tool doesn't modify VB source code. Instead, it creates a results repository that lists all tokens (that is, variables and constants) identified as possibly needing attention. The developer needs to examine these statements and determine which need to be updated.

Scheduling packages

Year 2000 projects are composed of a large number of individual tasks, some small and others much larger. Many tasks will be independent in that they can be performed at virtually any time. Other tasks can't be started until certain components have been completed. All these tasks need to be scheduled to maximize team member productivity and minimize the duration of the project. Another reason to use a scheduling package is to avoid letting tasks fall through the cracks.

Scheduling and updating a large number of tasks by hand is time consuming and difficult. A number of scheduling packages can help perform this duty. Three of the most popular are Microsoft Project, On-Target from Symantec, and Project Planner for Windows from Primavera Systems Inc.

As the deadline approaches, upper management will expect project reports. It's extremely important for the project manager to stay on top of the project's schedule. If the project starts to slip, corrective action must be taken quickly. An up-to-date scheduling package will allow you to quickly detect any slippage.

Software tools for scheduling projects aren't new to millennium conversion projects. They've been around for a long time. Following are some criteria you should consider when choosing a scheduling package:

- Will the product run on computers you already have?

- Do the computers you plan to run it on have adequate hardware (CPU, RAM, disk space, and so on)?

- What standard reports does it produce?

- If the standard reports aren't sufficient, how difficult is it to produce custom reports?

- Can the product be loaded on a network drive to allow multiple users access to it?

Configuration Management Tools

Controlling the changes made to software is the primary function of configuration management (CM). All modifications should be controlled, tracked, and distributed under strict control. Software version control products assist in tracking changes being made to software modules.

Year 2000 projects don't have unusual configuration management requirements. The only thing out of the ordinary is the quantity of programs and files being changed. If the pundits are right, approximately 80–90 percent of all programs will be affected by this problem. Tracking changes being made to this many modules requires the use of a source code management (SCM) tool.

One point worth considering is that year 2000 projects don't occur in a vacuum. It would be ideal to freeze systems during these efforts, but this isn't always possible. In most organizations, changes (emergency or otherwise) will be made to systems during the year 2000 project. When year 2000 modifications are finished, they will need to be integrated with these other changes. A software version control package can be of great assistance at this time. It will enable you to determine which modules have been changed by both efforts and how these changes should be merged.

Renovate2000 was developed by the makers of PVCS, one of the most widely used source code management systems in the industry. Renovate2000 draws on the experience of the people at INTERSOLV.

This tool enables you to control and coordinate changes made by developers working on different projects in the same application. This can help you avoid overwriting — and therefore losing — changes.

Some of the other features of Renovate2000 include:

- Defines, assigns, and schedules work packages for year 2000 project team members.
- Synchronizes source code changes between mainframe libraries and a LAN.
- Tracks progress being made by the team and converts this information into project metrics.
- Recovers source code that is lost or inadvertently overwritten.
- Notifies team members of all changes being made to year 2000 related modules.
- Automates the process of rebuilding software systems and applications. This shortens build cycles and can produce error-free builds.

Code Manipulation Tools

A code manipulation tool does just what it sounds like. It modifies the source code that computer programs are written in. A great number of code manipulation tools are on the year 2000 market, and most claim they can perform almost all corrections required to make programs year 2000 compliant.

This capability sounds wonderful, but there are potential problems. First, making "almost all" required changes isn't good enough. How do you know which changes weren't made? To find the last few changes might require that you examine the source code by hand — exactly the situation you were trying to avoid in the first place.

To be of maximum benefit, a tool must identify *all* year 2000 related changes. If there are any questionable changes, the tool should list them for someone to review.

Search tools

Tools can examine source code for date related variables in essentially two ways: scanning and parsing. I explain each of these methods in the following sections.

Scanning

A scanning tool simply searches source modules for variables that contain certain strings of characters, such as common words or combinations of characters used to refer to date fields. Many times, a scanning tool refers to a file with a large set of strings that it is scanning for. When the scanning tool finds a match in the source code, it's called a hit.

The following should help illustrate how a scanning tool identifies a date variable.

Assume that a scanner program searches for the following strings:

```
date, day, year, yr
```

Now assume that the following code snippet was passed to the scanner:

```
while((result_code = dbresults(dbproc2)) !=
        NO_MORE_RESULTS)
  {
    if (result_code == SUCCEED)
      {
/*    Bind program variables to local variables.      */
      dbbind(dbproc2, 1, NTBSTRINGBIND, (DBINT) 0,
          price_eff_date);
      dbbind(dbproc2, 2, NTBSTRINGBIND, (DBINT) 0,
          price_update);
      dbbind(dbproc2, 3, SMALLMONEYBIND,(DBINT) 0, (BYTE
          *) &base_price);
      dbbind(dbproc2, 4, NTBSTRINGBIND, (DBINT) 0,
          price_act_est_ind);
      dbbind(dbproc2, 5, FLT8BIND,(DBINT) 0, (BYTE *)
          &commodity_adjustment);
      dbbind(dbproc2, 6, NTBSTRINGBIND, (DBINT) 0,
          commodity_adjustment_ind);
      dbbind(dbproc2, 7, SMALLMONEYBIND,(DBINT) 0, (BYTE
          *) &commodity_price);
      dbbind(dbproc2, 8, SMALLMONEYBIND,(DBINT) 0, (BYTE
          *) &adjustments);
      dbbind(dbproc2, 9, SMALLMONEYBIND,(DBINT) 0, (BYTE
          *) &dayrate);
      dbbind(dbproc2,10, NTBSTRINGBIND, (DBINT) 0, (BYTE
          *) price_reference);
      dbbind(dbproc2,11, NTBSTRINGBIND, (DBINT) 0, (BYTE
          *) price_reference_date);
      dbbind(dbproc2,12, NTBSTRINGBIND, (DBINT) 0, (BYTE
          *) price_reference_prod_type);
    while (dbnextrow(dbproc2) != NO_MORE_ROWS)
      {
```

(continued)

(continued)

```
        base_price_ind[0] = 'Y';
        new_day_flag = 'Y';
        strcpy(price_eff_date2, price_eff_date);
        strcpy(price_source_ind2, price_source_ind);
        base_price2 = base_price / 10000.0;
        strcpy(price_act_est_ind2, price_act_est_ind);
        commodity_adjustment2 = commodity_adjustment /
          10000.0;
        strcpy(commodity_adjustment_ind2,
          commodity_adjustment_ind);
        commodity_price2 = commodity_price / 10000.0;
        adjustments2 = adjustments / 10000.0;
        net_price2 = net_price / 10000.0;
        strcpy(price_reference2, price_reference);
        strcpy(price_reference_dt2,
          price_reference_date);
        strcpy(price_reference_prod_type2,
          price_reference_prod_type);

    } /*  End of while (dbnextrow(dbproc) !=
          NO_MORE_ROWS) */

  } /*  End of if (result_code == SUCCEED)  */

} /*  End of while result_code != NO_MORE_RESULTS */
```

The scanner would declare hits on the following strings:

```
price_eff_date
price_reference_date
price_eff_date2
```

It would also incorrectly hit the following strings:

```
price_update
new_day_flag
dayrate
```

The scanner missed the following date related string:

```
price_reference_dt2
```

A hit may or may not represent a variable that actually contains a date value. The programmer who wrote the code may not have used common sense or consistency when naming variables. Therefore, a date related variable may be named after, say, the programmer's pet snake.

Parsing

Parsing is simply the process of making multiple passes through the source code and learning from each pass. Parsing takes longer than scanning because it attempts to "understand" what the code is doing. A parsing program can't gain this understanding in a single reading of the source code. The first pass through the source code, it may catch the most-obvious date fields. In the second pass, the parser recognizes variables loaded from or compared to the variables identified in the first pass. With each successive pass, the parser adds additional hits until it identifies all date related variables.

Assume that a parsing tool searches for the following strings:

```
date, day, year, yr
```

The following code is quite contrived. Its only purpose is to demonstrate some concepts instead of being logical or capable of being compiled. The code that will be parsed is

```
baseline_date = '1/1/98'
backup_baseline = baseline_date
if baseline_date > value_from_input_screen then
    output_value = backup_baseline
end
```

The parser's first pass identifies hits based on a list of target strings. It finds the following strings:

```
baseline_date
```

The parser's second pass identifies variables set to or compared with variables that have already been added to the hit list. The following variables were found:

```
backup_baseline
value_from_input_screen
```

A third pass of the parser finds variables set equal to hits found in the second pass. These variables are

```
output_value
```

Parsing tools and scanning tools differ only by their level of sophistication. Both parsing and scanning tools can make changes to the source code. Parsing is performed to enable the tool to find more, and one hopes all, occurrences of date related variables.

INTO 2000

INTO 2000 from INTO 2000, Inc., automates year 2000 conversions on AS/400 computers. INTO 2000 runs on PCs attached to an AS/400 host machine. Running the tool on PCs instead of directly on the host machine enables you to attach up to 999 PCs to a single host — your entire team can work on this project at one time.

INTO 2000 supports two of the major year 2000 solutions: windowing and date expansion. If a client chooses the windowing approach, INTO 2000 adds logic to programs that store dates with full century support without changing how they are displayed.

When INTO 2000 modifies a line of code, it can insert a modification marker of up to four characters. In that way, you can identify modified code later.

Another useful capability of INTO 2000 is its capability to convert existing databases. Data migration programs are created for each data file that has an expanded field. When these programs are executed, century values are inserted in the appropriate positions of each expanded field.

NA2000 SCAN

NA2000 SCAN is a programming language independent utility for dealing with the year 2000 problem. It finds and scans source program files on stand-alone PCs or LANs for date related references.

This utility can scan a list of up to 500 programs at a time. It can also search for and scan all files with specific file extensions.

NA2000 SCAN doesn't actually modify source code. (Strictly speaking, it doesn't belong in this "Code Manipulation Tools" section.) It creates a report listing programs and line numbers of statements that need to be changed. A project team member must manually change the statement. Another report is created that estimates the number of hours or years it will take to make the needed changes.

The vendor suggests a number of alternative uses for its product. One recommended application is to produce a second opinion to verify cost estimates from external consultants. Another suggested use is to verify that all the needed changes to your system have been made.

TransCentury Analysis

TransCentury Analysis for MVS and TransCentury Analysis AS/400 from Platinum Technology, Inc., work in the MVS and AS/400 environments. They identify all date occurrences by parsing the source code. The first pass identifies the more-obvious date references. Later iterations locate dependent code that also needs to be changed.

One output from TransCentury Analysis includes estimates of the time and resources it will take to make your year 2000 modifications, as shown in Figure 14-7. This particular tool allows users to define their own cost parameters, which can result in more-accurate estimates.

After TransCentury Analysis has identified all date occurrences, it can modify them. Date occurrences in source code can be substituted with a call to a TransCentury Calendar routine. Using a library of pretested calendar routines can reduce the amount of work required to convert an application. It can also drastically reduce the amount of testing that must be performed.

Text editors

Text editors aren't particularly glamorous and few seminars or user groups focus on them. They don't make a lot of promises about how they will make programmers 100 percent more productive. In fact, it is easy to completely forget about this line of tools.

It is a mistake, however, to overlook editors when choosing tools for a year 2000 project. Your team members will be editing a large number of files during this project. A good editor will make programmers more productive as well as cut down on the number of errors.

Following are some of the advantages of an advanced editor:

- Performs search and replace functions in multiple files
- Operates on multiple platforms

Figure 14-7: Sample output showing year 2000 compliance cost estimates.

```
IMPACT ESTIMATES                  S7.2:ESTIMATES FOR DATA STRUCTURE CHANGE
RPT   MEMBER      DIFF   TOTAL   --MAKE CHANGES-- ---COMPILES---   CREATE  ---
LINE  NAME        RATE   LINES   COUNT    WORKHRS   CNT   CPUHRS   TEST/HRS
----- ----------  ----   ------- ------  --------- ----- -------- ----------- --
   1   COPY/INCL                    45      2.3       2   .0022       7.0
   1   DATECALC    75     342     144       8.4      14   .0078       2.0
   2   FINPGM1     85     278      53       2.7       7   .0039       1.5
   3   FINSUB      95      77      41       3.0       4   .0022       1.0
   4   FINTEST     87     687     239      16.5      17   .0094       1.5
   5   MIDPGM1     95     147      15        .6       3   .0017       1.0
   6   MSSB0010    75     342     144       8.4      14   .0078       2.0
   7   TESTSUB     95      77      41       3.0       4   .0022       1.0
   8   TRANPGM1    85     278      53       2.7       7   .0039       1.5
   9   TRANTEST    87     687     239      16.5      17   .0094       1.5
           -------------------------------------------------------------------
          TOTAL:         2,915   1014      64        89   .05         20
PROGRAM AVERAGE:           324    113       7        10   .01          2
      TOTAL COST:$                        3,846           71       1,200
      GRAND TOTAL:$      10,012
===============================================================================
      AVERAGE COST:$                       427            8         133
%PCT TOTAL COST:                            38            1          12
```

- ✔ Uses color highlighting for a source file's different elements, that is, commands (key words), variables, and comments

- ✔ Displays values side-by-side in decimal and hexadecimal (This is useful when your method of handling the year 2000 includes encoding year values. It also enables you to display control codes embedded in data files or other types of files.)

- ✔ Opens and interacts with multiple windows, each showing a different source file

- ✔ Emulates other editors (such as vi, Brief, EMACS, or ISPC), enabling your project team to become productive immediately

- ✔ Handles very wide records and extremely large files (This is invaluable when your data contains very long records.)

PREDITOR

PREDITOR from Compuware offers a great deal of functionality in an editor. It includes most of the advanced features listed in the preceding section. Here are some of the additional features it provides:

- ✔ Includes built-in language support for many computer languages

- ✔ Correctly handles UNIX style end-of-line characters

- ✔ Preserves bookmarks across editing sessions

- ✔ Prints source files in portrait or landscape mode directly (Printing can include multiple columns, user-defined headers and footers, line wrapping, and line numbers.)

- ✔ Includes powerful find capabilities, such as forward and backward searches, and wrapping around the end of the buffer

ICE

ICE (Intelligent Code Editor) from Rasmussen Software is a text editor that is available for DOS and UNIX platforms. ICE runs as a DOS application in a Windows environment. Some of the features that ICE provides follow:

- ✔ File locking is available in ICE. If this is turned on and a file is already being edited, a second programmer can't edit the file.

- ✔ All menus, dialog boxes, and error messages can be translated into other languages. German, Spanish, French, and other languages are available.

- ✔ ICE accepts commands through the use of pull-down menus, the mouse, and Ctrl-key combinations.

- ✔ Multiple files can be open simultaneously.

✔ ICE allows different versions of the same file to be easily compared.

✔ ICE will match up control words and symbols in programming languages. Examples of these are IF/ELSE, begin/end, and matching sets of parentheses, braces, and quotation marks.

✔ Text files with lines up to 255 characters long are supported.

✔ Records delimiters (end-of-line control characters) for both DOS and UNIX are supported.

Although ICE can be used with any programming language, it has some features specific to COBOL. If your applications are written in COBOL, this editor will be especially valuable. Some of the COBOL-specific features follow:

✔ ICE makes periods in the source code especially visible.

✔ Source code can be formatted through an optional COBOL formatter to make it more readable.

✔ A single keystroke toggles the COBOL comment indicator in the current line.

✔ ICE can automatically flag any line that has been modified or added.

✔ Page numbers can be automatically numbered or renumbered.

✔ Search and replace operations can include or exclude comment lines.

Figure 14-8 shows ICE running on a PC in a Windows 95 environment.

Figure 14-8:
Editing
screen from
Intelligent
Code Editor.

Source recovery utilities

The Gartner Group estimates that corporate America has lost 3–5 percent of the source code in its libraries. This loss doesn't prevent the current version of the program from executing on a daily basis. If you don't need to modify the program, you can continue on the present course indefinitely. Unfortunately, the year 2000 problem requires that all source code in your organization be front and center.

If some of your source code is missing, you have few options. You can rewrite the source code from scratch. This choice isn't an attractive one. It requires that you document what the program does, write the code, and test it. Reproducing source code at any time isn't fun, but it's especially disconcerting in light of the year 2000 deadline. You have enough to do without this added task.

Another solution to this predicament is to try to recover the source code from load modules and executables. Source Recovery from The Source Recovery Company, Inc., can recover missing COBOL and assembler source code from object code in the following environments:

- ✔ COBOL
- ✔ CICS
- ✔ DB2
- ✔ IMS
- ✔ BMS MAPS
- ✔ Any MVS/VSE/VM program

Advantages to recovering source code instead of rewriting it are numerous:

- ✔ Recovering source code can be significantly cheaper than rewriting it. An article in the March 24, 1997, issue of *Computerworld* quoted a satisfied customer of The Source Recovery Company. He said it cost $500 to recover some COBOL source code. He felt it would have cost much more to rewrite it.

- ✔ Recovering source code can be significantly faster than rewriting it. This is especially significant in light of the upcoming year 2000 deadline.

- ✔ Source code recovered from object code will have fewer errors. Although both rewritten and recovered source code must be thoroughly tested, you can expect fewer errors in recovered code.

Date Utilities

This section describes two of the several types of utilities that deal directly with dates. One is used during the code modification phase of year 2000 projects. The other is useful during the testing phase.

Calendar routine libraries

Calendar related routines can minimize changes made to both program logic and data files. Such routines frequently reside in a library. Calls to these routines are made in place of the existing date related logic. In this way, you avoid the problems associated with comparing dates such as 111156 and 111100.

Platinum's TransCentury Calendar Routines are a library of standardized date routines containing more than 320 date processing functions. These routines recognize more than 150 date formats, multiple holiday tables, and a century indicator value. The routines can be used in any COBOL program.

The routines in this library can handle an enormous number of date related requirements. Some frequently confronted situations that the product can handle are listed here:

- Was 1996 a leap year?
- What is the third day before the end of the month?
- What is today's date in MM/DD/YY format?
- How many dates are between the day an account was opened and the day it closed?
- Reformat 01/23/97 into a format like January 23, 1997.
- What is the date 30 days from 12/15/1999?
- What day of the week is March 1, 2000?
- Is a given input date value valid?
- What is the last work day of the quarter?
- What is the next work day?

A user interface is available that organizes these routines into logical categories. Figure 14-9 is the first screen in this interface. The user (programmer) is presented with choices and is walked through a series of screens. When the programmer is satisfied with the results, the date logic generator creates a CALL statement in the original source code. This interface allows less-experienced staff to contribute to code repairs.

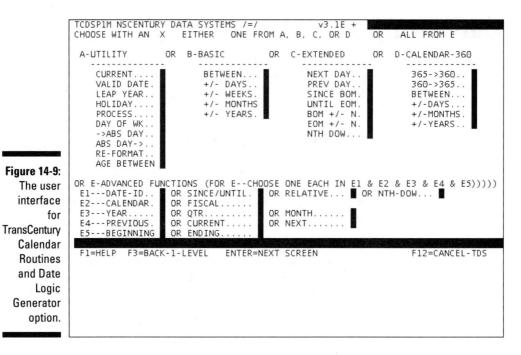

```
TCDSP1M NSCENTURY DATA SYSTEMS /=/              v3.1E +
CHOOSE WITH AN X   EITHER   ONE FROM A, B, C, OR D    OR   ALL FROM E

A-UTILITY      OR  B-BASIC        OR  C-EXTENDED     OR  D-CALENDAR-360
- - - - - - - - - - - - -   - - - - - - - - - - - -   - - - - - - - - - - - - -   - - - - - - - - - - - - -
    CURRENT....         BETWEEN...         NEXT DAY..        365->360..
    VALID DATE.         +/- DAYS..         PREV DAY..        360->365..
    LEAP YEAR..         +/- WEEKS.         SINCE BOM.        BETWEEN...
    HOLIDAY....         +/- MONTHS         UNTIL EOM.        +/-DAYS...
    PROCESS....         +/- YEARS.         BOM +/- N.        +/-MONTHS.
    DAY OF WK..                            EOM +/- N.        +/-YEARS..
    ->ABS DAY..                            NTH DOW...
    ABS DAY->..
    RE-FORMAT..
    AGE BETWEEN

OR E-ADVANCED FUNCTIONS (FOR E--CHOOSE ONE EACH IN E1 & E2 & E3 & E4 & E5)))))
    E1---DATE-ID..  OR SINCE/UNTIL.  OR RELATIVE... ▌ OR NTH-DOW... ▌
    E2---CALENDAR.  OR FISCAL......
    E3---YEAR.....  OR QTR.........  OR MONTH......
    E4---PREVIOUS.  OR CURRENT.....  OR NEXT.......
    E5---BEGINNING  OR ENDING......

F1=HELP   F3=BACK-1-LEVEL    ENTER=NEXT SCREEN          F12=CANCEL-TDS
```

Figure 14-9:
The user
interface
for
TransCentury
Calendar
Routines
and Date
Logic
Generator
option.

Programmers are not required to use the calendar routine's user interface. If
the programmer knows the format of the needed function, he or she can
simply insert it into the source code. The user interface is intended to help
beginning programmers until they become familiar with this product.

System date simulators

Testing year 2000 corrections is crucial. If you don't perform thorough
testing, you'll have no idea whether your changes are correct. To adequately
inspect these changes, you need to perform tests on a number of dates,
including the following:

- ✔ December 31, 1999
- ✔ January 1, 2000
- ✔ January 2, 2000
- ✔ January 3, 2000
- ✔ February 28, 2000
- ✔ February 29, 2000

- ✔ March 1, 2000
- ✔ December 31, 2000
- ✔ January 1, 2001

If you have dedicated test platforms, changing the system date frequently won't be a problem. If your testing must be performed on a nondedicated system, this might present problems. First, setting the date on a mainframe system isn't as simple as changing it on a PC. Second, any nontest application will be affected by the date change. Date simulator tools can overcome these problems.

A date simulator utility works by intercepting system date and time requests from application programs. Applications being tested are returned with simulated dates; all others are given the current (accurate) date information. This allows testing to coexist on the same machine with production applications.

Other uses of date simulation tools include testing programs on specific dates. For example, an accounting package might function differently at month-end, quarter-end, and year-end intervals. Tools that change the system time can allow these specific intervals to be easily tested at any time.

HourGlass 2000

MainWare's HourGlass 2000 is a date and time simulation package that operates on the MVS/ESA operating system. You can specify a list of job names or job name prefixes when you install HourGlass 2000. Only applications that are included in this list receive the simulated date and time. Other programs, that is, the ones not being tested, continue to receive the correct date and time.

HourGlass 2000 supports some of the following languages:

- ✔ BAL
- ✔ COBOL
- ✔ DB2 SQL
- ✔ IDEAL
- ✔ IEF
- ✔ LE/370 languages
- ✔ NATURAL
- ✔ PL/1

Online support for CICS and IMS DC environments is provided by HourGlass 2000. Altered date and time values can be limited to specific users, terminals, and transactions. The product even allows individual users to test under unique date and time combinations. This allows the many members of your project team to perform testing at one time.

TICTOC

Isogon's TICTOC is a date simulation tool for the OS/390 (MVS/XA and ESA) environment. It has been designed to introduce virtually no additional load on programs that receive simulated dates or are given the normal system date.

TICTOC runs at the operating system level, which enables it to be used by applications written in any language.

No code or JCL changes are required for programs to obtain test dates and times from TICTOC . An online interface allows you to identify the jobs that TICTOC will pass simulated dates to. You can identify job names explicitly or generically with wildcards (for example, all jobs beginning with ACCT*). You can use this interface also to specify the simulated dates each job should be passed.

VIA/ValidDate

Viasoft's VIA/ValidDate requires the IBM MVS/ZA or MVS/ESA operating system with TSO and ISPF to run. It allows you to execute an application and have it appear to be running on any date in the past or future. This enables testing to determine whether programs have correctly been changed to handle the year 2000 situation.

A logging facility tracks which jobs have been run with VAI/ValidDate. This is useful for verifying which applications have been tested and to assure that only authorized users are modifying the settings within ValidDate.

Data Management Tools

During your year 2000 project, you'll often find it necessary to modify data. Manually modifying vast quantities of data is impractical because it would be too slow and would introduce uncounted errors. It's also virtually impossible. Utilizing a tool to modify data is mandatory.

Data conversion utilities

At times, you'll need to convert data from one format to another. If you've chosen to deal with year 2000 dates using date expansion, most dates in your database will need to be modified. You'll need to add 19 in front of all existing two-digit year values.

Some organizations have millions and millions of data records. How long would it take to expand all these dates by hand? How many errors would be introduced in the process? The answers are "too long" and "too many." Using a conversion utility is the only practical method for dealing with this activity.

File-Aid

File-Aid from Compuware Corp. offers a great deal of functionality to deal with the year 2000. This tool runs under the MVS operating system. I describe the Reformat Utility in File-AID and its capability to modify data here.

Reformat enables the user to expand data to hold century indicators, initialize date values, and identify and use free space within data records.

Figures 14-10 and 14-11 show how two fields (EMP-HIRE-DATE and EMP-DATE-OF-BIRTH) in a hypothetical data file are expanded from six-character fields to eight-character fields. Figure 14-10 highlights the new area in the record that holds the century data for employee's birth dates. Figure 14-11 shows the century data for employee hire dates.

Figure 14-10:
File-AID expanding employee birth date fields.

Figure 14-11:
File-AID
expanding
employee
date of
hire data.

Vantage YR2000

Vantage YR2000 from Millennium Dynamics, Inc., provides a comprehensive solution to the year 2000 problem. This suite of tools can run on a mainframe or a PC computer. Most of the utilities in the suite are aimed at updating COBOL programs running on mainframe computers.

One of the tools it includes is a file converter. This utility provides a quick and easy way to upgrade data files to make them year 2000 compliant.

The File Converter can insert century values into existing data files. Both fixed and variable data files can be handled.

This utility can also be used to modify files back to their original state. This eases the effort it takes to perform regression testing.

Bridge programs

Bridge programs are used to convert data between one format and another. A date may be stored in a YYMMDD format, but a program may require that it be in a YYYYMMDD format. Without some conversion method, the program couldn't function.

Following are three examples of when a bridge program is necessary:

✔ Converting programs one-by-one. When the first program is modified, the data is reformatted. A bridge allows other programs to access the data until each program has been updated. When the last program is completed, the bridge program becomes obsolete.

✔ Accessing data from external sources. Other organizations may not resolve their year 2000 problems the same way you did, resulting in data formats that are incompatible with your programs. A bridge program could convert the data to a format that your programs can handle.

✔ Accessing historical or archived data. If your data format and programs change, you may not want to bother modifying historical data. You can leave this data in its original format and use a bridge to access it with updated programs.

The logic required to convert data between two different formats isn't rocket science. There is no reason why a bridge program can't be written in-house instead of obtained from a third party. The primary reasons for utilizing a package are speed and consistency.

Bridge 2000 from Viasoft runs in IBM MVS/XA and MVS/ESA environments. A dynamic method intercepts a program's request for data and translates it into the expected format. This logic is illustrated in Figure 14-12. To utilize Bridge 2000, the addition of a single CALL statement in an application is required.

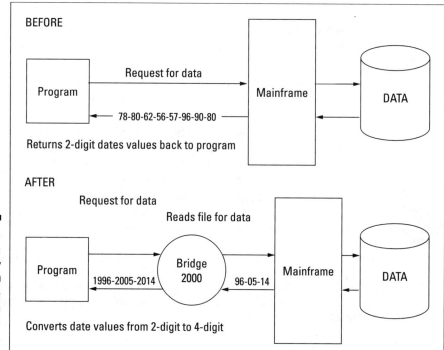

Figure 14-12: The logic used by Bridge 2000 to bridge between data and applications.

Many data files contain more than one date field in a single data record. Some of these dates might need to be converted and others might not need to be changed. Bridge 2000 allows you to handle each distinct field differently.

A bridge program is not the same as a data conversion program. Although they both convert data from one format to another, they perform this task at different times. A data conversion program typically performs its work once. It might be used at the end of the day or week or month to convert a large quantity of data. Because it is being accomplished after the fact, it is referred to as being offline. A bridge program, in contrast, performs its work when a program is trying to access the data. Because a production program is requesting the data immediately, a bridge program is considered online.

Year 2000 Suites

Unlike tools, which fill specific niches, suites attempt to do everything. Suites typically include tools that address each of the major categories of tools. They also frequently include guidelines or a methodology to follow. A few year 2000 suites on the market are Vantage YR2000 by Millennium Dynamics, Trans2000 from Transition Software Corp., SoftFactory/2000 from Micro Focus, and TransCentury from Platinum Technology, Inc.

Some advantages to using a suite include the following:

✔ Each tool is integrated with the others in the suite. The inventory piece feeds the impact analysis tool, which in turn provides a list of modules and priorities for the code manipulation tool, and so on.

✔ Dealing with a single vendor is significantly easier than dealing with multiple vendors. When the inevitable problem occurs, there won't be any finger pointing between vendors.

✔ Generally, a suite vendor has been in the business longer than a company with only a single tool. This gives you a little more assurance that when you call for support, you won't get an operator's voice saying that the number has been disconnected.

✔ A suite of tools frequently operates on a greater number of platforms than a stand-alone tool. If your organization has a diverse hardware environment, this capability can be very valuable.

If you thought there might be some disadvantages to using a suite, I won't disappoint you. Some vendors slap together a bunch of separate tools to compete in the high-end (that is, high-priced) suite arena. When this occurs, the tools won't be tightly integrated — thus negating one of the biggest advantages of using a suite.

The primary disadvantage to using a suite is that it is only as strong as its weakest link. Suppose the inventory tool in a particular suite is weak. The list of programs it will generate will likely omit a number of programs. No matter how excellent the remainder of the tools are, they can't compensate for the fact that not all programs are being corrected.

Many vendors will claim that their tools can be used with little or no training. Any experienced project manager will take such claims with a very large grain of salt. Assess whether training is necessary yourself. An investment in training up-front can have significant productivity returns over the life of the project.

Chapter 15

A Testy Situation

● ●

In This Chapter

▶ Understanding the importance of testing
▶ Using tools during your testing efforts
▶ Generating test data

● ●

*T*esting your year 2000 modifications is crucial. Following are some of the many reasons why this testing is especially important:

✔ You can't delay the deadline. If your system isn't ready on 1/1/2000, no amount of negotiating or explaining will buy you more time. A high percentage of software projects aren't completed on time — this can't be one of them.

✔ You have only one chance to get it right. On many projects, if the new version doesn't work, you can revert to the original system. Then you can correct the new version and reinstall it later. You can't do this when dealing with year 2000 projects.

✔ The year 2000 project will likely affect more applications and more lines of code than any previous projects. The amount of testing needs to be correspondingly high.

✔ In many cases, you'll be modifying code that hasn't been touched in years or decades. The original developers are probably long gone, and no one is familiar with the code. This alone dictates that testing be especially thorough.

✔ The year 2000 problem affects your systems as well as the computers of every organization you deal with. You need to test all data coming into your system as well as data you send out.

Until you have performed thorough testing, you can't be certain that your changes are complete or correct. You, management, your clients, and your users don't want any nasty surprises on the morning of Monday, January 3, 2000.

Estimating Testing Time

The amount of time devoted to testing will be a significant portion of your year 2000 effort. Year 2000 consultants and vendors estimate that testing will represent from 40–60 percent of the total time spent on these projects. If your project plan doesn't allocate roughly this amount of time for testing, you should reexamine it.

The year 2000 plan for the state of California estimates that testing will be 40 percent of the cost of the project. Table 15-1 lists cost and time estimates by project phase.

Table 15-1	California's Year 2000 Project Estimates	
Project Phase	**Percent of Project Cost**	**Time Frame (in months)**
Awareness	1	1
Inventory	1	1
Assessment	5	2
Solution design and handling	15	3–4
Development and modification	20	6–8
Testing	40	6–8
Implementation	10	4–5
Monitoring	8	6–10

Test Early and Test Often

"Vote early and vote often" was the advice on a campaign banner in the 1850s. I recommend taking this advice to heart, although in a slightly different context, during your year 2000 project. Following are two of the many positives to testing early:

✔ Testing will almost certainly take longer than expected. Starting early gives you a little more assurance that you'll finish in time.

✔ Testing early exposes problems earlier. Use this extra time to correct problems. If early testing exposes shortcomings in your project plan, procedures, or training, you will be better off the earlier you discover them.

Testing doesn't get any respect

It's time for me to get on my soapbox again. Testing software deserves more attention, resources, and respect than most organizations currently give it. Performed properly, testing is close to an art form. Not everyone can or wants to be involved in testing. Many developers look down on both testing and testers. They also look down on documentation and tech writers, but that's another story.

As the saying goes, it's a dirty job, but somebody has to do it. Testing shouldn't be something that should be assigned to your least experienced people. This assignment also shouldn't be given to team members who aren't working out as developers. Testing requires just as much skill, training, intelligence, and experience as developing — perhaps more.

Rigorous testing is absolutely necessary to produce error-free systems. The costs of errors in computer programs are always high. These costs are usually measured in lost revenue, dissatisfied customers, lost sales, and so on. The costs of a large number of errors on January 1, 2000, however, are likely to be much higher, and could include significant lawsuits, your job, or your organization's continued existence. Time to get off my soapbox.

Testing often also has many advantages. This project will affect a number of software components, such as operating systems, compilers, assemblers, link-editors, applications, and JCL scripts. Not all will be modified at the same time. Any one of these pieces has the potential to affect earlier changes.

For example, suppose that you've made modifications to a COBOL program and they pass the acceptance test. You receive a new year 2000 compliant version of the COBOL compiler and use it to recompile all of your programs. How can you be certain that it won't introduce errors into a program that was working previously? The only way to be certain this doesn't occur is to retest each program. This form of testing is called regression testing.

The real testing deadline isn't December 31, 1999

Articles and discussions that cover testing year 2000 projects strongly recommend that all changes be completed by December 31, 1998. The year 1999 should be reserved solely for testing. This allows an entire year to verify that the changes have adequately corrected the problems without introducing new ones.

Having your changes in place by December 31, 1998, has another important advantage. It allows you to use the year end as a testing opportunity. If year-end problems are going to occur, it's better to expose and correct them on 1/1/1999 than on 1/1/2000.

Planning Your Testing Activities

Earlier steps in your project will have broken the effort down to manage-able-sized chunks. These chunks are sometimes called upgrade units or partitions. You need to create a formal test plan for each piece. This section lists the components that should make up your test plan.

Acceptance tests

The objective of testing is to make certain that software performs as ex-pected. The acceptance test plan needs to lay out, in great detail, the steps of each test. These steps need to be clear enough that anyone can perform them correctly every time.

I once saw a *Perry Mason* show that had the following advice for trial lawyers: "Never ask a witness a question if you don't know how it will be answered." Actually, that might have been a *Matlock* program. The wisdom of this advice also applies to software testing. Successful testing means knowing in advance what the results of a test will be. Your test plan must describe the tests that will be run as well as the expected outcome. Other-wise, how will you know if the test has been passed?

Responsible parties

A number of members of your year 2000 team will probably be involved in the testing phase. The responsibility of each team member on each test must be outlined. Some roles follow:

- Designing the test
- Preparing the test data
- Executing the test
- Verifying that the test was successful
- Signing off that the test was successful
- Logging the results
- Assuming control of the source code after it passes the test

Test preparation

Effective testing requires that a number of pieces come together success-fully. Someone has to make sure that these pieces are all in the right place at the right time. Some of the pieces follow:

✔ Reserve test hardware for given tests. It may not be possible (or advisable) to run multiple tests on the same hardware simultaneously. Schedule time on the hardware just like you schedule conference rooms.

✔ Properly configure test hardware, making sure that the appropriate network connections, disk devices, modems, multiple terminals (to simulate multiple users), tape drives, and so on exist.

✔ Load all required software onto the test system, including the operating system, test tools, remote access software, and date simulation program.

✔ Make sure the most recent version of the software to be tested is available. This task must be carefully checked if you have many testers. Previous test efforts might have left uncertified software on the machine. Executing the wrong version of software wastes testing time and is extremely frustrating.

✔ Make sure that the correct test data is in place. Test data might exist for multiple time periods. Be certain that the desired data is loaded onto the system when tests are performed.

✔ Check the availability of all needed consumable items, such as computer paper, tape cartridges, and floppy diskettes.

✔ Have any required logging or tracking software in place. It's a waste of time to have to repeat tests because you didn't capture logging information.

✔ If local etiquette requires it, remove any software or data you loaded after you finish. This reduces the chance that subsequent tests will inadvertently run with your software or data.

Additional Hardware for Testing

You might have to buy additional hardware for your year 2000 testing. One example is if you can't risk changing software on a production system. Crashing a production job while running a test program isn't going to win you any friends with management, production staff, or users.

Another potential effect on production applications is performance. If systems are operating at their capacity now, adding testing activity might be the straw that breaks the camel's back. Extra processing might increase the response time that users experience to unacceptable levels. Batch jobs might not complete in their available windows.

Your current disk space might not be sufficient to add extra programs and data. Test data can be a significant consumer of storage space. To add new versions of programs and test data, you might have to add more disk drives.

Your business environment might require that year 2000 activities be performed during nonbusiness hours. This will require the team to work nights. Besides disrupting people's lives for a year or two, a schedule shift has other negative effects. While working nights, they won't be able to easily communicate with other MIS staff or users. This will cause problems if emergencies arise during the day while they are home asleep. If hardware is available that is dedicated to testing, your team can test during normal business hours.

In general, running year 2000 projects on production hardware is a bad idea. Although it will cost more to buy or lease additional hardware, not doing so is poor economy for several reasons:

- ✔ A lack of test hardware and testing time may cause your year 2000 project to be late. This alone is a powerful reason for acquiring test hardware.

- ✔ Performing testing on production systems may affect the performance your users experience. This may result in lost revenue.

- ✔ If testing gets behind schedule, you may be forced to increase the size of the year 2000 team. Additional team members raise the cost of the project.

- ✔ Running tests on production hardware raises the distinct possibility that production software or data can be corrupted. This may lead to lost data, downtime, and lost revenue.

Involving Users in the Testing Process

Users need to be involved in the year 2000 effort. Involving them in this process has definite advantages:

- ✔ The project becomes "our" project instead of an MIS project. Organization-wide acceptance of the year 2000 project is crucial.

- ✔ Users can provide insight into where dates are used, making it easier to identify programs that need to be explored and possibly changed. Don't rely on users remembering every date field in every system — you still need to search for date fields.

- ✔ Users know how the system is supposed to work. If the modified system deviates from expectations, they will be the first to know.

One area where users can make significant contributions is in the testing phase. Because users already know how the system functions, they can be very involved in developing test cases and running test scenarios. Getting users involved has the dual advantage of applying their expertise and freeing up developers so that they can focus on making changes.

Testing Year 2000 Changes

Testing software changes involves several different phases. This is true for development projects, year 2000 changes, and general fixes and enhancements. Each testing phase is geared toward testing certain types of errors. The combination of all types of testing is more likely to result in reliable software.

Skipping a testing phase isn't allowed — not even when the change is small or simple. How may times have you made a change that was so simple it couldn't possibly cause errors, but later you found that it caused one? It happens on projects I work on. Imagine dozens (or hundreds) of errors like this being introduced into your system.

Unit testing

Unit testing is the act of testing a single program module. Usually, the programmer who has made the modification performs the test because this person will be most familiar with the program and what was changed.

Unit tests are usually performed fairly soon after the changes are made. In that way, the change and its intended effects are fresh in the programmer's mind. It also allows the programmer to completely finish that task before moving onto the next one.

Useful tools during unit testing include the following:

- ✔ Debugger
- ✔ Coverage analyzer
- ✔ Date simulator

Chapter 14 discusses these and other tools.

All modified software should compile cleanly if the original code compiled cleanly. If the original source code generated compilation errors, the modified programs should produce the same errors.

After a module passes its unit test, the source code should be turned over to configuration management (CM) so that no additional (that is, unauthorized) changes are made to the code. If the programmer needs to make further changes, he or she must follow established procedures, which include the following:

1. Check out the module from configuration management's library. This ensures that only one person is making changes to it at a time. It also guarantees that the developer is working with the most recent version of the module.

2. Make the needed changes.

3. Unit test the module.

4. Have the test signed off by the appropriate authority.

5. Turn the module back to the configuration management group.

Integration testing

One meaning in the Random House *Webster's College Dictionary* for *integrate* is "to bring together or incorporate into a unified, harmonious, or interrelated whole or system." This is the intent behind integration testing. It attempts to verify that all individual modules in a subsystem will work together.

Unlike unit testing, integration testing isn't performed by the programmer. It's performed by the test team of the Quality Assurance (QA) group. One reason is that the programmer doesn't "own" the module any more — it was turned over to Configuration Management (CM) after passing unit testing.

Another reason is that the modules involved in integration testing may have been modified by many programmers. If five programmers were involved, would all five be involved during integration testing? It would get mighty crowded around that computer terminal.

One final reason programmers don't perform integration testing has to do with the level of knowledge required. For unit testing, the tester must understand the internals of the module, and only the programmer is likely to have this information. In contrast, integration testing focuses on how programs function rather than on their internal details. This testing is best accomplished by using a variety of data and observing how the application responds.

Useful tools during integration testing include the following:

✔ Date simulator

✔ Data aging tool

✔ Capture/playback tool

Chapter 14 discusses these test tools.

System testing

System testing is similar to integration testing but on a higher level. It tests the entire system at one time instead of just a single part of the system. The project test team or the Quality Assurance (QA) group performs system testing.

An example might help explain the difference among the testing methods. Assume a bank is upgrading its computer systems to make them year 2000 compliant. The following lists each of the test phases and the types of test that are performed during each.

Testing Phase	*Test Description*
Unit testing	Subroutine that performs interest calculations; function that generates new account numbers; report to print account summary information; routine that deducts funds from an account;
Integration testing	Creating a new customer checking account; making a loan to a customer; closing a savings account; generating monthly statements for customers; transferring funds from one account to another;
System testing	All testing performed during the integration phase

Useful tools during system testing include the following:

- ✔ Date simulator
- ✔ Data aging tool
- ✔ Capture/playback tool

Acceptance testing

Acceptance testing may or may not be necessary. Essentially, it is the same as system testing but performed by different people. System testing is performed by in-house or MIS personnel. Acceptance testing is performed by the client. With an internal client, the system test might be adequate. An external client will likely want to perform acceptance testing using its own personnel.

Useful tools during acceptance testing include the following:

- ✔ Date simulator
- ✔ Data aging tool
- ✔ Capture/playback tool

Regression testing

Alphonse Karr said, "The more things change, the more they remain the same." This saying definitely doesn't apply to computer software! For the software industry, the saying should be "the more things change, the more likely something will be messed up." Changing one part of a computer system often has the effect of creating errors in another part of the system. Unfortunately, the error is likely to be far removed from the original change. This makes these errors hard to predict and locate.

A personal example might be valuable here. A Visual Basic application I wrote recently developed an error when the client tried to use feature A. After some investigation, I discovered that the error had been introduced when I corrected a previous problem. To correct problem B, I overwrote a variable. The code for feature A needed this variable in its original state. After correcting problem B, I didn't sufficiently test the application and therefore didn't notice that A no longer worked.

Regression testing exposes problems like this. *Regression testing* consists of tests to make sure that a change doesn't create additional problems. If I had performed sufficient regression testing, I would have found that by fixing B, I inadvertently broke A.

Regression testing is a lot of work. Each regression test requires that every feature in an application be tested again. Performing this testing manually requires a massive amount of time and effort. Doing it by hand isn't practical.

A simple example demonstrates why regression testing can't be performed manually. Assume that a particular application has 50 screens, or windows, that a user can access. Assume that these windows have an average of 25 data entry fields. To adequately test each field, you might need to enter 20 different values. The total number of values that need to be entered is 25,000 ($50 \times 25 \times 20$). If it takes 15 seconds to perform each action, it would take 6,250 minutes, or 104 hours and 10 minutes, to test this application.

That's a lot of time to test one application a single time. If you retest the application after each significant modification, how many times will that be? Can you afford to devote that amount of time to this activity? On the other hand, can you afford not to perform this testing?

Another argument against manually performing regression testing is consistency. A regression test may take hours to perform. It may require that hundreds (or thousands) of separate values be entered, buttons pushed, and so on. Can you be certain that all this activity will be performed exactly the same way each time? Isn't it probable that someone will make a mistake at some point during the test? If a mistake is made, what effect will it have on the remainder of the test? An error can easily invalidate some or all of your tests.

Automating your regression testing is the only practical solution to these problems. Some of the advantages of automated testing include the following:

- Fewer human resources are required.
- Tests are more consistent.
- Tests can be run overnight or on the weekend.
- Results are logged to make a permanent record of whether each test passed or failed.

Creating Comprehensive Test Data

The quality of your test data can make or break your testing activity. Testing with inadequate test data can allow errors to remain undetected. As a result, you can deliver software that contains errors. On a year 2000 project, this is a very serious problem.

Quantity

Good test data must be similar to production data in both quantity and diversity. If a production system typically runs against 100,000 data records, testing with 100 records isn't good enough because it doesn't exercise the program enough.

Diversity

Data that isn't diverse can make a program look like it's correct when it isn't. Assume that a payroll program reads timekeeping data records and produces weekly paychecks. If all the test data consists of 40-hour weeks and nothing else, it isn't much of a test. Some of the data must be unusual or outright incorrect to fully test the program.

For example, you test for an employee who

- Worked -1 hours
- Worked 0 hours
- Worked 40 hours
- Worked 50 hours
- Worked 60 hours
- Worked 168 hours
- Worked 169 hours
- Logged 40 hours vacation
- Logged 41 hours vacation
- Logged 8 vacation hours but has no vacation hours left
- Claimed 41 sick hours
- Claimed a total of more than 40 hours of regular work, vacation, and sick leave
- Entered more than 40 hours of jury duty
- Logged 40 hours of reserve duty of National Guard training
- Has multiple timekeeping records
- Claimed 8 hours of holiday time during a week that has no holidays
- No longer works for the company
- Resigned in the middle of the pay period
- Never existed
- Has 0 dependents
- Has 99 dependents
- Has paid the maximum amount of FICA for the year
- Is having wages garnished
- Is part-time
- Is salaried, but has a timekeeping record

These examples of test data aren't exhaustive. They're simply an example of how test data must contain diverse and even unusual values. Test data also needs to contain some outright invalid data. If invalid data isn't provided, how can you be certain that error processing will be handled correctly? Testing is an attempt to prove that the program doesn't work properly. Invalid test data must be included to test this assertion.

Specific year 2000 data

Test data for a year 2000 project must reflect that goal. It must include dates before and after 1/1/2000. Your test data can include the following dates:

- December 31, 1998
- January 1, 1999
- December 31, 1999
- January 1, 2000
- January 2, 2000
- February 28, 2000
- February 29, 2000
- March 1, 2000
- December 31, 2000
- January 1, 2001
- February 28, 2001
- February 29, 2001 (invalid date)
- March 1, 2001
- December 31, 2001
- January 1, 2002
- February 29, 2004

Generating test data

How can you generate acceptable test data? Following are potential sources for this data:

- **Generate it manually.** This is the least desirable source because you'll most likely end up with an insufficient quantity of data that isn't varied enough and took too long to produce.

- **Obtain a data generating tool.** These tools are fed the layout of a data file and can generate the requested number of records. They can create a rich variety of data for flat files or relational database systems.

- **Capture existing production data and manually modify the dates to test the year 2000 situation.** This approach has the advantage of being based on realistic data. The only disadvantage is that manually modifying the data might introduce errors.

✔ **Use a data manipulation tool to age current data.** This approach is probably the most desirable because the data will be representative of the production environment, and using a tool to modify the data will result in fewer errors than doing it by hand.

Day-of-week calculations

Many programs need the answer to questions like "What day of the week will January 1, 2000 be?" If your system handles leap year in the year 2000 incorrectly, it might affect day-of-week (DOW) calculations for the remainder of the year. Verify that the DOW calculation for March 1, 2000, shows that it is a Wednesday. Any errors here have the potential to surface throughout your systems. They can affect when backups are run, when reports are generated, and when files are deleted.

Windowing data

If your solution to the year 2000 problem is a windowing approach, test that aspect sufficiently. Make sure that test data include dates on the edges of the window. Test with a minimum of the following dates:

✔ Just below the lower edge of the window

✔ Right on the lower edge of the window

✔ The upper edge of the window

✔ Just above the upper edge of the window

For example, suppose that your window extends from January 1, 1930, through December 31, 2029. Data to test the edges includes the following four dates:

✔ December 31, 1929

✔ January 1, 1930

✔ December 31, 2029

✔ January 1, 2030

Obviously, you want to test for more than these four dates. All testing, however, emphasizes these four "edge" dates.

Examining Other Aspects of Testing

A number of areas in testing don't fall into any neat categories, and I cover these in this section.

A testing opportunity

Most systems have different processing performed at certain intervals. Common intervals are

- Month end
- Quarter end
- Year end
- Fiscal year end

Of these intervals, year end has the most significant amount of processing that isn't performed at any other time. You can use the end of 1998 as a grand experiment. If your changes are in place, you can use this opportunity to verify that modifications are both complete and correct.

One method is to run the old and new systems in parallel during this period. You wouldn't have to do this for an extended period — several days or a week should be adequate. Compare the results between the two systems. If errors occur, you've learned a valuable lesson. If no errors occur, you'll have a high degree of confidence in your changes.

Leap year

The year 2000 is a leap year, so the month of February of the year 2000 will have a 29th day. All software testing must verify that applications will handle this day and this month. Testing should also check that the first day of March is a Wednesday.

Third-party software

Vendors will likely supply you with year 2000 compliant versions of their products. You can't afford to rely on their assurances that it will correctly handle the year 2000. You should thoroughly test all new versions, therefore you need to establish test cases and test data.

You should do this as quickly as possible. If you expose any problems, contact the vendor immediately! Why the urgency? It will take the vendor time to identify and correct the problem, and it will take even more time to get an updated version back to you.

Backup procedures

Backup and restoration procedures are very dependent on dates and date processing. Backups are made at intervals determined by dates. Here's one example schedule: Make a complete backup every Saturday at 2 A.M., with incremental backups Monday through Thursday at 11 P.M., and a system-wide backup on the last business day of every month.

Restoration processes are also heavily date dependent. Suppose that a system crashed on the 10th of the month at 9 A.M. The backup must restore the most recent complete backup. It then needs to apply the incremental backups for every day since the complete backup. All of this information is driven by dates and day of week (DOW) logic. Any mistakes here can cause the restoration to fail. Even worse, it can damage your backup tapes.

Test your backup and restoration procedures. Make sure that these scripts, programs, and so on will correctly function in the next millennium. If your backups don't work when you need them, you are in deep yogurt.

Integrating other changes

After you have made and tested your year 2000 changes, you might think you are finished. (It's time to stop working the 16-hour days and catch up on your life.) Unfortunately, you might need to perform one more little step. If non-year 2000 changes were made to the software, you need to integrate these with your year 2000 modifications. After these changes are complete, you must perform regression testing to be certain that errors weren't included.

Testing Tools

Testing your year 2000 changes isn't practical without using test tools. The amount of work to do is simply too great to perform it manually. This section is an introduction to the great variety of software testing tools. I've attempted to include descriptions of the most-significant types of tools available.

Debuggers

A debugger is a test tool that enables a programmer to observe exactly what happens as a program executes by inserting breakpoints in the source code. When a breakpoint is reached, execution of the program stops. The programmer can then "look around" the program and do the following:

- Examine contents of variables
- Alter the contents of variables
- Modify the source code from within the debugger
- Display the contents of any memory location

Other features available in some debuggers include the following:

- ✔ Enables the tester to step through the program one line at a time.
- ✔ Hides statements being executed if the tester doesn't want to see details of a subroutine call.
- ✔ Builds a list of variables to be watched. The contents of these variables are displayed at all times.
- ✔ Clears or disables all breakpoints.
- ✔ Displays the stack (list) of all function calls that have not returned.
- ✔ Continues execution until the statement that the cursor is on is reached.
- ✔ Halts when a variable contains a specified value.
- ✔ Halts when a loop has been executed a specified number of times.
- ✔ Continues execution until the program completes.

Debuggers enable a programmer to observe and to some extent control program execution. Debuggers are included in some programming environments but must be purchased from a third-party vendor in other environments. Most PC client/server GUI development tools include a debugger. They are also frequently used with mainframe-based programming environments.

Because debuggers require that you dig into the source code, they are used almost exclusively by developers. They will most likely be used during unit testing. If problems occur later in the project, a developer might require a debugger to locate and correct the problem.

Features offered by debugging tools differ significantly, especially between different hardware and software platforms. The capabilities available on a Windows platform are considerably different than those available on a mainframe environment.

Visual Basic debugger

Figure 15-1 is a screen shot of the debugger included in Microsoft's Visual Basic. The background window is the application form currently being executed. The middle window is the source code where the breakpoint was encountered. The foreground window shows the watch list of variables being observed.

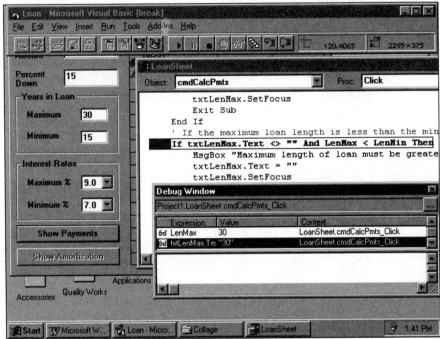

Figure 15-1:
The Visual
Basic
debugger.

VIA/SmartTest

VIA/SmartTest from VIASOFT is a debugging test tool for the IBM mainframe environment. It requires the IBM MVS/XA or MVS/ESA operating system with TSO and ISPF (Release 3.1 or higher). You can use VIA/SmartTest when testing the following languages:

- PL/1
- Assembler
- APS
- COBOL
- CICS

Some of the debugging features available with VIA/SmartTest follow:

- Debugging can step through programs one statement at a time or entire paragraphs at a time.
- Breakpoints can be based on the value in a variable.
- A histogram is generated that tracks the number of times each statement, paragraph, or section is executed. Histogram data can be summarized and printed.

✔ Code can be added to the program during debugging. This enables the user to perform dynamic testing.

✔ Changes made during dynamic testing can be applied to the source code if desired.

Date simulators

A date simulator simulates the system time on a computer, usually a mainframe computer. Date simulators operate by intercepting system date requests from applications. Usually date simulators maintain a list of programs that should be given the simulated time. All other calling programs are passed the true system time. This makes it possible to test a specific set of programs at a given time. Figure 15-2 illustrates how a date simulation program functions.

A simulator allows you to test software on a certain date before that date arrives or after the fact. For instance, you can set the system time to December 31, 1999. By executing test programs, you can see how the system will react when it rolls over to the year 2000.

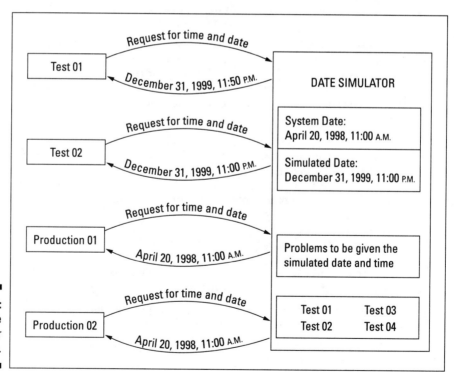

Figure 15-2:
How a date
simulator
operates.

Date simulators can enable you to perform repeated testing with the same set of test data. Test data might be a snapshot of production data from a certain time period, say 12/31/1996 through 1/6/1997. To obtain valid test results, you might need to set the simulator date and time to somewhere within that period. You can continue to use this data indefinitely if the date simulator is set to return a date in the 12/31/1996 through 1/6/1997 range.

If you have a dedicated test computer, you can simply set the clock to any time you want. This will work, but using a date simulator has advantages over this approach. When setting the date ahead, watch out for the following potential pitfalls:

- ✔ Changing the system time on a mainframe frequently requires an IPL (initial program load). Performing an IPL will certainly take longer than changing the time in the simulator.

- ✔ If the system time is set forward, accounts and their passwords may expire. But someone with the access to restore them may not be immediately available. This little problem may cost more time than you'd expect.

- ✔ Product licenses of third-party software may expire when the system time is set forward. Simply returning the clock to the current time may not correct this situation. The software might interpret this as an attempt to violate the license agreement. Contact the vendor if this occurs.

- ✔ Frequently, files and datasets are given an expiration date when they are created. They are deleted when the system time advances beyond that date. If the time is advanced for testing, these datasets might be deleted. You can avoid the problem by removing expiration dates or setting them to a future date, such as 1/1/3000.

TicToc

TicToc from Isogon is a date simulation tool that runs on mainframe computers running the MVS/XA or MVS/ESA operating system. This tool enables you to test how programs will run on any date. When loaded onto your computer, it is completely transparent to all applications. No code or JCL (job control language) changes are required.

Some of the features that TicToc offers follow:

- ✔ A simple interface is provided that enables you to determine which programs receive the simulated date and time.

- ✔ Programs that aren't on the simulated date and time list are unaffected by TicToc.

✔ Security allows you to limit who can make modifications to the simulated time and the list of programs that receive the simulated date and time.

✔ TicToc supports all programming languages (COBOL, PL/1, assembler, and so on).

✔ TicToc supports multiple clock formats (decimal, binary, time units, microseconds, and TOD clock format).

VIA/ValidDate

VIA/ValidDate from VIASOFT enables a tester to evaluate how programs will function under any date scenario. This tool operates in the IBM MVS/XA or MVS/ESA operating system with TSA and ISPF (Release 3.*x* or above). The following languages are supported:

✔ OS/VS COBOL

✔ VS COBOL II

✔ PL/1

✔ C

✔ CICS

✔ IMS/DC

Following are some of the features offered by VIA/ValidDate:

✔ Simulated dates can be set to any desired value. These dates and times can be in the past or the future.

✔ A logging facility enables you to track jobs that have been passed a simulated date.

✔ Installation time is less than half an hour.

✔ Security prevents unauthorized users from modifying the simulated date and list of programs that receive simulated dates.

Data aging tools

A data aging tool "ages" data. To use it, you copy data to a separate file, volume, and so on. You then instruct the tool to change specific date fields by adding a value of, say, 20 years to them. This allows you to use genuine data without manually modifying it.

Capture and playback tools

Capture and playback tools enable you to reproduce test sessions easily and consistently. The gist of this class of tools is as follows:

1. Set up the testing environment.

2. Turn on the capture program.

3. Execute the test, including any user interaction (data entry, button clicks, code entry) with the program being tested. Each user action and application response is captured.

4. After the test is complete, terminate the capture program.

5. To reproduce the test, simply set up the testing environment and initiate the playback program.

When you walk through the application being tested, every user action is recorded and written to a script file. This includes every keystroke, data entry, mouse movement, menu selection, function key pressed, and so on. The application's responses are also captured and stored.

Later, when you want to reproduce the test session, the playback part of the tool feeds these actions into the application. The application can't tell that it is being driven by a program instead of a user. The script faithfully reproduces every action that was taken during the original session.

This capability is extremely valuable. Some of its advantages include the following:

- ✔ Test sessions are replayed exactly like the original session.

- ✔ Without user hesitations and pauses, replays of test sessions run much faster than the original session.

- ✔ Some tools allow scripts to be tied together, that is, run sequentially. This enables you to rerun dozens or hundreds of individual test scripts.

- ✔ Test sessions can be run unattended. You can initiate a test session and have it running overnight or over the weekend.

- ✔ When the results are different from the original session, the differences are logged.

- ✔ Scripts are created without any programming. Users can be taught to capture their test sessions.

As wonderful as these tools are, they have their drawbacks. They don't replace the need for people to be involved in the testing activity. They simply make some of the steps easier. Some of the shortcomings are as follows:

- A person has to run the test originally.

- This tool doesn't increase the quality or thoroughness of the test. It simply runs the test faster the second (and later) time around. If you didn't test a particular feature the first time, it won't be tested during subsequent test runs.

- Test data must remain consistent. Changes to the data can make the application's responses differ from the original responses. The playback tool will interpret such differences as errors and declare the test a failure.

- Some skill is required to tie multiple scripts together. If one script leaves the application in a certain condition (that is, on a certain screen or expecting a specific input operation), the next script must pick up from exactly that point.

- Significant changes to an application might require that you rerun tests for that screen or group of screens and generate new test scripts.

Capture and playback tools are most valuable when performing system and regression testing. System testing can be accomplished by creating and saving test scripts made during integration testing. Pulling all these scripts together will test all aspects of the system.

Regression testing can be accomplished the same way. Build a master test script once. To perform regression testing, you simply rerun that script. This will test the entire system and compare it to the original test session's results. Any differences represent regression errors and will be logged.

Workbench/2000

Workbench/2000 from MicroFocus includes a recording facility that captures program execution for replay. This tool records screen output, whether it is a sysout display, a 3270 CICS screen, or an IMS screen. Workbench/2000 executes on Intel-based PCs.

Some of the features provided by Workbench/2000 follow:

- Screen results of every test are saved to disk files.

- Files produced by multiple tests can be compared to determine whether the application has changed.

- Tests can be executed multiple times.

Coverage analysis tools

Estimates of the percentage of code that will be directly affected by the year 2000 problem range from 1–5 percent. A medium-sized corporation may have 10,000,000 lines of source code. The lines of code affected range from 100,000 to 500,000. Even if the lower estimate is more accurate, we're still talking about an enormous number of lines of code.

These estimates include only programs maintained by the MIS department. Additional applications that users have developed (or contracted out) aren't included. Examples of such user-created applications include spreadsheets and programs based on personal database packages.

After these statements have been modified, they must be tested. How can you be sure that each of them will be tested? The answer to this question is to perform a coverage analysis.

Tools are available that monitor the lines of source code executed during every test. This information can be accumulated across all test sessions. The composite data enables you to identify which lines haven't been tested at least once. This tells you what additions need to be made to your tests.

Workbench/2000

Workbench/2000 is described in the "Capture and playback tools" section. It performs coverage analysis as well. The lines of code executed during each test session are logged to an analysis file. This file can be used to verify that all year 2000 code changes have been tested.

VIA/SmartTest

I discuss VIA/SmartTest in the "Debuggers" section. VIA/SmartTest also provides a coverage analysis facility. Each test session you perform records the lines executed during that session. These results can be summarized and printed.

Performance analysis tools

Year 2000 compliant programs will probably execute more slowly than the original versions for a number of reasons, including the following:

- ✔ Data records may be longer now. It takes more time to read longer records from disk because fewer records can be contained in one read operation.
- ✔ Additional logic has been added to programs. More statements to execute means slower programs.

> ✔ Larger data records and programs consume more CPU memory. This can result in more swapping activity between memory and disk swap areas.

You need to determine, in advance, how much of a performance effect these changes will make. It is much better to identify and correct performance problems well in advance than find out about them the day after cutover.

Tools are available that measure the performance characteristics of programs. They might measure CPU time used, disk I/O performed, average response time, and so on. Acquiring and using such a tool lets you measure the affect of your year 2000 changes.

Run the performance tool on your original applications and document its performance. Then install the year 2000 modifications. Rerun the performance tool and compare the results with the original statistics. If there is no change or the difference is marginal, you probably have nothing to worry about. If a large discrepancy exists, you need to address this potential land mine.

Many capture and playback tools record the time that it takes a test to complete. You can use this capability to document performance degradation, as follows:

1. Develop the test scripts that will be used to test an application.

2. Execute the tests on the original (that is, unchanged) version of the application.

3. Record the time it takes to execute the test.

4. Install the modified, year 2000 compliant version of the application.

5. Execute the tests on the modified version.

6. Record the time it takes to execute the test.

7. Compare the two execution times. ***Note:*** For this comparison to be valid, the background activity during both tests should be the same. The easiest way to assure this is to have the test script be the only system activity.

Part IV
The Good, the Bad, and the Ugly

The 5th Wave   By Rich Tennant

"OH SURE, IT'LL FLOAT ALRIGHT, BUT INTEGRATION'S GONNA BE A KILLER."

In this part . . .

The chapters in this part deal with topics that will last beyond the completion of your year 2000 project. As the title of this part implies, some topics are good, some are bad, and some are downright ugly.

The good is that your efforts to clean up code, retire unused applications, and delete duplicate versions will pay dividends for years to come. These efforts will make ongoing maintenance easier and possibly reduce licensing costs.

The bad is that you may not be finished with date problems yet. Some other date related problems are lurking just over the horizon. Your choice of solutions for the year 2000 problem may have added one more problem to this list.

The ugly is that many experts expect that the year 2000 problem will create a tremendous amount of litigation. The chapter on this topic should provide you some insight into how to protect yourself and your organization from a tidal wave of litigation.

Chapter 16

The Good Side of the Year 2000 Situation

*E*very cloud has a silver lining — at least that's what poets, optimists, and refrigerator magnets say. Solving your organization's year 2000 problems does indeed have a positive side. In fact, it has a number of significant advantages. Try to remember this when you're sweating it out during that final stretch.

You're Still In Business

The first and foremost silver lining of dealing with your year 2000 problems is that you'll still be in business. On January 1, 2000, you'll still be able to receive orders, send out invoices, cut paychecks, and maintain your inventory.

Your competition may not be so lucky. A significant number of companies will go out of business if the experts are to be believed. Capers Jones, Chairman of Software Productivity Research Inc., predicts that mid-sized corporations — those with 1,000 to 10,000 employees — are at the greatest risk. Here are his estimates for failure rates based on the size of the organization:

Size of Organization	Number of Employees	Predicted Failure Rate
Small	< 1,000	3%*
Medium	1,000 to 10,000	5%–7%
Large	> 10,000	1%

* This 3% is above and beyond the normal attrition rate for small businesses.

Creating a Software Inventory

Performing a software inventory should be among the first steps of every year 2000 project. A software inventory compiles information on every program, like what data it uses, how often it runs, and where the data comes from. This knowledge is extremely valuable for both this project as well as future projects.

An inventory enables you to better understand how many programs exist, how they interact with each other, and which computers they run on, among other things. Documenting all your software, the versions you are running, and what machine each runs on is valuable in many situations. For example, with a software inventory, you can do the following:

- ✔ Identify different versions of third-party software packages running on your computers. Upgrading all computers to a single version simplifies training and maintenance, and reduces confusion brought about by discrepancies between versions.

- ✔ Track which programs are running at each of an organization's computer centers. If a program is modified at one site, the inventory can identify other sites where the program needs to be modified.

- ✔ Determine what programs are currently running on an old version of an operating system when upgrading. The inventory helps you identify and test for problems that you may encounter while making the transition.

- ✔ Highlight how data flows between programs and computers within your computer systems.

- ✔ Get a jumpstart with the next project that affects a large number of programs. One such project on many organizations' horizon is the need to handle the new Eurocurrency. Changes to computer programs to handle the European Monetary Unit (EMU) don't rely on year 2000 corrections. If both changes are made simultaneously, it isn't likely that either will be successful before January 1, 2000.

✔ Check that all related components (such as source code, libraries, and data files) are identified and deleted when an application or system is being abandoned. This helps prevent unused objects from accumulating again.

Developing a Data Dictionary

A data dictionary is a database that documents information on the data maintained by an organization. Details on every field (column) in every database file or table needs to be collected and stored. Each of these fields is referred to as a *data item*. Every computer shop should have a thorough and up-to-date data dictionary. Following are some of the pieces of information you should store in a data dictionary for each data item:

✔ Name

✔ Description

✔ Type (for example, character, integer, real, money, or date)

✔ Size (for example, character 24, short integer, or double real)

✔ Originator of each field (that is, the department or program that "owns" or generates this data)

✔ Where it exists (that is, the name of the database and the specific table or the data file where the item is located)

✔ Where it is used (that is, which programs, reports, input screens, or exported data streams)

✔ Range of values (that is, an integer greater than 0, the 50 state names, valid zip codes, or ID numbers of current clients)

✔ Synonyms (that is, other names by which this data item is known)

After a data dictionary has been put into place, it has many valuable uses. You can, for example, use it to answer questions that would otherwise require a great deal of research to resolve. Some examples of these questions follow:

✔ Which data fields contain dates?

✔ Which programs access a particular data item and what is the type of access (read, write, modify, or delete) each performs?

✔ What are all the data fields on a given input screen?

✔ To which users is a given report distributed?

✔ If a data item is expanded from six to eight characters (does this sound familiar?), which database tables, data files, reports, and screens will be affected?

✔ If all date fields are expanded from six to eight characters, how much additional disk space will be required?

TIP

A data dictionary will be a valuable management tool during your year 2000 project and afterwards. If your organization doesn't currently have a data dictionary, creating one with the data you collect during your year 2000 project is a great idea. A data dictionary can be built internally or a commercial product can be obtained and installed.

Removing Unused and Duplicate Code

Many organizations will find that they have a significant number of obsolete programs. These programs were developed to fulfill a business need. As the organization evolved or the business needs changed, the program was no longer necessary. Unfortunately, nobody ever bothered to tell MIS (management information systems) to delete the program. As this scene occurred many times over the years, the number of obsolete programs, libraries, and data files accumulated. Truly obsolete programs can be deleted from your computers without affecting users in the least. If they notice any change at all, it will likely be a faster response time.

The amount of code the obsolete programs represent will vary widely among installations. Isogon, a vendor that markets a software auditing package, estimates that the percentage of unused source and load modules will average about 30 percent.

One organization has documented their year 2000 experiences in a paper published on the Internet. This company, a nationwide automotive dealer in Europe, performed an inventory of disk files on their IBM AS/400 computers. The amount of disk space consumed by old versions of source code, object modules, and data files amazed them. Their disks had been 92 percent utilized (full) before the project. Afterwards, in spite of expanding date fields by two digits, the disk utilization rate dropped to 56 percent. All of this reduction was attributed to the deletion of obsolete files.

Much like obsolete programs, a significant amount of duplicated code can be found in many computer shops. A software inventory can help identify and eliminate duplicate versions of the same program. If a duplicated program was developed internally, you will save on disk space. If the program is one you have licensed, you can save on both disk space and licensing fees.

Creating More Efficient Code

Most experts recommend that year 2000 projects shouldn't include other objectives. I completely agree with this advice. Having multiple objectives can result in all of them being performed at a mediocre level, instead of one task being performed well.

This doesn't mean that your team shouldn't go into this project looking to make other changes. Sometimes, however, code can be so inefficient that it jumps out at you, begging to be corrected. In these situations, it makes sense to address the problem as long as the programmer is already making modifications in that program.

It isn't clear where the line should be drawn between what should be changed and what should be left alone. Each project team will have to define it for themselves. My suggestion is to correct only truly significant errors. Cosmetic errors should be deferred until you complete the year 2000 project.

If you decide that your team won't make any changes, the programmers can instead log examples of inefficient code that they come across. After your year 2000 project is complete, a mop-up team can begin correcting the most egregious inefficiencies. The code may not be corrected right away, but at least it will have been identified and put on somebody's to-do list.

Consolidating Date Handling

Computer programmers are without a doubt an independent lot. Many of them just want to be left alone to do their jobs as they see them. This particular trait has both a good side and a bad side. One of the negative aspects is that programmers generally prefer to write their own code instead of using available library routines. The "not invented here" syndrome is alive and well in many computer shops. Some of their arguments for continuing this practice are:

- No library function is available for what this code needs to do.
- My code is written more efficiently than the code in the library.
- I know that my code is correct, but I can't be certain that the library's subroutine is.
- My routine is more flexible than the subroutine in the library.
- Making a call to a library will increase the size of my executable.

Most of these arguments just don't hold up. Libraries, for the most part, are accurate, flexible, and written efficiently. The real answer is that programmers would prefer to do it themselves than rely on code written by someone else.

What does this have to do with date routines? Plenty! In my opinion, library functions dealing with dates are among the most diverse and inconsistent in the industry. Functions vary enormously from library to library. What one operating system, database system, or compiler provides isn't likely to be offered by another vendor's product. Many programmers feel that it's easier to write their own code instead of finding a library routine that does what they need. In many cases, they are correct. The industry would be doing everyone a favor if date data and date related functions were standardized.

Some project plans call for modifying the code to call functions in year 2000 compliant libraries. Changing all date related code to call standardized, consistent subroutines will be a significant improvement over the individualistic approach now in place. Doing this will cut down significantly on the errors and maintenance in your code. Besides making the code year 2000 compliant, it will make the code easier to understand and modify in the future.

Recovering Source Code

Estimates by the Gartner Group state that from 3–5 percent of the source code used by corporate America has been lost. Year 2000 projects need to rewrite or otherwise recover this source code before they can continue. Future projects will likely need this missing source code as well. Any source code that is recovered now represents one less module that needs to be rewritten or recovered during a future project.

Upgrading Technology

Upgrading technology may involve both hardware and software. You may buy new hardware for testing, and move it into production when testing is completed. Or you may buy replacement hardware if you can't make the existing hardware year 2000 compliant. Perhaps you'll buy new hardware if you anticipate performance problems. In any event, you may end up with newer, faster hardware on your computer room floor. This will be an advantage for years to come.

During your year 2000 efforts, you may also acquire new software, such as new compilers, new operating systems, or the most current versions of application software. As a result, your operations will run smoother, or faster, or both.

Building a Testing Foundation

Experts and consultants estimate that from 40–60 percent of your year 2000 efforts will be associated with testing. Being able to apply this testing expertise or information in the future would be a tremendous advantage.

If you use testing tools, such as capture/playback tools, you will create a lot of test scripts. With a little planning, you may be able to reuse test scripts. Suppose that you write a particular script to test a function during integration testing. If you write the script properly, you can use it again during system testing. You can likely use it many times during regression testing.

Reusing a test script this many times speeds up the testing process because you'll need to write and debug that many fewer test scripts.

Test scripts and data represent a significant investment of an organization's time and resources. It would be a shame if you didn't make the most out of this investment. Test data and test scripts built for a year 2000 project can form a baseline for long-term testing. This baseline of tests, however, would need to be well documented.

These tests could be used under a variety of circumstances, such as the following:

- Resolving performance problems
- Determining whether a system can handle additional users without experiencing performance problems
- Determining whether a new version of an operating system, a compiler, or development software will cause a problem
- Testing the impact of extensive changes in application software, both internally developed software and software acquired from third parties

Reusing Tools

You can apply the tools that you use to correct your year 2000 problems to other problems. You can leverage your experience with these tools into improved productivity and accuracy on your next large software project. Some examples of these situations are the following:

- Modifying software to handle the new Eurocurrency
- Migrating all applications to another platform with different system calls
- Changing your method of handling millennium problems from date windowing to date expansion at some future time

Reducing Future Maintenance

Many year 2000 projects will include upgrading to more recent versions of vendor-supplied software. Other projects will replace date related logic with calls to a standardized library. Both of these efforts have a positive side effect: reducing future maintenance needs. This should enable you to direct more of your resources toward enhancing your systems instead of fighting fires.

Gaining a Competitive Advantage

One thing your organization will gain as a result of its year 2000 project is a much deeper knowledge of its systems and the software in them: what they can do, what they can't do, and what is required to change them. This knowledge should enable you to react more quickly when new systems or changes to the existing system are called for.

This combination of knowledge and experience can place you in a competitive advantage in your industry. You will be in a better position to exploit new technologies than competitors who aren't as familiar with their systems.

Chapter 17

Just When You Think Your Date Problems Are Over

● ●

In This Chapter

▶ Reexamining your year 2000 solution

▶ Encountering date problems other than the year 2000

▶ Accessing historical data

● ●

*O*ne solution to the year 2000 problem is to expand two-digit year values to four digits. If you use this solution, your system is set until December 31, 9999. Personally, I wouldn't be losing sleep worrying about what's going to happen in the year 9999.

If your solution wasn't to expand the dates, your system may break down eventually. You need to keep this in mind and be prepared to deal with it. You may have a few years or a few decades before you are forced to address this problem, but don't forget about it until it's almost too late. After all, that's how we got into this situation in the first place!

Fixed Windowing Solution

If you chose a fixed windowing solution, your system can reference a fixed 100-year window. As you come closer to the end of the window, you'll need to reexamine how you are handling this situation. See Figure 17-1. At that time, you may choose to expand dates to four digits or to change the fixed window to a sliding one.

You may encounter problems before the end of the window occurs. For example, if the scope of your business or the data you retain expands, you may need to enter a date outside this window. An alternate solution would be to expand all dates in your system to four digits.

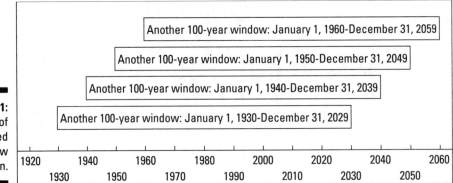

Figure 17-1:
Endpoint of
your fixed
window
solution.

Sliding Window

A sliding 100-year window is another solution to the year 2000 problem. This technique requires that two-digit year values be within a 100-year sliding window. Each two-digit year value is translated into a four-digit year in the 100-year period.

One major aspect of this solution may create problems in the future. How do you handle data that slips off the front end of the sliding window? Each time the calendar flips over to a new year, data in the most distant year is no longer accessible.

For example, suppose your sliding window originally encompasses the years from 1940 through 2039. Five years from now, the window will have advanced to include the years 1945 through 2044. What happens to the data between 1940 and 1944? If you attempt to access it, the translation now interprets 40 to mean 2040 instead of 1940. Dates that originally meant 1940 are now interpreted as 2040. This could cause significant misunderstandings and problems. Figure 17-2 illustrates this problem.

One type of data susceptible to this problem is data retained on people. If you are keeping data on people's ages, you will have problems storing it in a 100-year window. People are living longer than ever before. If your systems deal with this type of information, you will be encountering increasing numbers of dates that exceed a 100-year window.

Eventually, if the problem of losing your data makes the system unworkable, you'll have to consider another solution to your year 2000 problems. Two such solutions are date expansion and date compression (encoding).

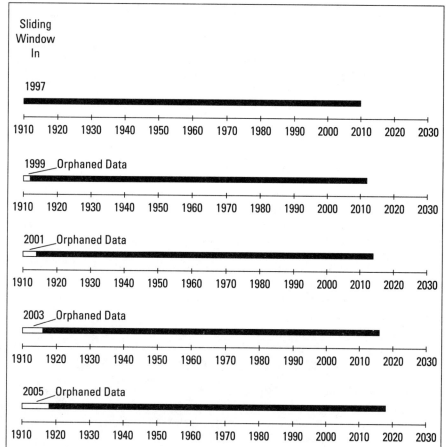

Figure 17-2:
A sliding
window
solution
leaves
orphan data
every year.

Date Compression

Date compression, also called date encoding, is a year 2000 solution that compresses a four-digit year and stores it in two digits. This value is used as an offset from a base year. Typical examples of base years are 1800 or 1900. The year being represented is obtained by adding the base year to the encoded year value stored in the data record. The advantage of this approach is that you don't need to expand the size of the field holding the year.

By expressing the year value in a number system other than decimal, significantly more values can be represented. Some of the number systems that you may use are base 16 or base 256. But even years compressed into other number systems have an upper limit. Table 17-1 shows the maximum value that you can express in each number system.

Table 17-1	Several Compression Techniques and the Last Year They Will Work			
Base Being Used	Maximum Value Expressable in Two Digits	Maximum Year with a Base Year of 1800	Maximum Year with a Base Year of 1850	Maximum Year with a Base Year of 1900
Base 16	255	2055	2105	2155
Base 36	1295	3095	3145	3195
Base 62	3843	5643	5693	5743

If you have implemented date encoding to address your year 2000 problem, you can probably sleep easy for the next few decades. Base 16 is the smallest number system suggested. If you use base 16 and 1850 as the base year, your computer system won't encounter date problems until 2105. I'd bet dollars to donuts that all your computers and their software will have been replaced by that date. Even if they haven't, it's not likely that you'll be exhumed to correct the problem.

A growing number of centenarians

Individuals who have achieved an age of 100 years are referred to as *centenarians*. (No, this isn't the same as the *centurions* in B-grade movies about ancient Rome.) It's estimated that the number of centenarians alive in the United States is 56,000. The number of people with this distinction is expected to expand. The elderly in the United States are the fastest growing segment of the population.

The U.S. Census Bureau estimates that the following number of centenarians were alive in each of these years:

1950	4000	1980	15,000	2000	72,000
1960	6000	1990	28,000	2040	1,300,000
1970	10,000	1995	56,000		

Other Date Related Disasters

Most people are focusing on the year 2000 situation. Organizations are striving to make sure their hardware and software will be ready in time for this January 1, 2000, deadline. The year 2000, however, isn't the only date related crisis on the horizon. As you find out in this section, a number of other date oriented problems are lurking just out of our collective sight.

UNIX

The UNIX operating systems runs on computers ranging from PCs to midrange computers to supercomputers around the world. UNIX stores the date and time as the number of seconds that have elapsed since 0000 UTC, January 1, 1970. This count is stored in a 32-bit signed integer. On January 19, 2038, the number of seconds will reach 2,147,483,647. The next tick of the clock will cause this value to overflow.

Virtually every version of the C and C++ languages will be affected by this problem as well. The libraries used by these languages use the same format to store date and time fields. Both the UNIX operating system and programs written in C and C++ are embedded in the infrastructure around the country. This problem has the potential to be more serious than the year 2000 problem. If your organization is a heavy user of UNIX, you have been put on notice.

Macintosh

The original Mac operating system used a long word (double-sized storage location) to store the number of seconds since January 1, 1904. This location will overflow at 6:28:15 A.M. on February 6, 2040. At that point, Macintosh computers using the original operating system will be in trouble.

More recent versions of this software use a 64-bit signed word to hold date information. This allows the system to access dates between 3008 B.C. and A.D. 29,940. If you're running a recent version of MacOS, you can rest easy for the next few thousand years. A posting on the Internet indicates that all Apple computers manufactured since 1988 handle this 32,000-year range of values. If your computer hardware still includes Macintosh computers that run the original operating system, you'll need to replace them in the next 40 years.

Global Positioning System

The Global Positioning System (GPS) is a network of 24 satellites orbiting the globe. They constantly emit radio signals that give their positions and the date and time. A GPS receiver receives signals from three, or preferably four, satellites. By comparing the exact times each signal was received, a GPS receiver can determine its exact location to within 350 feet.

More and more uses are being found for the Global Positioning System, including the following:

- Precision farming
- GPS integrated with mapping systems for delivery trucks, rental cars, and so on
- GPS units small enough to be carried by hikers and backpackers
- Battlefield uses such as more accurate targeting
- Aviation navigation
- Tracking whales and other animals for scientific studies

The revenue from GPS-oriented systems is expected to mushroom in the next few years — from $1.5 billion in 1996 to $8 billion by the year 2000.

What does this have to do with the year 2000? The Global Positioning System contains a binary field called a week number. This field represents a count of the weeks that have passed since a reference date. Time zero of the GPS system time is 00:00:00 UTC 6 January 1980 (UTC is Universal Time Coordinate). A GPS cycle is 1,024 weeks, or 7,168 days, so the first GPS rollover will occur at 00:00:00 UTC 22 August 1999. The result could be inaccurate date and time values and incorrect coordinates. GPS receiver manufacturers need to examine their receivers to verify that they will function correctly after August 21, 1999.

If you employ this technology in your personal or corporate life, you need to contact the manufacturer. If your organization produces hardware that uses this technology, you need to gear up to address this potential problem.

Retaining Access to Archived Data

Historical, or archived, data is typically stored on reels of magnetic tapes. Your organization may have accumulated an entire library of such tapes over the years. In many instances, this data is retained for legal, accounting, or tax requirements. For the most part, this data probably hasn't been touched in years.

You've probably heard the saying that data is an organization's greatest asset. Well, you're about to hear it again. The data your organization has built up over the years represents a reservoir of information about your business, your industry, and your clients.

This information can help you recognize and capitalize on emerging trends, so it is too valuable to simply throw away. Projects to develop data warehouses are attempts to assemble all this data and make access to this information easier.

Your year 2000 solution — whether you are making modifications to store the date with a four-digit year, or encoding the year value, or using a sliding or fixed window — will probably make archived data inaccessible to current programs.

If an audit or litigation comes up, you won't be able to provide data to substantiate your position. If the CEO wants information that requires access to historical data, you'll have to explain why you can't fulfill the request.

Part of a year 2000 project needs to address this potential problem. One solution is to convert all archived data to make it compatible with the new data format. This approach makes all your data immediately available to production programs. It also eliminates the need for conversion or bridge programs. Converting this data, however, represents an enormous amount of work, directly proportional to the amount of archived data that exists. In addition, your conversion program had better be perfect. If it contains errors and you neglected to make backups, you may be wiping out or deleting some of this valuable resource.

A second approach is to develop and test bridge programs that allow the current versions of your programs to access archived data. The advantages to this approach are that you convert archived data only when you need to access it. And, because the archived data is never modified or deleted, there is less of a chance that it will be damaged or destroyed. This approach does have disadvantages. Data won't be available immediately. To access data, you must apply the bridge program. In addition, if the current programs or data formats are changed, the bridge program must be modified also. It would be very easy to overlook this necessity.

One solution that you shouldn't consider is to maintain both the old and the new versions of the programs. In the long term, this idea is extremely impractical. It requires that you maintain twice as many programs. Inevitably, changes to the old programs will become out of sync with the new programs, and you won't be able to access archived data the same way that you can access current data.

Chapter 18

Legal Ramifications of the Year 2000 Problem

In This Chapter

▶ Understanding legal issues

▶ Predicting who will get sued

▶ Protecting yourself and your organization

▶ Examining other legal situations

*T*he legal fallout costs from year 2000 problems may be greater than the cost of correcting the problem. The Gartner Group estimates that it will cost up to $600 billion to correct the problem. An article in the June 1997 issue of *ABA Journal* projects that legal costs and business disruptions arising from year 2000 problems may exceed a trillion dollars. No one knows whether either of the estimates will come close to the real costs, but the amounts should make you stop to think.

Key Legal Issues

The year 2000 has a number of potential legal considerations that need to be considered. Listed here (in convenient alphabetic order) are some of the more significant issues you need to be aware of.

Acquisitions

Suppose you started early and have dealt with all year 2000 related problems in your organization. You think you'll be able to sleep nights between now and January 1, 2000. Not so fast! If your corporation acquires another organization, you may be inheriting a whole new year 2000 mess. The newly aquired organization's systems may not be ready for this event. In the worst-case scenario, you may have to repeat all previous efforts — but with less time available to you.

How can you prevent yourself from falling into this quicksand-like situation? During the "due diligence" phase of the acquisition process, ask a lot of questions. Ask to see their year 2000 project plan. Ask to meet the project team. Ask to check out their test platforms. Ask which tools they are using. Determine where along the schedule they are right now.

Contracts

A software contract may involve lengthy negotiations between equally powerful industry heavyweights. Or it may be consummated when a buyer breaks the seal on a shrink-wrapped package containing a diskette.

Regardless of the contract's format, the contract itself may involve warranties (implied or otherwise), disclaimers, and maintenance agreements. Whether the vendor will be liable for year 2000 related problems may be left unsaid in the product's contract. When this occurs, it will be more difficult to determine who is liable for the problems. Your best advice is to have competent legal counsel examine the contract to determine the vendor's liability.

Another contract consideration revolves around the number of copies of the software that you can legally possess. Normally, a licensee is allowed to run the software on a single computer and make one backup copy of software. Many organizations will be acquiring new computers for year 2000 testing. Running existing programs on this test platform will likely violate your contract. Check your software contracts for these limitations. If necessary, request permission to run the software on your test installation.

Copyrights

Computer programs are frequently copyrighted. If your organization modifies a copyrighted program, the result may be considered a derivative work. This has the potential to open your organization up to infringement litigation.

It is possible to obtain permission to modify the program. You need to contact the vendor to obtain their agreement. Explain that you need to modify the software to make it year 2000 compliant. Assure them that this isn't an attempt to develop and market a competitive product.

If you choose to go this route, make sure that you know who can access and modify the software. In many cases, it would violate nondisclosure provisions of the contract to allow your year 2000 service provider to decompile, disassemble, or reverse engineer the software. Be extremely careful of the information and assistance you provide without the vendor's permission.

Vendors may be willing to allow an employee to modify their software, but might draw the line at a consultant or contractor doing this work. Their legitimate concern is that a consultant is more likely to violate nondisclosure restrictions than the original customer.

Employment contracts

Qualified personnel to deal with the year 2000 problem are expected to be in short supply. Companies without sufficient staff will likely offer above-average compensation to recruit qualified individuals. Your organization might find itself in this situation before the year 2000 project is completed.

These qualified people have to come from somewhere. That "somewhere" just might be your competitor. If so, this may open you up to legal problems. Accusations may be raised that you're hiring to acquire trade secrets about your new recruit's previous employer.

Another angle on the employment contract situation is shutting down a completed project. If you staffed up for a project with permanent employees, what will you do with the staff when the project ends? If this isn't handled properly, you might be in for wrongful termination litigation.

Financial disclosures

For most organizations, costs to correct year 2000 related problems will be significant. Financial disclosure statements may require that you reveal these costs. Failure to do so may subject the company, including directors and officers, to fines or litigation from stockholders.

Insurance

Although it's possible that existing insurance policies will cover the cost of correcting your year 2000 problems, I wouldn't bet the farm on it. Insurance companies aren't likely to pay for problems that their policies don't unequivocally address.

A number of companies have developed policies specifically to cover the year 2000 situation. These policies can help to pay for the costs of year 2000 related expenses. They can also handle the costs of unexpected expenses such as business disruption or loss of income.

Don't expect that you'll be able to snap up these policies without any questions being asked. Insurers will be very wary of adverse selection, a situation in which policyholders buy insurance only when they are certain they can collect from it. (An example of adverse selection is a homeowner trying to buy flood insurance just as the dam is bursting.) To avoid this situation, insurers will want to review your efforts to deal with the year 2000 problem. If you aren't actively working to solve it, they aren't likely to want to pay for it for you.

Mergers

Mergers bring up some of the same situations as acquisitions. The right questions regarding computer systems and the year 2000 need to be asked. Otherwise, the merger may not be as harmonious as expected.

Taxes

There are questions as to whether costs associated with year 2000 problems can be capitalized or expensed. In the United States, a Financial Accounting Standards Board task force has recommended that these costs be expensed. At the time of this writing, the IRS has not yet stated a position on this topic. As the magic date comes closer, this situation will certainly become clearer.

The difference will have a significant effect on a corporation's bottom line. Corporations would prefer that these costs be a current year deduction. If the costs must be capitalized, corporations would prefer that they be amortized over as short a period as possible. The federal government may resist current year deductibility. This would minimize tax revenue deductions associated with these expenses.

Year 2000 compliance

Many vendors were shipping systems that weren't year 2000 compliant as recently as 1997. Can they legitimately claim that this problem was unexpected? Shouldn't they have tested their product with dates beyond January 1, 2000?

On the other hand, what liability do consumers have? A great deal of publicity has surrounded the year 2000 problem lately. Shouldn't consumers be expected to ask vendors for a statement regarding compliance? It might be tough to argue that a software vendor should pay for a problem that clients chose to ignore.

The mother of all lawsuits

Experts predict that the litigation generated by the year 2000 will be unprecedented. An article in the June 1997 issue of the *ABA Journal* quoted a lawyer with experience in this area who said legal costs could easily exceed a trillion dollars. It is predicted that this situation will surpass any litigation in history.

When you think of large lawsuits and class action suits, what comes to mind? Significant cases that I remember include:

- Asbestos removal
- Savings and loan debacle
- Cleanup of toxic waste dumps
- Tobacco litigation

How much publicity did these incidents get? How long were they covered on the nightly news? How many congressional investigations did they spawn? Now imagine if experts are correct and the year 2000 is bigger than all of them!

Should an upgrade that corrects a year 2000 problem be covered under an existing maintenance contract? Should the vendor be required to correct year 2000 problems even without a maintenance contract because the software is defective?

The answers to these questions are unclear, and it's likely that they will be argued in courtrooms for years to come.

Lawsuits and the Year 2000

Litigation requires a defendant. The list of potential defendants in the year 2000 situation is long and varied. Some are listed here. In our litigious society, you can let your imagination run wild with potential defendants.

Software vendors

Companies that produce software are perhaps the most obvious defendants in year 2000 related litigation. A typical claim will probably be that the calendar rolling over to the year 2000 is an expected occurrence. Everyone knows that it will follow the year 1999. Therefore, there is no reason why software shouldn't be capable of handling this situation.

One point to consider when suing a software vendor is that you can't sue what you can't find. This is particularly true if the software was purchased long ago and there has been little or no contact with the vendor since then.

Perhaps the software vendor went out of business. Maybe the firm changed its name and location. Or it may have merged with another company or been acquired by a larger company. Any of these reasons may contribute to it being difficult or impossible to find your vendor.

Even if you're successful in finding and suing the vendor and winning your case, don't start counting your money yet. If the vendor doesn't have any assets, you won't be able to collect anything.

Year 2000 solution providers

Many organizations will engage year 2000 solution providers to help them overcome these troubles. After paying good money, they will expect their problems to be solved. If problems occur on January 1, 2000, they will be looking for blood.

Not all upgrades will be perfect. Despite everyone's best efforts, there will be problems. Some of these problems will cause more problems and cost more money. When this happens, the client is likely to sue the solution provider.

The year 2000 situation has become big business, with an enormous number of potential customers worldwide. Many are desperate to update their systems. As the panic level rises, customers are likely to ask fewer and fewer questions regarding the background of a service provider.

The cost of getting into this business is fairly small. It can be as little as renting an office, putting in phone lines, and running some advertisements. The combination of eager customers and easy entry makes this field ripe territory for crooks, scam artists, and other questionable characters. If legitimate solution providers get sued, imagine how many problems the less reputable companies will have. If you later attempt to sue a less than reputable company, don't be surprised if they are no longer in business.

System integrators

Value Added Resellers (VARs), or system integrators, put together, market, and install complete computer systems. They provide both the hardware and software needed to build a system. The software may or may not have been written by them. In many cases, they simply purchase and perhaps customize an existing software package.

Many business and other organizations (especially smaller ones) acquire their computer systems from VARs. Examples of the kinds of systems a VAR may develop are local area networks, accounting packages, personnel systems, inventory control programs, and small databases.

The liability of VARs and system integrators is uncertain. On the one hand, they didn't create the problem in either the hardware or software. They may not even be aware that a piece of hardware or software will have a problem with the year 2000. To solve this problem, they must rely on support from the original product vendor.

On the other hand, VARs and system integrators did market and profit by selling a computer system. They frequently provide maintenance contracts or warranties of their systems. This may cause them to be liable in court.

Auditors

Auditors examine the books of organizations and certify that they have followed standard accounting practices. Many people rely on the accuracy of this certification, including:

- ✔ Stockholders
- ✔ Potential stockholders or investors
- ✔ Banks considering loans to the organization
- ✔ Bondholders
- ✔ Firms that supply materials on credit
- ✔ Landlords

If the auditors don't identify and publicize potential problems, any of these groups could lose money. The auditors could potentially be held liable for failing to provide accurate information.

The year 2000 adds a great number of unknowns to the auditing stew pot. Because the year 2000 has never happened before, it raises many uncertainties regarding what auditors should examine. Until these questions are resolved, ask a lot of questions about year 2000 expenses and how they are treated.

Corporate officers and directors

One group that can potentially be held personally responsible for year 2000 problems are directors and officers of a corporation. As the leaders and makers of policy, they should have foreseen this problem coming and addressed it. If the stock value of the corporation declines, they could potentially be held personally responsible.

Many corporations are incorporated in the state of Delaware. The standard that this state has adopted regarding negligence of directors is the following:

"Directors of a corporation, in managing the corporate affairs, are bound to use that amount of care which ordinarily careful and prudent men would use in similar circumstances. Their duties are those of control and whether or not by neglect they have made themselves liable for failure to exercise proper control depends on the circumstances and facts of the particular case."

If the stock price dropped significantly, stockholders could sue the directors and officers of the organization. Their claim would be that a prudent individual would have foreseen this problem in time to correct it. In light of all the publicity on the year 2000 problem, it would be difficult to claim that the problem wasn't anticipated.

Consultants

Expert consultants are frequently retained to advise an organization when it acquires a new computer system. These experts claim to be familiar with both the needs of the organization and the available systems. They provide up-to-date expertise that the organization doesn't have or normally need. This expertise assists the organization in obtaining the software package most suited to their needs.

What if the consultant isn't aware of potential year 2000 problems? Who is liable if the consultant recommends a product that later experiences significant year 2000 related difficulties? An expert would have a difficult time later claiming that he or she had overlooked this important consideration.

Taking Steps to Protect Yourself

The legal exposure of the year 2000 problem can haunt your organization for years. To protect yourself, the best defense is a good offense. Perform the following actions immediately to avoid or minimize problems later.

Examine your potential liability now

Does your organization sell software? Does it export data to other organizations? Does it provide a service to external clients that can't be interrupted? Does it possess data that can't be lost? Do any of your systems have the potential to harm or endanger human life?

Only by asking probing questions like these can you determine your potential liability. The time to ask these questions is now. It will take longer to get the answers (and to act on them) than you expect.

Build a paper trail

Normally I don't suggest that people spend time covering their flanks. I feel you should do your best and let the chips fall where they may. Unfortunately, the year 2000 problem isn't a normal situation. If there is the slightest chance that you or your organization can be sued, you should protect yourself. One way to do this is to maintain records demonstrating your activities. This paper trail can be used to prove that prudent and prevailing precautions were put into place.

Be aware that a paper trail can prove to be a double-edged sword. You may think that it demonstrates that you took proper and sufficient steps when dealing with the year 2000 problem. An opposing attorney may try to use the same information to show that your activities were inadequate. If you take the trouble to document your activities, be sure that they are worth documenting.

Potential year 2000 litigation

Many year 2000 situations involve legal issues that aren't immediately obvious. For example, suppose that a bank makes a substantial loan to a certain organization. This organization doesn't become year 2000 compliant in time and goes out of business due to year 2000 problems. The loan isn't repaid. Should the bank have lent the money? Who's to blame for this poor decision?

As another example, suppose that directors or officers of a corporation sell stock just before negative year 2000 disclosures are made. After the release of this information, the stock price declines. Have they taken advantage of insider information?

Suppose that some of your current computer systems were purchased from ABC, Inc. They don't have sufficient personnel to make your installation year 2000 compliant. To make sure that the system will continue to function, you contract with XYZ, Inc. for this work. XYZ converts the same system for a number of organizations. All this experience enables them to offer long-term support for this particular package. ABC views this disclosure as a violation of your contract. They sue you, XYZ, and everyone else who signs with them.

A final example: A large manufacturer has instituted a "just in time" system for the parts it uses on its assembly line. This corporation solved its year 2000 problems in plenty of time. Unfortunately, not all of its suppliers were as proactive. Shortly after the turn of the century, the computer systems of the suppliers crash. They can no longer deliver the contracted parts. Who is liable here? Can the manufacturer sue the vendors for lost income? The problem could have been avoided if the manufacturer had aggressively verified that its suppliers were year 2000 compliant.

Require year 2000 compliance in all new software contracts

It's bad enough that your old software may not be year 2000 compliant. Don't compound this mistake by acquiring new software that isn't year 2000 compliant. Any new software contracts should include a standard year 2000 compliance clause.

The vendor may claim that the current version isn't year 2000 compliant but an upcoming version will be. Don't simply take the vendor's word for it. Insist on getting answers to the following questions:

- ✔ What is their definition of "year 2000 compliant"?
- ✔ What version of the package will be compliant?
- ✔ When is that version expected to be delivered?
- ✔ What if it is late?
- ✔ When it's delivered, how difficult will it be to install it and perform any needed conversions?

Perform due diligence

If your organization acquires any other entities, you need to do your homework. Determine whether their systems will have a year 2000 problem. Some of the questions you should be asked are:

- ✔ Have they developed a year 2000 project plan?
- ✔ What will it cost to become compliant?
- ✔ How realistic is their schedule and their cost estimates?
- ✔ What are the project's potential bottlenecks?
- ✔ What will happen if the project isn't finished in time?

If the year 2000 correction ends up costing more than expected, you may want to write an escape clause into any agreements.

Verify the qualifications of contractors

You may end up contracting with outside groups or individuals to assist with the year 2000 problem. Before you sign on the dotted line, you need to get a number of assurances. Some of the questions to ask include the following:

- ✔ What experience does the group have?
- ✔ Are they willing to provide references? Make sure you contact them!
- ✔ What guarantees or warrantees do they provide?
- ✔ What assets do they have to back up their promises?
- ✔ If the project falls behind, can they provide additional personnel to attempt to catch up?
- ✔ Is there a relationship between the consulting group and any tool vendor they use? You want them to use the best tools available, not what the home office wants them to use.
- ✔ Is there a relationship between the consulting group and any of your competitors? Are they owned by the same company? Do they have a long-term partnership? If such a relationship exists, you may be reluctant to engage that consulting group.

Part V
The Part of Tens

The 5th Wave   By Rich Tennant

"WELL, SYSTEMS INTEGRATION ISN'T PERFECT. SOME DEPARTMENTS STILL SEEM TO GET MORE INFORMATION THAN OTHERS."

In this part . . .

The Part of Tens is my favorite part of ...*For Dummies* books. It gets valuable information to you quickly.

This book, like every book ever printed, can contain only a limited amount of information. The ten online sources of information in this part, however, can provide you and your organization with virtually unlimited information on the year 2000 situation. You should plan on creating bookmarks for many of these invaluable sites.

One chapter in this Part of Tens lists some questions you should be asking yourself, your management, and any potential vendors you are thinking of doing business with.

Another chapter in this part has a more personal touch. It's a listing of local year 2000 user groups. Joining and becoming active in such a user group will make your life easier in the upcoming, hectic months. If nothing else, it will connect you with people in a similar situation who can sympathize with your woes.

The final chapter in this part will, I hope, lift your spirits a bit. Just remember, no matter how bad it seems to be, it could always be worse. Good luck, and I hope the following chapters are helpful to you during your year 2000 endeavors.

Chapter 19

Ten Online Sources of Year 2000 Information

*T*he year 2000 problem is beginning to capture the attention of the world. More and more information is being published in books, magazines, and newspapers as well as being aired on TV. Scarcely a day goes by that I don't hear or read something about this topic. An even greater amount of year 2000 information is available online. Each reservoir of year 2000 knowledge can provide a needed piece to the puzzle you are dealing with. With so many sources, though, finding the best ones takes time and initiative.

Most of the sources listed here are Web sites that anyone can access. All contain articles, white papers, or discussions related to the year 2000. Most contain links to other Web sites. Be sure to bookmark the pages you find most useful.

Although the following Web sites were active when I wrote this chapter, some might not be when you read this book. Links that I mention may no longer exist, and some of the Web pages may have been changed. On the bright side, you'll probably find more Web sites dedicated to this topic with even more information and advice. These sites are just a starting point. Do a little searching and you are bound to turn up considerably more sites than I have listed here.

www.year2000.com

Web site www.year2000.com, shown in Figure 19-1, is the mother of all year 2000 Web sites. It represents an enormous collection of information on the year 2000 problem. This Web site is provided by de Jager & Company Limited and The Tenagra Corporation. Peter de Jager is perhaps the most widely recognized expert on the year 2000 situation. He has been raising the awareness of this problem around the world.

It's hard to summarize all the information this site provides. Some of the categories of information available follow:

- ✔ A schedule of upcoming year 2000 related conferences
- ✔ A list of vendors that offer year 2000 related products or services
- ✔ An archive of current and past articles and press releases
- ✔ A year 2000 FAQ (frequently asked questions) file that is about 75 pages
- ✔ Job listings and résumés of people looking for positions
- ✔ A list of year 2000 user groups

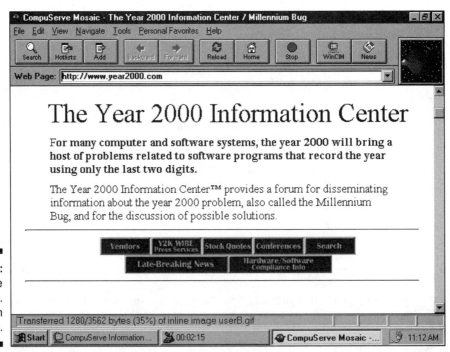

Figure 19-1:
First page
of the www.
year2000.com
Web site.

✔ The option of being added to their mailing list

✔ Links to other year 2000 sites

The list of articles on this site is especially thorough. Figure 19-2 is an example of some of the articles listed on this site while I write this book.

This should be your first stop on the Net. The first item you should download is the FAQ file. After reading this file, you'll be able to hit the ground running on a year 2000 project.

www.software.ibm.com

The `www.software.ibm.com` Web site should be your second stop. The information available on this site is slightly less general than de Jager's site. Figure 19-3 is a screen shot of the opening page of this IBM site.

To access IBM's year 2000 information, click on the icon labeled "Visual Age 2000 Y2K Solutions." The tools and advice listed on this site concentrate mostly on IBM products, both software and hardware. The listing of tools provides an overview of what is available, as shown in Figure 19-4.

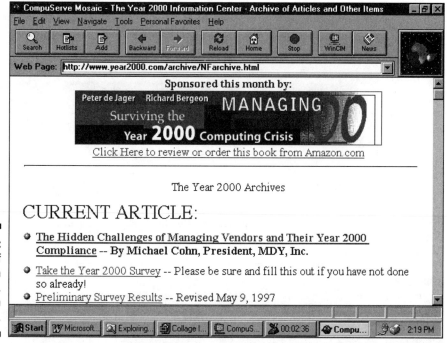

Figure 19-2:
List of
articles on
the www.
year2000.com
Web site.

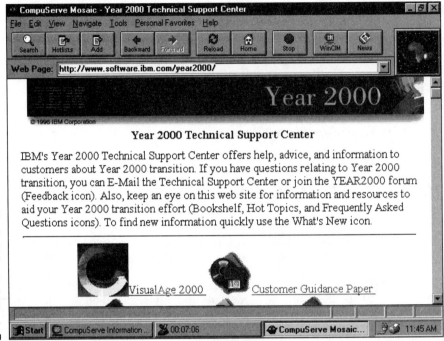

Figure 19-3:
Opening
page of
IBM's
software-
related
Web site.

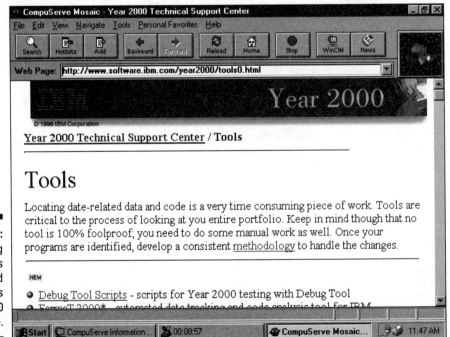

Figure 19-4:
A listing
of tools
described
on IBM's
year 2000
Web site.

A number of items on this site are general enough to be used by anyone involved in a year 2000 effort. The information included can be applied to any (that is, non-IBM) hardware and software. The most valuable of these is a paper outlining IBM's recommended methodology for dealing with a year 2000 problem. Some of these generic resources are

- IBM's methodology for dealing with the problem at `www.software.ibm.com/year2000/method0.html`
- A discussion of bridge programs; see the Methodology page
- A presentation on testing considerations lists tips on testing
- Testing stages that list three stages for year 2000 testing
- "Getting Started," a list of things you need to identify in your organization
- "Categories of Tools," a general listing of the types of tools available
- "Date Simulator Uses and Explanations" document on how and when to use date simulator tools

A page of frequently asked questions addresses IBM hardware and software. Some of the year 2000 related topics listed on this page are

- Programming languages: COBOL, RPG, others
- Operating systems: MVS, OS/400, VSE, others
- Databases
- Hardware: AS/400, System/3x, others
- Testing: AS/400, general
- Methodology

www.y2k.com

Most year 2000 Web sites concentrate on the technical aspects of the year 2000 situation. The `www.y2k.com` Web site focuses on the financial, legal, and other managerial aspects of the year 2000. Figure 19-5 shows the opening page of the site.

Some of the topics covered on this site are diverse and not likely to be discussed on other sites, such as

- Convincing company directors and senior officers of the gravity of the year 2000 problem
- Investment risks and opportunities that the year 2000 situation creates
- Educating in-house legal counsel on the year 2000 and its legal ramifications

Figure 19-5:
Opening
page of the
www.
y2k.com
Web site.

> ✔ The liabilities of corporate directors and officers
>
> ✔ Sample contracts, notices, and disclosures
>
> ✔ Management related articles and presentations

Specific examples of articles and presentations that you can access on this site include the following:

> ✔ "The Role of Legal Counsel in Year 2000 Remediations," by Greg Cirillo
>
> ✔ "'Sharks & Pigs' Rating Y2K Liability," by Dan Hassett & Greg Cirillo
>
> ✔ "Time to Beat the Computer Clock," by Gregory Cirillo & Ira Kasdan
>
> ✔ "Surviving the Year 2000," by Daniel Hassett
>
> ✔ "Memo to In-House Counsel," by Ira Kasdan
>
> ✔ "For Risk Managers the Year 2000 Is Now," by Andrew Pegalis
>
> ✔ "Negotiating Your Y2K Assessment/Remediation Contracts," by Greg Cirillo
>
> ✔ "Sequel: Y2K Remediation Contracts: When Your Back Is Against the Wall, You Do Not Need Leverage to Succeed," by Greg Cirillo

www.spr.com

The Software Productivity Research (SPR) Web site, at www.spr.com, provides a wealth of information on software measurement, assessment, and estimation. The chairman of the Software Productivity Research organization is Capers Jones, who is one of the most respected authorities in the industry on the topic of software measurement. Figure 19-6 shows SPR's initial Web page.

The most valuable piece of information on this site is a paper by Mr. Jones titled "The Global Economic Impact of the Year 2000 Software Problem." This paper contains extensive information on the year 2000 situation, including the following topics:

✔ The volume of software installed in the United States expressed in function points

✔ Potential business failures that the year 2000 situation could cause — broken down by company size, industry, and financial health of the organization

✔ Year 2000 repair costs broken down by company size, industry, programming language, and state

✔ Benefits of solving your year 2000 problems

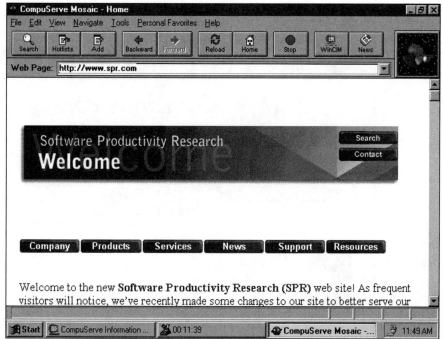

Figure 19-6:
Web site of the Software Productivity Research organization.

✔ Costs of correcting this problem by city, by country, and worldwide

✔ Fallacies associated with the year 2000 situation

✔ Year 2000 terms and concepts explained

✔ The costs of repairing databases, repositories, and data warehouses

✔ Litigation that might be generated by the year 2000 situation

This paper can be used to convince your management that the year 2000 problem really exists. It also provides concrete examples of what it will cost to correct the problem, how much time the corrections should take, and the implications if the problem isn't addressed. If this information isn't able to gain support for the year 2000 effort, you should consider turning in your resignation and taking your skills elsewhere. If management isn't willing to act now, a job with this organization might not exist for long.

www.comlinks.com

ComLinks is an online media community that contains a large number of valuable year 2000 oriented resources. These resources are geared more toward management than the programmers who will be making the changes. Figure 19-7 shows the ComLinks opening page.

Figure 19-7:
The
ComLinks
opening
Web page.

The Y2K Issues, Y2K FAQ, and Library buttons on the home page take you to screens that list a number of articles, including the following:

- "What Management Needs to Know About the Year 2000 Computer Date Problem," by Leon Kappelman and Phil Scott

- "Accrued Savings of the Year 2000 Computer Date Problem," by Leon Kappelman and Phil Scott

- "Triage for Year 2000 Efforts," by David Eddy

- "OMB Report — Getting Federal Computers Ready for 2000"

- "It's All a Matter of Communication," by Alan Simpson

- "Legal (Y2K) Issues Confronting the Federal & State Governments," by Jeff Jinnett

- "Testing for Year 2000," by Richard Warden

- "Computer Software and Year 2000 Compliance," by William A. Tanenbaum

- "Motivating for Year 2000," by Richard Warden

- "Immediate Action at the Highest Corporate Levels," by Steven L. Hock

www.itpolicy.gsa.gov

Many people believe that the government will be affected by the year 2000 even more heavily than the private sector. The government has an enormous number of computers and is highly dependent on them to fulfill its daily functions. The government doesn't have the best reputation for approaching problems proactively.

You'll be pleased to know that government at the federal level is actively working on the year 2000 situation. A number of government Web sites are dedicated to this problem. The General Services Administration (GSA) has a fairly extensive Web site at www.itpolicy.gsa.gov, as shown in Figure 19-8.

From the initial Web page, select the year 2000 information directory. The screen in Figure 19-9 is displayed.

This site serves a number of purposes, including the following:

- Publishes the best practices for dealing with the year 2000 situation

- Presents links to other year 2000 sites on the Internet

- Lists year 2000 tools, products, and services

- Provides access to documents and white papers dealing with the year 2000

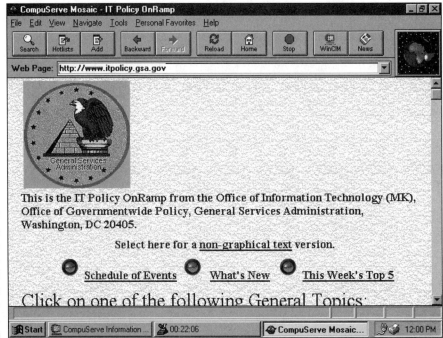

Figure 19-8:
Initial Web page of the General Services Administration.

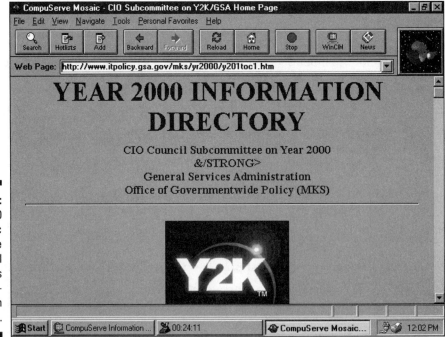

Figure 19-9:
Year 2000 specific page of the General Services Administration Web site.

One collection of information that isn't readily available are hyperlinks to how governmental bodies are dealing with this problem. Some of the government bodies linked to are

- Air Force Year 2000 home page
- Department of the Army page
- Defense Information Systems Agencies
- Federal Aviation Administration (FAA)
- U.S. Marine Corps
- National Institute of Standards and Technology (NIST)
- Department of the Navy
- Department of Veterans Affairs

This site also contains links to Web pages sponsored by individual state governments.

www.gartner.com

The Gartner Group is a highly respected consulting organization when it comes to analyzing, understanding, and predicting trends. The year 2000 situation is certainly one that they are covering. The first page of its Web site, which is at www.gartner.com, is shown in Figure 19-10.

You can use its Web site to search its extensive library of articles, papers, and presentations, as shown in Figure 19-11. When I searched for the string "year 2000," a list of 100 documents was quickly returned to me.

Some documents included in this list of 100 follow:

- "Time Marches On — Less Than 900 Working Days to January 1, 2000"
- "Executive Edge: Year 2000 Solution"
- "'Year 2000 Problem' Gains National Attention: Gartner Group Advises U.S. Congress on Issue"
- "Overcoming the Twin Pressures of EMU & Year 2000"; EMU is the acronym for European Monetary Unit
- "PCs and the Year 2000 Problem: Minor Complications or Major Crisis?"
- "Year 2000 ESPs: A Market Segmentation"

Figure 19-10:
The Gartner Group's initial Web page.

Figure 19-11:
The Gartner Group's search page.

www.computerworld.com

Computerworld is the computer industry's weekly newspaper. It covers all aspects of computer hardware and software. As one would expect, a number of year 2000 oriented articles show up in this newsweekly. *Computerworld* also supports a Web page. When you first log onto `www.computerworld.com`, you see the Web page shown in Figure 19-12.

Click the Year2000 selection, and — because *Computerworld* is a weekly publication — you are presented with the most recent year 2000 articles. Some of the ones I accessed in mid-July, 1997, follow:

- ✔ "IS Chief: Year 2000 a Fraud"
- ✔ "Year 2000 Muck Mires Midrange"
- ✔ "Client/Server Users Must Push for Year 2000 Tools"
- ✔ "Numbers Add Up to a Bigger Year 2000 Disaster"

Another useful feature of the Computerworld Web page is the Year 2000 Scoreboard, which presents the latest in year 2000 trends, issues, and statistics. If you're not a regular *Computerworld* subscriber (and you don't snitch it off a coworker's desk), scan through this page — I'm sure you'll find it worthwhile.

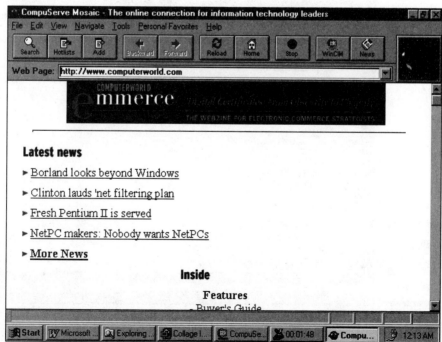

Figure 19-12: The Computerworld home page.

www.mitre.org/research/y2k/

The Mitre Corporation does a lot of consulting for the government, especially the military. Consequently, it is very involved in updating computer systems to make them year 2000 compliant. The Mitre Web site, at www.mitre.org/research/y2k/, contains a large collection of year 2000 related information. Their year 2000 home page is displayed in Figure 19-13.

You can find valuable veins of information within the enormous amount available at this site. Some of the items follow:

- A downloadable list of year 2000 vendors and their products
- Steps you should take now to begin your year 2000 project
- Cost estimations for making an organization year 2000 ready
- Testing for year 2000 compliance
- Sharing and collaboration for the year 2000
- Global Positioning System (GPS) and dates
- Overview of the seven viable solutions to the year 2000 problem

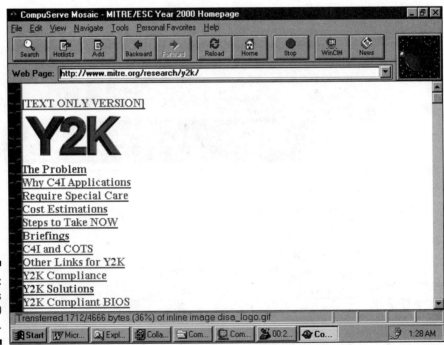

Figure 19-13: Mitre's Year 2000 home page.

I found an especially informative document at `www.mitre.org/research/y2k/docs/PHASES.html`. It described the six phases of a successful year 2000 project. The opening graphic on this page, shown in Figure 19-14, presents these phases and an estimate of the percentage of time that you should spend on each.

Although this Web site isn't the easiest to negotiate, it certainly is informative. Two areas that helped me find my way around were the Index and the What's New hot spots.

CompuServe

CompuServe isn't a Web site like all the other online sources listed in this chapter. To access this online service, you must subscribe to it. Then, after you subscribe and log on, you can get to the year 2000 forum by entering GO YEAR2000.

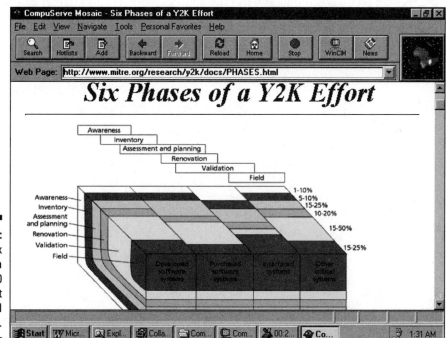

Figure 19-14: The six phases of a year 2000 project posited by Mitre.

You can view ongoing discussion threads on the year 2000 topic or search their library for papers, articles, and past discussions on the year 2000. A few of the sections available in this forum follow:

- ✔ Year 2000 News
- ✔ PCs: Tech Issues
- ✔ Mainframes: Tech Issues
- ✔ Consumer Issues
- ✔ Tools & Methods
- ✔ Jobs & Classifieds
- ✔ Seminars/Speakers
- ✔ Predictions

The capability to search one or all sections for specific phrases is also available.

I recommend that you use the sources listed in this chapter extensively for guidance and tips. I also suggest that you log back into your favorite sites periodically. New material is added to some of them daily.

Chapter 20

Ten Questions to Ask Prospective Consulting Firms

. . . .

In This Chapter

▶ What experience do they have?

▶ Are they willing to provide references?

▶ How long have they been in business?

▶ How much year 2000 experience do they have?

▶ Do they have experience with large projects?

▶ How large is their staff?

▶ Is their work guaranteed?

▶ Can you reject staff personnel?

▶ When can they start?

▶ How much will it cost?

. . . .

*M*ost year 2000 projects will be large and difficult undertakings requiring expertise and programmers that many companies don't currently have. Because few individuals have the skills and experience necessary, organizations will be looking for outside assistance from consulting firms or vendors who either do the majority of the project or provide additional staff. Other clients will be looking for some guidance; after the project is mapped out, these clients will do the work themselves.

Organizations looking for help won't have to look far! A great number of consultants, consulting firms, and vendors are already available in this arena. Like mushrooms after a morning rain, more are springing up all the time. The problem will be selecting the correct one. Making the wrong choice can have a catastrophic effect on your project.

You need to ask the right questions to determine whether a prospective consulting group will be able to handle your project. The following ten questions represent a starting point.

Experience?

One blunt question you need to ask is whether the prospective consultants have undertaken and succeeded on a year 2000 project. If they have this experience, they will be happy to discuss it at great length. If they hesitate, use weasel words, or seem reluctant to give you a straight answer, interpret this as a no.

It's great if the prospective consultants are honest, hard-working, intelligent, and brush their teeth three times a day. Maybe these characteristics would allow them to pick up the needed skills quickly, but experience counts for an awful lot. Do you really want them to be learning their skills on your nickel? Wouldn't you rather have a consulting firm that is honest, hard-working, intelligent, hygienic, *and* experienced?

You'll never know whether they have experience unless you explicitly ask. If you don't ask, they certainly won't tell.

Obtain information about their experience in writing. If you ever need this information, perhaps in a lawsuit, it will be useful only if it has been committed to paper. An oral description of their experience isn't worth the paper it isn't written on.

Who?

Who have the prospective consultants worked for on year 2000 projects? Are they willing to provide references of past clients? If they do provide a list of clients, contact each one. Ask whether the objectives were achieved. Were deadlines met? Were the consultants professional?

If a consulting firm isn't willing to provide references, be somewhat leery of them. They may have a good reason for this reluctance, but they may have many bad reasons as well. For example:

- They don't have any previous clients.
- Their previous clients may be dissatisfied with the quality of the job that they performed.
- Their former clients may warn you about negatives that the firm would prefer stay hidden, such as cost overruns, missed deadlines, or bait-and-switch tactics.

In these days of litigation, former clients may be reluctant to come out and clearly say negative things about a consulting firm. You may have to listen very closely to understand what they are really trying to say. If this is how the message is passed on to you, be even more cautious of the firm.

How Long?

How long have the consultants been in business? In general, the longer they've been in business, the better. The failure rate of new businesses is pretty high. It's reasonable to assume that companies that have survived for a number of years are among the fittest. At a minimum, being in the business for a while demonstrates the following:

- ✔ They've developed some marketing skills.
- ✔ Clients must be satisfied with the job they do. This is especially true if they receive a lot of repeat business.
- ✔ They're likely to have some financial assets. These reserves will allow them to survive the inevitable highs and lows of consulting.
- ✔ They have a certain amount of tenacity. Otherwise, they probably would have folded the first time the going got tough.

How Long? (Part Deux)

Another duration-related question to ask is how long they have been in the year 2000 business. A consulting firm may have been around for a long time. They may be quite successful in their own niche. But this doesn't guarantee that they will be successful when dealing with year 2000 problems.

Again, it boils down to experience with this type of project. If you're willing to take a chance on an established firm with no year 2000 experience, know what you're getting into.

Large Project Experience?

Do you have a recipe for a favorite dish? Have you ever doubled the recipe to make more of it for a party or pot-luck supper? It wasn't as easy to make a double batch, was it? Your pots and pans probably weren't big enough. It probably required more time to bring it to the desired temperature without scorching it. It was harder to stir it and thoroughly mix the ingredients. You likely didn't have a serving dish that was big enough. Have you ever made a batch ten times larger than your normal recipe? How much harder do you think that would be to handle?

Restaurants, college dorms, and other institutions routinely serve hundreds or even thousand of meals. What's the difference between them and you? They have experience with larger quantities, and they have the proper equipment. These concepts affect software projects the same way they affect cooking. Dealing with software projects of a certain size is fairly easy. If you double the size of the project, dealing with it is more than twice as hard. To handle very large projects, you need both the experience and the proper tools.

Most year 2000 projects will be on a significantly larger scale than other projects. Do the consultants you're interviewing have experience with projects of this size? As always, if you don't ask, they're not likely to volunteer this crucial information. If they don't understand and don't have experience with the potential problems with extremely large projects, I suggest that you steer clear of them.

Staff Size?

One reason for turning to consultants for help on a year 2000 project is that you don't have enough people to do the job. You may not hire additional permanent staff because

✔ You'd need to release them at the end of the project.

✔ You can't find people to hire with the desired skills and experience.

✔ The rules and procedures in your organization make it easier to hire contractors than to hire permanent employees.

One or more of these reasons may have swayed you to hire a consulting firm to assist with this project. A question you must ask them is whether their staff is large enough to handle your needs as well as their current client base. How many people do they currently have? How many are assigned to existing projects? How many will your project require?

If they don't have adequate staff, think twice about hiring them. Why? They, too, will have trouble finding experienced individuals to hire. If they have to increase their staff too quickly, the experience and knowledge base of the current staff will be severely diluted.

Are You a Victim of Bait and Switch?

Have you ever seen an advertisement on TV or in a newspaper that seemed too good to be true? When you went into the store, the clerks said they were so sorry, but they had just sold the last sale item. They did, however, have a better model for just a few dollars more. You walked out of the store with what they had instead of what you wanted.

They just pulled a bait and switch on you. The bait was the sale item for a very low price. The switch was getting you to buy something that wasn't on sale. You were taken! Bait-and-switch operations are illegal.

Retail operations aren't the only places that use a bait-and-switch ploy. Service industries, such as consulting firms, are also capable of tricking you with this tactic. In these cases, the bait isn't a toaster, a microwave oven, or a clock radio. It's a person.

Bait and switch by a consulting firm works like this: When you first start talking to the firm, they trot out the most experienced, impressive individuals in the firm. These men and women have advanced degrees from first-rate universities. They have tremendous experience on cutting-edge projects. They are so impressive they make you drool. You've just been shown the bait. The firm may not actually promise that these people will be working on your project, but they imply it. While in this vulnerable state, you sign the contract.

You've taken the bait, and you're about to see the switch. When you meet your project team for the first time, guess what? It won't include those impressive individuals you met in the office. When you ask about them, you'll receive assurances that they will be assigned to your project as soon as they finish up another project. I've got news for you: It isn't going to happen. Those people will never see the inside of your offices. The firm had no intention of assigning their best people to your project. They are kept in the office as bait for the next client (sucker).

Another possibility is that those impressive people are put on your project for a very short time and then quietly transferred off your project. The explanation may be that they are needed to handle an emergency on another project. Despite these promises, you won't see them again in this lifetime.

How can you avoid getting taken in by this deceptive tactic? Insist that the contract specifies exactly who will be working on your project. Have your legal department look the contract over for loopholes. Be extremely suspicious of phrases such as "or individuals with similar experience" and "when the individual becomes available."

If a consulting firm balks at your insistence on specifying people by name, you should be dubious of their intentions. Don't let them talk you into deviating from your stance. They may make promises or give you verbal assurances, but those mean nothing if it isn't in writing. Walk away from a firm like this.

An even better protection is to include damages clauses in the contract stating that if they take key personnel off your project, they will be subject to a fine. Unfortunately, you're even less likely to get a contract with such a clause in it.

Guarantees?

Anyone can make a lot of promises at the start of a project. A consulting firm must be willing to put their promises down on paper with clearly defined criteria of what constitutes a completed and successful project. Otherwise, you could end up squabbling in court.

Assume that the worst happens. The consulting firms fails to accomplish what you both agreed to. You take them to court and win. Will you be able to collect the amount you sued them for? Do they have any assets that can be seized?

If they have no assets, a judgment against them is worthless. Before you sign a contract, have your legal staff and accountants examine their books to find out their current assets and liabilities.

Staff Disputes?

The staff provided by a consulting firm is composed of individuals. Some will be pleasant and others will be abrasive. Some will be hard-charging go-getters, and others will be more laid back. Some will be extremely competent, and others will be only mediocre.

During the course of the project, you may become dissatisfied with a few people on the consulting firm's staff. You may think they aren't pulling their weight or are causing too much trouble. Can you have them removed from the project?

Did you ask for this right in the contract? If not, you may be out of luck. You can request it anyway, but don't be surprised if such a request is treated lukewarmly.

If you were farsighted enough to require that this be in the contract, congratulations. Make sure that the contract specifies that the individual will leave the project immediately upon your request. You should also include a provision that gives you the right to approve any additions to the project staff. This will prevent them from slipping in some less experienced people when you are paying for people with a great deal of experience.

Don't think for a minute that this can't happen to you! A number of years ago, I was on a project where this occurred. The vendor sent over an individual who had never logged onto a computer terminal before! All his experience was on computers that used cards as the sole input medium. Unfortunately, the contract didn't give the client the right to reject staff members.

When?

You've developed your year 2000 project plan. You have upper management's support. The funding is finally available. The tools have been ordered, delivered, and installed. A contract has been signed with a consulting firm. You're all set to go, but nothing is happening. What's the holdup?

The consulting team isn't available yet. They're still on another project. Did you remember to specify when you planned to begin the project? Does the contract require them to field their staff at that time? If not, you'll probably have to sit on your hands for awhile.

How Much? (A Bonus Item)

How much is this assistance going to cost you? Does the contract specify whether you'll be paying a flat amount for the entire project? Can certain items cost you extra? Are you paying for expenses? If people are traveling to your site from out of town, expenses could be considerable: weekly airfare, hotels, rental cars, and meals.

What if you discover some applications or data that aren't specified in the original contract? How much will it cost to have the consulting firm handle those additional changes as well? Will you negotiate a flat rate for them or will that work be performed on a time-and-materials basis? If you go the time-and-materials route, what is the hourly rate? Can this rate increase as you get closer to the year 2000?

Don't be surprised if a consulting firm tries to get in the door with a surprisingly low bid. They may be hoping to low-ball the bid and make their profit from change orders. This tactic calls for them to make a big fuss over every simple deviation from the original specifications. The number of changes on a normal project is high. When a consulting firm uses this tactic, the number of change orders is abnormally high.

The best defense against this is to talk to former clients of this firm. If these tactics were used on a previous client, don't be surprised if they try it on you as well! You should be suspicious of any bids that are significantly lower than others.

Chapter 21

Ten Year 2000 Gotchas

● ●

In This Chapter

▶ Failing to get support from upper management

▶ Understanding the values 00 and 99

▶ Being unaware of license expirations

▶ Backing up in the twenty-first century

▶ Starting your year 2000 efforts now

▶ Avoiding copyright violations

▶ Paying as little in taxes as legally possible

▶ Handling PC problems

▶ Overlooking data conversions

▶ Locating troublesome desktop applications

● ●

Not Obtaining Support from the Highest Levels of Management

Any year 2000 project will have a significant affect on all parts of an organization. It's easy for a project manager to forget how wide the ripples will spread from this project. Some of the ways this project could affect an organization are listed here:

✔ It will cost a boatload of money. The costs increase depending on the number of computers and programs, the amount of data, and so on.

✔ Fixes or enhancements to production programs will likely be delayed for at least two reasons. One, programmers will be very busy correcting year 2000 problems. Two, MIS folks will push to freeze changes to production software so that they don't have to try to hit a moving target.

✔ Programmers and users might require training. Programmers will need to be trained on new tools, techniques, and possibly computer languages. If changes are made to the user interface, users will need to be trained on the new version of the system.

✔ If the in-house MIS staff isn't large enough or skilled enough, you'll probably hire or contract with consultants. This will affect a number of parts of the organization, such as security and office services.

✔ If this problem isn't adequately addressed, directors and officers may be exposed to litigation. They may be held personally responsible if a jury determines that they didn't act in a prudent manner to protect the organization's assets.

Not everyone will be delighted with these changes. It will make many people's jobs more confusing or difficult, especially when they learn that all this effort is the result of a decades-old programming problem.

To get everyone's assistance, you need support from the highest level of management. Only this support will enable you to get the funding necessary to make the project a success. This support will be necessary to convince (force?) users to accept a freeze of the current systems.

Alternative Meanings for the Values 00 and 99 in Your Data

The average lay person assumes that values of 00 or 99 in a date field mean just what they say. The first is the value zero and the second is the value ninety-nine. If you are just such a person, you're grossly underestimating the ingenuity of the wily programmer.

Over the years, a great number of data fields have been overloaded with more than one meaning. If the value is less than 99, the value represents a year. If the value is 99 or 0, it represents something else. When logic in the code reads a value of 99 in a particular date field, the program doesn't handle it as a "normal" date. Following are a few examples of the logic that might be performed:

✔ The current record is the end of the data file. The program will not attempt to read another record.

✔ A value of 99 indicates that the current record is the end of the data file. Relational databases have NULL values for this purpose, but traditional data files had no such value.

✔ A value of 99 or 00 can indicate that the file or tape should never be destroyed. When the year 2000 or 2001 arrives, the "never destroy" date will be less than the current date. This could result in the deletion of files (even ones created recently).

This logic has come to pass for a number of reasons. Here are a few:

- ✔ It was easy. The proper way to handle the programming change might have required adding a new field to the record. This would require modifying all programs that access the data file. It would require also the conversion of all existing data records to the new format. This represents an enormous amount of work. Is it really such a surprise that someone might have taken a shortcut by using a single field to serve two purposes?

- ✔ It was expedient. Virtually every computer operation has a backlog of changes to be made. Sometimes the backlog is measured in years. When making changes, programmers frequently have two choices. One, do it correctly and take a long time to complete the request. Two, take a shortcut and get it completed more quickly. If pressure is being applied to make modifications quickly and move onto the next request, which do you think will be chosen?

- ✔ The programmers didn't anticipate what would happen when the year 1999 or 2000 arrived. Even more likely, they didn't think that the program being modified would be in use in 10 or 20 or 30 years.

The prospect of values being interpreted differently than one would expect presents a significant problem. The dilemma is that year 2000 automated tools can't automatically correct the problem. A tool might recognize that a date field is involved, but it can't understand the logic in the source code. Most likely, the tool wouldn't even attempt to modify the code. This might create some of the following problems:

- ✔ A large number of files might be deleted on 1/1/1999, 1/1/2000, or 1/1/2001.

- ✔ An application might terminate when it encounters the first data record with a year value of 1999.

- ✔ Perfectly valid values of 99 and 00 might be ignored because the program takes them to be a nonvalue.

- ✔ An application might attempt to read beyond the last record in a data file. This would occur because it keeps reading until it finds a record with a 99 value. Your year 2000 project might have changed all 99 values to 1999.

The last situation is a prime example of why you can't rely on tools alone. Without a person looking at the code, you'll never be sure that unusual programming logic is being handled correctly.

Expiring Software Licenses

Software vendors provide a product in return for a fee. There's nothing wrong with this — it's called capitalism. Most commercial software products aren't purchased; they're licensed. Your organization probably doesn't own the copy of Acme Inventory System that it runs on its computers. You have a license to run a certain number of copies of the product under certain circumstances. You're not allowed to give it away, show it to competitors, or run it on additional machines.

Software vendors may have taken certain steps to protect their investment. This might be accomplished by including logic in the product to prevent the software from being used illegally. Code might check that the computer's ID is the same as the ID of the machine for which it has been licensed. Or it might request a code or a password when the system is installed or starts up. Perhaps it checks that the system date hasn't exceeded the licensing period.

Many software products include logic to warn you — or terminate the product — when your license expires. Will all these products function correctly on 1/1/2000?

Even if date related security checks weren't included on purpose, they might have been included accidentally. Perhaps a developer used a year value of 00 or 99 to signify something other than the date.

If the vendor is still in business, this problem will be an inconvenience. It could shut your system down until you are able to reach them. The best case is if they can provide you with a password or other method to override the problem. A less desirable solution requires them to modify the program and distribute the new version to you.

If the software vendor is not in business, this problem could be a catastrophe! You might be left to fend for yourself. The available options aren't particularly appealing. Some things you can consider:

- ✔ Modify the source code yourself. If your contract with the vendor required it to deliver the source code, you can examine and modify it yourself. After making changes, you will need to test it thoroughly! The reason for such an emphasis on testing is that your programmers aren't likely to be familiar with the code. Another reason for testing is that the source code you have may not match the executable version.

- ✔ Obtain the source code from an escrow account. Frequently, vendors aren't willing to release their source code, but they are willing to turn it over to an escrow account, in which a third party holds the source code. It is released to the customer when pre-agreed-to conditions are met. If the vendor is no longer in business, you should be able to obtain the source code. *Note:* Obtaining source code from an escrow account may be a way to deal with a vendor who isn't being cooperative on year 2000 issues.

✔ Reverse engineer the software. You can attempt to develop source code from object code if you can't obtain the original source code. You might attempt to do this yourself, or you might engage the services of a company that specializes in reverse engineering.

✔ Attempt to find the vendor. Perhaps the vendor isn't really out of business. Investigate whether the vendor has moved, is operating under a different name, or has been acquired by another corporation.

✔ Contact user groups to determine how other users are handling this situation. Perhaps they've solved the problem. If they aren't able to help, at least you'll all have each other's shoulder to cry on.

✔ Replace this application with another. The replacement could be something developed in-house or purchased from another vendor. Make sure that the replacement is year 2000 compatible!

You should contact all software vendors and obtain assurances that their products' licenses won't cause trouble when the calendar rolls over to 2000. Try to badger them into providing information that proves they have dealt with and solved this potential problem.

You may be tempted to test this potential problem yourself. You may think that all you need to do is set the system clock forward to January 1, 2000, and run the application. DON'T DO IT! The program may or may not work in the year 2000 — but you may encounter problems when the clock is reset to the present time. Some programs will detect this and assume that it's an attempt to get around the licensing requirements. This might shut down the program. If you still want to attempt this, contact the vendor first to make sure that this activity won't cause unexpected problems.

Not Backing Up Your Data

Backing up data on a regular basis is a thankless job. It can be time consuming and boring. Ninety-nine percent of the time, the data is copied to tape and never seen again by human eyes or a magnetic tape drive. However, one of the corollaries of Murphy's law states that the system will crash the one time the backup isn't performed or ABENDs. (ABEND is geek talk for when a program ends abnormally.) When this happens, no one will remember the hundreds of times the backups were performed correctly. They'll be thinking about the one time it didn't run correctly.

Data backups are frequently driven by dates. They are also commonly controlled by day of week (DOW) values. On the last day of the month, quarter, or year, every file is copied to tapes and retained for a long, long time. On Sundays, the backup might copy every file in the system. This particular tape might be reused after a number of weeks. On Monday through Saturday, the backup might copy only the files modified on that day. The daily backup tapes might be overwritten after a few weeks.

Does your backup logic use special code values in the date fields? Does a year of 99 in a field represent a special code instead of the year 1999? Does a value of 00 have a special meaning? It might mean that this file or tape should be retained indefinitely.

Does logic in the backup process store year values as two digits or four? If your answer is two digits, will year comparisons be performed correctly in the next few years? Suppose that a tape is made on 1/1/96 and should be retained for five years. The year when the tape can be reused is stored in two digits as 01. A comparison between this year value and the current year might return unexpected results. When the logic compares 01 to 98, it might determine that the tape can be reused immediately. This will result in the loss of valuable files. If this occurs many times, you might be completely without any backups.

Examine the logic in backup programs or scripts. Don't let this issue drop through the cracks. Otherwise, you might be unpleasantly surprised when the last thing you need is a surprise!

Starting Too Late

If you remember only two words after reading this book, I hope they are "start now." The longer you put off solving the problem, the bigger it becomes.

One reason this is true is because your system is collecting more data every day. You also might be adding more computer programs. Each day you delay results in more data or more programs that must be examined and possibly converted. Starting now means that you'll need to convert fewer programs and data.

I'm no oracle, but I'll make a bold prediction. Your year 2000 effort will take longer than you anticipate. I'm willing to step out on this shaky limb for many reasons:

- You'll find programs that were overlooked when the original project estimate was made. Addressing them will take additional time that isn't built into the schedule.

✔ Personnel assigned to this project will be sidetracked to correct operational problems. This will happen because these problems must be corrected for the company to continue to operate. All you can hope to do is to keep these interruptions to a minimum.

✔ Attrition will affect your year 2000 team. Some of your team members, maybe the best ones, will be lured away by another organization. It will take time and money to locate, hire, and train new personnel.

✔ It will flat out take longer than expected to accomplish some of your tasks. Computer projects are known for taking longer than estimated and this project won't be any different.

✔ Data originally overlooked will be "discovered" and will need to be converted. This data might come into your organization from an outside source.

One last reason to start early is that many of your tasks won't be entirely in your control. If you are forced to rely on another party, you won't be able to control or predict how long it will take them to fulfill their promises. A few examples should help to illuminate this point:

✔ It will take you longer than expected to convince management that this is a real problem. While they are mulling it over, you won't be able to gear up to attack the problem.

✔ You will almost certainly be contacting software vendors to determine whether or not their products are year 2000 compatible. If they aren't compatible, you'll want to know when an updated version will be available. I'm sorry to be the one who breaks the news to you, but your correspondence won't be at the top of their to-do list. If they answer you at all, it will probably be with a form letter. You'll need to contact them many times before you get a satisfactory response.

✔ If source code is lost, you can contact an organization that recovers source code from executables or object modules. You won't be the only ones looking for this assistance. It could take the vendor longer than anticipated to finish the task.

✔ Consultants and consulting organizations will be swamped. They won't be able to respond to your requests as quickly as you hoped.

✔ Ordering additional hardware for testing or replacement may take longer than expected.

Violating Copyrights

Most shops have licensed applications from third-party vendors. If you read the license carefully, you'll discover that you don't own the software. You have the right to use it under certain conditions. You most definitely do not have the right to disassemble or modify this product. Doing so would violate their copyright on the software.

Your vendor may not be planning on addressing the year 2000 problem. More specifically, the vendor might not be planning on updating the version of the program you are running. If you are using version 1.1, for example, and the current version is 4.1, there is very little (that is, zero, nil, no way Jose) chance that the vendor will correct your version.

You have two choices. First, you can upgrade to the latest and greatest version. Although this might solve the problem, any upgrade entails time, effort, expense, and risk.

The second solution is to convince the vendor to allow you to modify the program. This also takes time and effort and has its risks and complications. Perhaps the vendor doesn't have the source code for outdated versions of the product. Or, if you can obtain the source code, it might be in a computer language that is unfamiliar to your staff.

Paying Too Much in Taxes

Costs to correct your year 2000 problems are likely to be significant. For some organizations, these costs will be tens of millions of dollars. Any prudent management team will try to minimize these costs in any possible (legal) way.

The tax implications of costs associated with your year 2000 project need to be investigated. If your year 2000 related costs can be written off, the after-tax profit can be increased. Not addressing this topic from the very beginning might cost your organization a lot of money.

Overlooking PC Problems

The majority of press coverage on the year 2000 problem centers on mainframe computers. Most of the coverage deals with the problem of storing year values as two digits instead of four digits. Many mainframe computers and a huge number of programs must be examined and corrected. This is certainly going to be a big problem, but it's not the only problem.

Just because most of the attention is on mainframes and COBOL programs, don't overlook potential problems with your PCs and the software running on them. They will also be affected even if they don't get as much coverage. Some potential problems:

- ✔ The BIOS in computers will have problems rolling over to the year 2000.

- ✔ Software your organization has written won't properly handle the transition between 12/31/1999 and 1/1/2000.

- ✔ Software your organization has written won't recognize that the year 2000 is a leap year.

- ✔ Software you've purchased from a third party won't handle either the 1999/2000 transition or the leap year in 2000.

Each individual PC might not be difficult to modify, but the problem presented by PCs is their sheer number. Many large organizations have tens of thousands of PCs. Many times these PCs are distributed in locations around the world. If each PC takes 30 or 60 minutes to test and correct, how much time will it take to correct tens of thousands of them? If you don't begin your efforts early enough, you won't be able to complete testing in time.

Another aspect of PCs that is frequently overlooked is software developed outside the control of MIS, such as small databases, spreadsheets, macros, and DOS batch files. If these were developed by individual users, there's no telling whether they comply with any standards. There's probably no inventory or estimate of how many of these programs exist. Users aren't likely to consider the year 2000 impact on these programs until they start failing. By that time, MIS will have developed a project plan and allocated staff to it. It will be difficult to get MIS to reallocate its staff without adversely affecting the project's schedule.

Misjudging Data Conversion Requirements

Organizations tend to accumulate large amounts of data, and the rate at which they collect it seems to be accelerating. Several trends tend to drive this increase. For example:

- ✔ It's becoming easier than ever to collect large amounts of data. Data is now entered into many systems electronically. Point of sale (POS) computers document who bought what, when, and at what store. Data files are exchanged electronically between organizations.

✔ It's cheaper to store data now. The prices of disk drives are sinking. The cost of retaining data indefinitely is affordable. Some very large databases are in the 10 terabyte range. (A terabyte is 1,000,000,000,000 bytes.)

✔ Data warehouses are being built that allow extremely large databases to be searched, sorted, diced, and sliced. Because the data can be useful, it has become economically realistic to acquire and retain it.

This section explains why and how the size of data has increased. Year 2000 projects will need to examine, understand, and perhaps convert this data. Don't underestimate the time, effort, or unanticipated difficulties involved in converting your data. Seriously misjudging this part of your year 2000 project could have a potentially fatal effect on your schedule.

Neglecting Desktop Applications

Keeping track of the software on mainframes and servers is a difficult job. It takes time and persistence to maintain an accurate, thorough list of all the applications an organization is running. Even when someone is assigned to maintain this information on a full-time basis, it's easy to get behind. This sort of task is easy to put on the bottom of a to-do list.

If it's difficult for MIS to track software, how much more difficult will it be to track applications running on individual desktop PCs? It will be very difficult if not impossible.

It's easy to overlook an application running on a desktop PC. Perhaps it's one that MIS never heard of. Perhaps an employee developed it in a spreadsheet or a single-user database system. It's been used faithfully every since, but the employee has long since moved on. Users specify two-digit year fields when entering data, so you can't be certain what four-digit year value is stored internally.

Will this particular application work in the next century? Probably not. Will you find out about this application before it blows up in the year 2000? Probably not. Is there any documentation available on it? Probably not. Is the source code available, and will it compile under the most recent version of this tool? Probably not. The "probably not's" win four to nothing.

Another potential problem is PC database packages that have been acquired over the years. You're undoubtedly familiar with the ones I'm talking about. They are used for keeping track of inventory, invoices, client lists, and time card data. In shops, these are the lifeblood of the company. What were they originally written in? Will they work after 1/1/2000? Does the vendor still support them? Can you find the vendor?

This situation is more likely to affect smaller organizations than big ones because larger organizations are more likely to have an MIS group. The MIS group has likely instituted some formal procedures for acquiring software. If the procedures are followed, the MIS group will at least have been informed of the purchase. Smaller organizations, without such a group, probably have few or no such procedures. Software purchases may not have been listed or catalogued.

Start investigating these potential disasters now. The first step is to thoroughly inventory the contents of the hard drive of every PC. You should also inventory the drives on all file servers. After you have a list of the programs, you should investigate where they came from. If they were developed internally, find out who wrote them. Otherwise, find out where they were purchased.

I think a strong correlation exists between the size of the software vendor and the likelihood that they are still in business. The smaller the company, the less likely that it is still in business. This knowledge (or prejudice) leads me to think that you should talk to your smaller vendors now. If they have indeed gone out of business, the sooner you learn about it, the better.

Chapter 22

Ten Year 2000 User Groups

*T*he year 2000 problem can be intimidating. No change of this nature and extent has ever occurred before. This project has a deadline that you can't delay or avoid. Your project is probably underfunded and was started too late. The litigation potential of this situation dwarfs anything in our legal system's history. If your efforts fail, it could cause your organization to go out of business. No pressure whatsoever on this project, is there?

Fortunately, you don't have to face it alone. Many others are facing the same problems as you are. By helping each other out, we might just make it through this predicament. As Benjamin Franklin said at the signing of the Declaration of Independence, "Yes, we must, indeed, all hang together, or, most assuredly, we shall all hang separately."

User groups are formed to enable members to help one another. By sharing their experiences, they can assist others who might not be so far along the year 2000 path. If you run into a problem, you can call up someone you met at last month's meeting and see whether he or she encountered a similar situation. Almost invariably, people will be happy to relate how they solved their problem.

What do user groups typically do? The Y2K meetings I have attended, heard about, and read minutes from have common elements, such as the following:

- ✔ These groups typically have a speaker. Sometimes the speaker is someone who has firsthand experience dealing with the year 2000 problem.

- ✔ These groups frequently invite representatives from other disciplines (attorneys, accountants, and experts in the field) to speak.

✔ Many user groups reserve a time period for members to actively participate in a question-and-answer session or a panel. Members might ask the group in general if anyone has run into a problem like one they are encountering.

✔ The membership list of a year 2000 group is usually fairly accessible. Most groups distribute their membership list freely. This enables members to easily contact other group members who might be working in the same environment. This type of networking is exactly what the group is intended to generate.

Frequently, user groups invite a vendor representative as a speaker. The vendor's presentations can provide new insights. Be aware, though, that vendors are looking at the problem from a slightly different angle than you are. That is, you are trying to solve a problem, and they are trying to make a sale. Listen to what they say, but remember where they're coming from. Most of all, never forget these magic words: There is no silver bullet for the year 2000 problem!

A large number of year 2000 user groups exist in the United States and around the world. More are springing up all the time. Choosing which ones to list here wasn't easy; I decided to select a variety of offerings and locations.

If a user group has a Web site, I include its address and a screen shot. It's possible, though, that a Web site will no longer exist or will have changed locations by the time you read this book. If the Web address is no longer current, try locating it using the suggestions at the end of this chapter.

Atlanta, Georgia

The Web page for the Atlanta area's user group is

```
www.se.commerce.net/atlyear2000/
```

You can e-mail this group from its Web site, which is shown in Figure 22-1.

Kansas City, Missouri

The address of the Kansas City Y2k Group is

```
www.triplei.com/3mc/kcy2k.htm
```

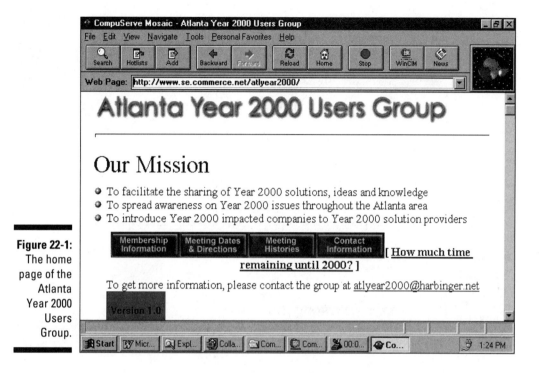

Figure 22-1:
The home
page of the
Atlanta
Year 2000
Users
Group.

The contact name for this group is Andrew Ellner. His phone number is 913-262-6500, extension 2047, and his e-mail address is aellner@triplei.com. A screen shot of this Web page is shown in Figure 22-2.

San Francisco, California

The contact person for the San Francisco Bay Area Yr2000 User Group is Anthony M. Peeters. The telephone number provided for him is 415-673-1075. The fax number that you can use to contact this group is 415-673-7635. The e-mail address for this group is info@sf2000.com. Their Web site is at

```
www.sf2000.com
```

Figure 22-3 shows a copy of this Web page.

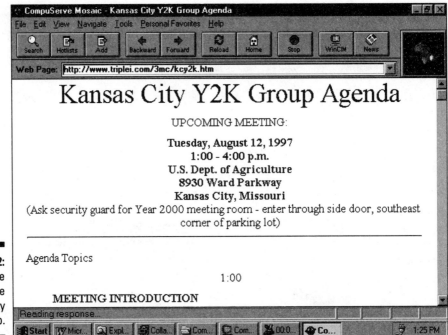

Figure 22-2:
Home page
of the
Kansas City
Y2K Group.

Figure 22-3:
Web page
of the San
Francisco
Bay Area
Yr2000 User
Group.

Delaware Valley

If you live in the Delaware Valley area, you should be looking for the Delaware Valley Year 2000 Special Interest Group. The Web page is shown in Figure 22-4, and the Web address is

```
www.libertynet.org/~dpmaphil/dvy2ksig/index.html.
```

Washington, D.C.

With the convergence of government, military, education, and business in the Washington, D.C. area, it's not surprising that the area has a Year 2000 user group. This site is sponsored by the Fannie Mae Corporation as a service to both government and private sector groups in the area.

The Washington D.C. Year 2000 Group has the home page shown in Figure 22-5. The Web site is at

```
www.bfwa.com/bwebster/y2k
```

For more information on this Web site, contact Bruce F. Webster at bruce_webster@fanniemae.com or bwebster@btwa.com.

Portland, Oregon

The scenic Pacific Northwest is home to the Portland Year 2000 Ready User Group. This group meets on the first Wednesday afternoon of the month from 3:30 to 5:30. The meeting place is at Consolidated Freightways, Inc., at 1717 NW 21st in Portland. For comments or questions or to be put on the mailing list, contact Patrick Canniff at canniff.patrick@cnf.com.

Figure 22-6 shows a shot of the home page. The Web address is

```
http://pdxweb.ci.portland.or.us/y2k/
```

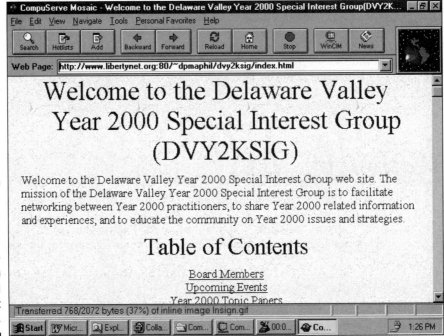

Figure 22-4:
The home
page of the
Delaware
Valley Year
2000
Special
Interest
Group.

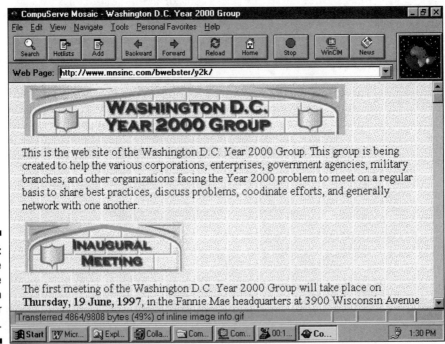

Figure 22-5:
The home
page of the
Washington
D.C. Year
2000 Group.

Figure 22-6:
Home page
of the
Portland
Year 2000
Ready User
Group.

Utah

In Utah, people involved in a year 2000 effort can participate in the Utah Year 2000 Users Group. This group meets on the second Thursday of each month. A contact address for this organization is HortonJL@chq.byu.edu.

The Web address is

www.governor.state.ut.us/sitc/usergroup/usergroup.htm

Figure 22-7 shows a shot of the home page.

Tampa Bay, Florida

If you're located in Tampa Bay, Florida, you can join the Tampa Bay Area Year 2000 User Group. This group meets the first Tuesday of each month. For more information about this group, contact Richard Saulsgiver at 813-935-7332, extension 115. The e-mail address is Data_Solutions_2000@ bigfoot.com.

The Web site address for the Tampa Bay Area Year 2000 User Group is

```
www.galleria.net/date2000/
```

Figure 22-8 shows a screen shot of this organization's home page.

Dallas/Ft. Worth, Texas

If you live in the Dallas/Fort Worth area and you have the year 2000 on your mind, you can join the Dallas Year 2000 Prep group. This group is sponsored by the Dallas/Fort Worth Data Administration Management Association. For more information, contact Bill Wachel at 214-333-6221. His e-mail address is wmwachel@onramp.net.

The Web address is

```
www.dfwdama.org/y2ka.htm
```

Figure 22-9 shows a shot of this group's home page.

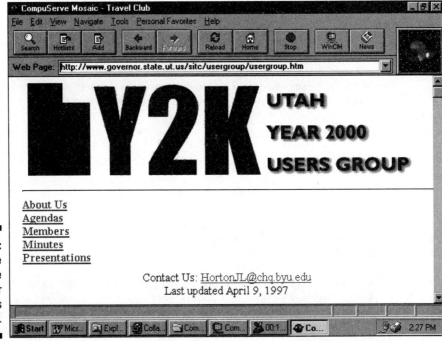

Figure 22-7:
The home page of the Utah Year 2000 Users Group.

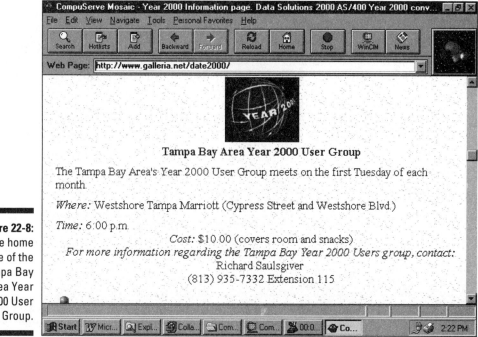

Figure 22-8:
The home page of the Tampa Bay Area Year 2000 User Group.

Figure 22-9:
The home page of the Dallas Year 2000 Prep group.

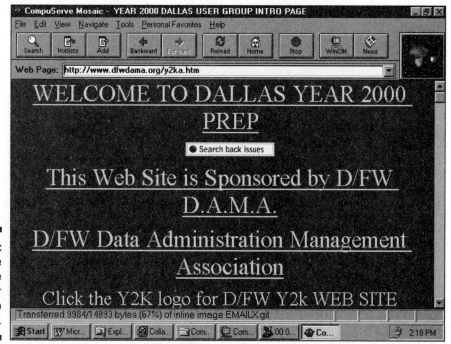

Nebraska

Last but not least is the Nebraska Y2K User Group. This group meets on the second Thursday afternoon of each month from 4:30 to 6:00. The meeting location rotates between several corporate sites in Omaha, Nebraska.

The Web address of this organization is www.omahafreenet.org/metro/computers.html. When you're on this page, click the label titled "Nebraska Year 2000 User Group."

Finding a User Group

If I haven't listed a user group in your area, how can you find one? Following are some of the ways to locate a user group in your locale:

- ✔ Ask your coworkers. They might know or they might know somebody who knows.

- ✔ Look in the paper. The business section of local newspapers frequently contains announcements. A listing of year 2000 user groups may well be listed here.

- ✔ Contact a local computer professional society, such as IEEE or ACM. User groups dedicated to particular software products might also be able to help you.

- ✔ Get online! Many of the year 2000 online resources in this book provide a listing of year 2000 user groups. One that certainly does is www.year2000.com.

- ✔ If none of the previous methods works, fire up your favorite Internet search engine and search for the phrases "year 2000" and "user group." Doing this showed me a few groups that the year 2000 oriented Web sites didn't include.

If there isn't a year 2000 user group in your area, consider starting one. Although starting a user group is more work than simply attending the meetings, it will be a rewarding experience. As your junior high gym teacher probably said, "It builds character."

Chapter 23
Ten Things to Do to Get Ready

● ●

In This Chapter

▶ Publicizing the year 2000 problem

▶ Writing only year 2000 compliant code

▶ Requiring new software to be year 2000 compliant

▶ Joining a year 2000 user group

▶ Modifying manuals and materials

▶ Establishing a priority among programs

▶ Replacing forms

▶ Communicating with suppliers

▶ Canceling vacations during the critical period

▶ Controlling software changes

● ●

*H*ave you ever gone on vacation and *not* forgotten something? Maybe it was sunscreen, film, bug spray, extra diapers, traveler's checks, or a pacifier. It seems like something always gets left behind.

Your year 2000 project will be the same. The list of steps you must take is long. Invariably, something won't make it onto the project schedule. These ten items are tasks that you might forget along the journey.

Increase Awareness of This Problem

The year 2000 problem isn't going to affect just the MIS group. It will affect everyone. Whether they know it or not, their professional lives are on a collision course with destiny. Every person in your organization needs to know about this problem so that they will

- ✔ Understand when they are asked (or forced) to modify their habits, hours, and so on.

- ✔ Be aware of what's going on if they are asked to participate in the testing phase.

- ✔ Think about and look for unforeseen year 2000 problems.

- ✔ Understand why their change requests aren't being handled immediately.

- ✔ Understand why the hordes of contractors have been hired and seem to be taking over the building.

I hope I've convinced you that the year 2000 situation needs to be widely publicized. But how can you accomplish this? Here are a few ways to increase awareness:

- ✔ Does your organization have a newsletter? If so, include year 2000 articles on a regular basis.

- ✔ Distribute copies of this book! In fact, buy everyone in your organization their own copy. I personally feel that this would be beneficial to all concerned, particularly me.

- ✔ Use the corporate e-mail system. On a regular basis, e-mail little tidbits of year 2000 information to the staff. Don't overuse this particular delivery method, however, or you'll annoy people.

- ✔ Put on brown-bag lunch seminars. Everyone brings their own lunch, or you spring for pizza. Your project manager or another suitable speaker discusses the year 2000 problem in general and how the project is going.

- ✔ Display year 2000 posters around the building. They don't have to be everywhere. Just use a few to keep the problem in people's minds.

- ✔ Copy articles from magazines and newspapers and distribute them. For added credibility, use magazines from diverse disciplines. Lawyers would receive articles from publications from their field, accountants would get articles from publications in their field, and so on.

- ✔ Establish a contest for identifying potential year 2000 problems. Each bona fide problem discovered earns a prize. The prizes could be a gift certificate, lunch, special parking space for a month, or company shirt. The grand prize would be a week's vacation on January 1, 2000!

- ✔ Distribute year 2000 screensavers to everyone (whether they want one or not). That way, they can be reminded on a daily basis that this problem is on its way.

Stop Writing Code That Isn't Year 2000 Compliant

It seems obvious that any new code or modifications to existing code should be year 2000 compliant. One hand is spending money and effort to correct a problem, so why would the other hand be enlarging the problem? Although this may seem obvious, it might not be happening.

The development group and maintenance groups may not be focusing on this problem. They may be carrying on the way they always have, including writing code that won't work correctly when 1/1/2000 arrives.

How can this situation be corrected? You simply need to communicate the situation to everyone who develops or modifies software. Schedule a training session for all developers and maintenance programmers. Explain the problem and describe the techniques being used to handle it. Be sure that what you're teaching them is consistent with the overall techniques being used to deal with this problem.

Year 2000 Compliant Clauses

Some third-party programs will have year 2000 problems. You already know that this problem exists in some of the software on the marketplace. Why would you purchase software that adds to your problem list? Any software you acquire should be guaranteed to be year 2000 compliant.

One way to achieve this objective is to add year 2000 compliant clauses in all your software contracts. Get your legal department to write up an explicit definition of what you consider "year 2000 compliant software."

For assistance on this, you can check some year 2000 Web sites. One potential source is the state of Washington's conversion guide, which is titled "Year 2000 Conversion Process Guide." This paper contains a sample clause that requires software products to be year 2000 compliant. The home page for the Washington State Department of Information Services is

```
www.wa.gov/dis/2000/y2000.htm/
```

Join a Local Year 2000 User Group

Although you may sometimes feel isolated on this project, you aren't alone. Many other programmers and project managers are struggling through the same process. User groups are being established so that each of us can gain from one another's experiences.

The title of this section could have been "Misery Loves Company." Instead, I kept to the high road. I chose to be more optimistic than that.

If no one is willing to share in a user group, everyone will end up reinventing the wheel. We need to develop an attitude that we're all in this together. Helping someone else doesn't cost you anything. Be willing to share with other organizations any tricks or tools you have found.

Update Manuals and Training Materials

It's almost certain that your year 2000 corrections will be visible to the users. Some of the changes they might see include the following:

- ✔ Date fields on input screens might expand from two digits to four. This might require users to enter the two century digits for the first time.

- ✔ Programs might be coded to handle century values on the screen in a certain way (that is, if century values are always assumed to be 19). These assumptions might be displayed on the screen or they might show up only on reports.

- ✔ Reports might have their date fields expanded to include century values.

- ✔ Backup procedures might be changed.

No matter what the exact changes are, it is imperative that you inform users *in advance*. If they aren't told about these changes before they occur, they will resist them. As a rule, people hate to have things crammed down their throats. I sure hate it. Don't you?

You can short-circuit this problem by informing users about it in advance. Update manuals and training materials to reflect any modifications in the user interface. Establish training sessions if the changes are significant enough.

Manual changes and training aren't applicable only for users. Also update any documentation for developers, database administrators, systems analysts, and maintenance programmers. After the project is over, the project team will begin to forget why they did certain things. Documenting these decisions and changes right away will result in fewer problems due to fuzzy memories.

Prioritize Your Systems

An obvious statement about the year 2000 situation is that the later you start, the less time you'll have to correct it. What if you didn't start in time to correct everything? What if your organization has so many programs and so much data that you won't be able to complete it all in time?

The answer to these questions is to prioritize the programs that must be modified. If there isn't time to convert all of them, you'll need to focus on the truly crucial ones. Handle less-critical programs later.

Right about now, you might be claiming that all your systems are critical. Stop for a second and examine your list of programs. Aren't some a little more critical than others? Can't some be delayed?

After this moment of introspection, you may sincerely conclude that many or most of your systems are critical and you can't function without them. If this is truly the case, you must add resources. This is the only way to make all critical programs compliant by the required date. You say this isn't possible? You say that management won't support spending more money? Then I guess your programs weren't all that important after all, were they?

Use Outdated Consumables

Does your organization use preprinted forms? How many different ones do you have? Probably more than you can remember offhand. There are job application forms, insurance forms, invoices, accounts payable forms, travel reimbursement forms, and more. Your organization probably uses dozens of different preprinted forms.

How many of these preprinted forms have a date field with 19 already filled in for the year? You need to order new ones with 20 as the leading characters. This might not make or break your organization, but it is one thing you can address easily enough.

Confer with Your Suppliers

If your system is year 2000 compliant in time, congratulations. Unfortunately, your success may be jeopardized if your suppliers are not compliant as well. How well will your fully compliant system function if all the dates passed to it are 00 instead of 2000? How well will your business function if your suppliers can't take your orders? Suppose that your customers can't pay you because their systems don't work. How long will it be until cash flow becomes a problem?

A chain is only as strong as its weakest link. Your organization is but a single link in a very long chain. Suppliers are on one side of you, and customers are on the other. Don't forget to include banks, credit unions, insurance companies, and government entities in this chain. If any of them aren't compliant in time, the ripple effects will reach all of you.

Contact all the entities that your organization does business with and ask them when their systems will be year 2000 compliant. Obtain details on how far they are and what type of solution they are implementing. If your solution differs from theirs, all of you will likely need to convert the data that flows between you.

You need to gain assurances that they are working on the problem because it will affect your organizations. If they supply you with raw materials or subassemblies, you depend on them to fulfill your orders. If their failure causes you to break a contract, you might not be able to blame them, especially if they have little or no assets. Your customer might try to show that you were negligent because you didn't research this avenue.

You should also contact the manufacturers or suppliers of equipment that includes embedded controllers. If the embedded chips need to be replaced or reprogrammed, you will need to contact these organizations as soon as possible.

Cancel All MIS Vacations

Cancel all MIS vacations? Is this a joke? No, it isn't a joke, and it isn't funny. Even after your best efforts, you will probably have last-minute problems. If problems do occur, you will want to deal with them immediately. Your MIS staff must be available to handle these problems. Canceling vacations for MIS personnel during late December of 1999 and early January of 2000 will help assure that the staff will be available.

Establish a policy regarding vacation time during this period as early as possible. Today isn't too early. After it is on paper, it will be easier to enforce. Otherwise, you'll end up dealing with staff members' requests over and over.

Establish Software Configuration Management

Software configuration management (SCM) is the process of controlling modifications made to software libraries. The simplest version of software configuration management is referred to as check in/check out.

This process allows only one programmer to work on a module at a time. If I have checked out module XYZ, you can't check it out until I'm finished with it. You may be allowed to look at it, but you can't alter it. When I'm finished with XYZ, I check it back in. It's now available for you (or whoever gets there first) to check out. This level of control has the following advantages:

- ✔ Establishes a definitive version of every module in the library. Each time you check out a module, you are assured that you have the latest and greatest version of the source code.

- ✔ Cuts down on the number of copies (usually different copies) of a single module that are floating around. This reduces the amount of disk space dedicated to storing source code.

- ✔ Prevents two programmers from working on the same module at the same time. If this is allowed, someone's changes will be lost.

More-advanced versions of software configuration management have additional features. One common feature is the capability to roll back changes. Suppose that a module is working perfectly. Programmers Bob, Ted, Carol, and Alice make changes to the program, in that order. Then a user notices an error in the program. Whose changes made the error?

Sophisticated SCM packages enable you to remove the changes one set at a time. You would first remove Alice's changes and test the program. If the error still exists, it wasn't due to Alice's modifications. Next you would back out Carol's changes. The bug still exists, so it wasn't her. Ted's alterations are rolled back next. Aha, the error is no longer there. Ted's changes are the culprit. Ted needs to correct his programming errors and save them. If testing shows the program is now correct, Carol's and Alice's changes are reinstalled. This feature can be very handy when an error isn't immediately noticed.

The more changes you make to your systems, the more valuable a software configuration management system will be. We've already established that year 2000 changes can be extensive. An SCM package will be invaluable during this project.

If you don't already have software configuration management in place, the sooner you install it the better because

- ✔ It will take you time to research SCM packages. Acquiring and installing the package will take even more time. The sooner you start, the sooner it will be finished.

- ✔ An administrator will need to be chosen and trained on this package. This will take time.

- ✔ Programmers will need to be trained to use these packages. Their training won't need to be as extensive as the training administrators receive, but it will still take some time.

- ✔ It would be best if the package is completely installed and training is completed before your year 2000 project kicks off. You don't want to add one more variable in the middle of the project because it would tend to unnecessarily confuse team members.

Ten reasons why you don't need to worry about the year 2000 problem

#1 My company has already filed for bankruptcy.

#2 Someone else always comes up with a solution at the last minute.

#3 All the programmers on my staff who aren't on vacation during the week of January 1, 2000, will be on call.

#4 The newspaper at the checkout stand in the grocery store says that the world will end before 2000.

#5 My company has a history of killing the messenger who bears bad news.

#6 I think someone else is working on it.

#7 I'm a big-picture type. Problems like this are for other people to worry about.

#8 January 1 falls on a Saturday and Monday's a holiday — I'll have lots of time over the weekend.

#9 My company doesn't have any programmers — the competition hired them away from us last week.

#10 My friend on the Psychic Friends Hotline told me not to worry about it.

In case you haven't found a good enough reason, here are ten more.

#1 I've been working here only a little while. I'll blame any problems on my predecessor.

#2 Everyone knows this is a scam perpetuated by consultants to jack up their rates.

#3 A guy on the news said this problem isn't as bad as people are making it out to be.

#4 Most of the source code seems to be misplaced.

#5 If I really have to deal with it, I'll outsource it overseas.

#6 What year 2000 problem?

#7 All of my company's maintenance is outsourced. Let them take care of it.

#8 My company downsized all my coworkers, and I'm working 18-hour days already. I don't care whether it goes out of business.

#9 I was planning to phase out computers before then anyway.

#10 All of my systems are new, so they couldn't possibly be affected by the year 2000 crisis.

Glossary

· ·

ABEND: Stands for *abnormal end*. Indication that a program or job has terminated abnormally.

acceptance test: A set of test runs by the customer or client before accepting a system.

ASCII: American Standard Code for Information Interchange. A code for translating numeric values into characters.

assembler language: A second-generation computer language. Assembler is used to program computers at a very low level.

BASIC: Beginner's All-Purpose Symbolic Instruction Code. A computer language developed for use by nonprogrammers. BASIC is the language used by Visual Basic.

BIOS: Basic input/output system. Used by the computer to interface with hardware devices.

bridge: A temporary (or maybe not so temporary) program that translates data between formats.

byte: Eight binary digits of computer storage. A byte can be used to store a single character or a small integer value.

C: A computer language created by Brian W. Kernighan and Dennis M. Ritchie at Bell Labs.

C++: An object-oriented computer language.

centenarian: A person who has lived for 100 or more years.

century window: A 100-year interval, usually crossing a century boundary.

CICS: Customer Information and Control System. A transaction-processing system developed for mainframe computers.

client: A computer that requests servicing or information from a server computer.

client/server: A method of dividing computer applications into three components: a client, a server, and a network connecting them together.

CMOS: Complementary Metal-Oxide Semiconductor. A type of computer chip that retains its contents even when the power is turned off. CMOS chips are frequently used to hold the BIOS instructions.

COBOL: Common Business Oriented Language. A computer language frequently used for business applications.

compiler: A program that translates computer source code into a language the computer can understand.

configuration management (CM): Procedures put into place that protect against unplanned or unauthorized changes to computer software.

copybooks: Documentation that describes fields in data files.

coverage analyzer: A tool that documents which statements in a program have been executed during a testing session.

CPU: Central processing unit. The hardware chip that controls processing in a computer.

critical event horizon: A time by which computer programs must be corrected to prevent errors from occurring.

CSP: A computer language used on mainframe computers.

cutover: The act of moving from the current system to a new system.

DAT: Digital audiotape. A storage medium used to back up data.

data aging: The practice of modifying date values in data to generate test data.

data conversion: Converting data from one format to another. Frequently used during testing operations.

data dictionary: A database that documents all database files, tables, and fields (and explanations of them) used by an organization.

data source: A source of data (frequently from an external source) used as input to a computer application.

date aging: The practice of modifying date values in data to generate test data.

date compression: A method of dealing with the year 2000 problem by compressing four-year digits into the spaced previously occupied by two digits.

date encoding: Another term for date compression.

date expansion: A method of dealing with the year 2000 problem by expanding two-digit year values into four digits.

date simulator: A utility used to pass a simulated date and time value to applications that are being tested.

DB2: DataBase 2. A relational database management system for mainframe computers available from IBM.

debugger: A test tool used to observe and control source code statements executing in an application program.

direct access storage device (DASD): A fancy term for a computer hard drive.

DOS: Disk operating system. An operating system frequently used by personal computers (PCs).

EDI: Electronic data interchange. The exchange of data by electronic means. A significant advantage of EDI is that you avoid having to reenter data into a second computer system.

EEPROM: Electrically erasable programmable read-only memory. A type of ROM (read-only memory) chip that can be erased and written to while still on a circuit board.

embedded controller: A microchip used to control a device or process.

encapsulation: A method of dealing with the year 2000 problem. It takes advantage of the fact that the Gregorian calendar repeats itself every 28 years.

European monetary unit (EMU): A new currency that will become the currency of all members of the European Common Market.

event horizon: The date on which a hardware or software component first fails to process dates properly. Each application can have a unique critical event horizon.

FAQs: Frequently asked questions.

fixed window: A method of dealing with the year 2000 problem that allows applications to access any year in a fixed 100-year window.

FORTRAN: Formula translation. A computer language frequently used for scientific and engineering applications.

function: A routine that a program calls to execute a commonly performed set of instructions.

GPS: Global Positioning System. A system that allows precise geographic positioning to be calculated.

Gregorian calendar: Calendar system put into place by Pope Gregory XIII in 1582. It corrected errors that the Julian calendar system had allowed to accumulate.

GUI: Graphical user interface. A user interface that provides objects (menus, buttons, list boxes, sliders, multiple windows, and so on) that users interact with.

hexadecimal: A numbering system that uses base 16. Its digits are 0–9, A, B, C, D, E, and F.

HRIS: Human resource information system. An application used by many personnel departments to maintain information on employees.

I/O: Input/output. That part of a computer or computer program concerned with reading in data or exporting data.

IMS: Information Management System. A nonrelational database system from IBM.

Initial program load (IPL): The reboot process for a mainframe computer.

integration test: Testing performed to ensure that programs within a system work together properly.

ISO: International Standards Organization.

JCL: Job control language. Programming statements used by mainframes to control how and when a job (batch program) runs.

Julian calendar: Calendar system put into place by Julius Caesar in 45 b.c.

Julian date: A dating system that contains the number of days that have passed since a set date. The reference date is frequently January 1, 4713, b.c., but it can be another date.

K: Kilobyte. A measurement of computer memory or storage. 1K equals 1024 bytes.

LAN: Local area network. A network of computers in a relatively small area, such as a building or a floor of a building.

library: A repository of modules that can be called by many programs.

LOC: Lines of code. Measurement of the size of a program or group of programs by counting the number of executable lines of code.

lunar year: A division of time equivalent to 12 lunar months.

MB: Megabyte. A measurement of computer memory or storage. 1MB equals 1,048,576 bytes.

millennium: A period of 1,000 years.

MIS: Management information systems. One term for the people in charge of an organization's computers.

MVS: Multiple virtual storage. An operating system for very large IBM mainframe computers.

Not Invented Here (NIH): The tendency to discount the value of solutions discovered elsewhere in favor of locally developed solutions.

packet: A group of data sent at one time across a computer network.

PL/1: Programming language/1. A programming language developed by IBM.

platform: The hardware that a computer program runs on.

quality assurance (QA) group: The group charged with testing and ensuring the quality and accuracy of software in many organizations.

RAM: Random-access memory. Computer memory that can be read from or written to.

regression test: Testing performed to ensure that errors aren't inadvertently introduced when changes are made to a system's software.

relational database management system (RDBMS): A database package that organizes information into tables.

RPG: A computer language used to generate reports.

RTC: Real-time clock. A chip in a PC that uses a battery to maintain the current time whether or not the computer is turned on.

SCADA: Supervisory control and data acquisition. Computer systems used to monitor and control pipelines, utility networks, railroads, and so on from a single control center computer.

server: A computer that fulfills the requests of other computers on a network. Examples of servers are database servers, file servers, and fax servers.

silver bullet: A methodology or product that promises to solve all your problems.

sliding window: A method of dealing with the year 2000 problem that allows applications to access any year in a sliding 100-year window.

software inventory: A list of all programs, modules, data, and so on that are used by an organization's computer systems.

solar year: The time it takes the earth to travel around the sun once. This is approximately 365 days, 5 hours, 48 minutes, and 46 seconds.

source code management (SCM): A product that allows MIS staff to maintain control over source code used at their organization.

SQL: Structured Query Language. A computer language frequently used to access relational databases.

standardization: The enforcement of standard date formats, names, and routines.

subroutine: A routine that a program calls to execute a commonly performed set of instructions.

surge protector: A device that protects equipment from variations in AC power.

system: A combination of computer hardware and software that fulfills a user's computing needs. A system can be as simple as a desktop PC or as complex as a supercomputer and its software.

system integrators: An organization that builds computer systems by assembling them from preexisting hardware and software components.

system test: Testing to verify that the entire computer system functions correctly.

T1 line: A high-speed communications line that can transmit 1.544 Mbps.

T3 line: A high-speed communications line that can transmit 44.736 Mbps.

tool: A program or a utility that is used to develop or test a computer program.

unit test: Testing to verify that a single source module is error-free.

UNIX: A computer operating system that runs on hardware ranging from PCs to supercomputers.

UPS: Uninterruptible power supply. A device that guarantees that equipment will continue to receive power even if the AC power goes out.

UTC: Universal time coordinated. A worldwide time standard.

VAR: Value added reseller. A company that builds systems by assembling hardware, existing software, and programs they have developed.

VAX: A minicomputer manufactured by Digital Equipment Corporation (DEC).

Visual Basic: A GUI development product developed by Microsoft.

VM: Virtual machine. An operating system for IBM computers that allows one computer to simulate multiple separate computers.

VSAM: Virtual sequential access method. A method of storing data on disk drives that allows rapid access.

VSE: An operating system for IBM mainframe computers.

WAN: Wide area network. A network of computers that communicate with each other over a wide area.

Index

●●●

IDG BOOKS WORLDWIDE REGISTRATION CARD

Visit our
Web site at
http://www.idgbooks.com

ISBN Number: 0-7645-0241-7

Title of this book: Year 2000 Solutions For Dummies®

My overall rating of this book: ❏ Very good [1] ❏ Good [2] ❏ Satisfactory [3] ❏ Fair [4] ❏ Poor [5]

How I first heard about this book:

❏ Found in bookstore; name: [6] _____ ❏ Book review: [7]

❏ Advertisement: [8] _____ ❏ Catalog: [9]

❏ Word of mouth; heard about book from friend, co-worker, etc.: [10] ❏ Other: [11]

What I liked most about this book:

_____

_____

What I would change, add, delete, etc., in future editions of this book:

_____

_____

Other comments: _____

Number of computer books I purchase in a year: ❏ 1 [12] ❏ 2-5 [13] ❏ 6-10 [14] ❏ More than 10 [15]

I would characterize my computer skills as: ❏ Beginner [16] ❏ Intermediate [17] ❏ Advanced [18] ❏ Professional [19]

I use ❏ DOS [20] ❏ Windows [21] ❏ OS/2 [22] ❏ Unix [23] ❏ Macintosh [24] ❏ Other: [25] _____

(please specify)

I would be interested in new books on the following subjects:

(please check all that apply, and use the spaces provided to identify specific software)

❏ Word processing: [26] _____ ❏ Spreadsheets: [27]

❏ Data bases: [28] _____ ❏ Desktop publishing: [29]

❏ File Utilities: [30] _____ ❏ Money management: [31]

❏ Networking: [32] _____ ❏ Programming languages: [33]

❏ Other: [34] _____

I use a PC at (please check all that apply): ❏ home [35] ❏ work [36] ❏ school [37] ❏ other: [38] _____

The disks I prefer to use are ❏ 5.25 [39] ❏ 3.5 [40] ❏ other: [41] _____

I have a CD ROM: ❏ yes [42] ❏ no [43]

I plan to buy or upgrade computer hardware this year: ❏ yes [44] ❏ no [45]

I plan to buy or upgrade computer software this year: ❏ yes [46] ❏ no [47]

Name: _____ Business title: [48] _____ Type of Business: [49]

Address (❏ home [50] ❏ work [51] /Company name: _____)

Street/Suite# _____

City [52] /State [53] /Zip code [54]: _____ Country [55] _____

❏ **I liked this book!** You may quote me by name in future
IDG Books Worldwide promotional materials.

My daytime phone number is _____

IDG BOOKS WORLDWIDE™

THE WORLD OF COMPUTER KNOWLEDGE®

☐ **YES!**

Please keep me informed about IDG Books Worldwide's World of Computer Knowledge. Send me your latest catalog.